D0400382

STEPHANIE WINSTON is also the author of *The Organized Executive*, a highly acclaimed business guide to organization and time management. The founder and director of The Organizing Principle, a New York based consulting firm, she travels throughout the country on behalf of private clients and corporations, lectures extensively, and conducts workshops and classes on the subject of organization.

also by Stephanie Winston

The Organized Executive

Getting Organized

Updated and Revised

The Easy Way to Put Your Life in Order

STEPHANIE WINSTON

Revised edition prepared with the assistance of
Marnie Winston-Macauley

WARNER BOOKS

A Time Warner Company

Photograph on page 208 used with permission of the California Closet Company.

Copyright © 1978, 1991 by Stephanie Winston
All rights reserved.

Warner Books, Inc., 666 Fifth Avenue, New York, NY 10103

w A Time Warner Company

Printed in the United States of America

Library of Congress Cataloging-in-Publication Data
Winston, Stephanie.
    Getting organized : the easy way to put your life in order /
Stephanie Winston. — Updated and rev., Rev. ed. / prepared with
the assistance of Marnie Winston-Macauley.
      p.   cm.
    Includes bibliographical references and index.
    ISBN 0-446-39173-5
    1. Home economics. 2. Housewives—Time management.
I. Winston-Macauley, Marnie. II. Title.
TX147.W75 1991
640—dc20   90-21800
                                             CIP

Cover design by Bob Antler
Illustrations by Susanne Strohbach

Contents

Preface

When *Getting Organized* was first published, it answered two different kinds of questions about being organized. The purpose of the original book was, for the first time, to offer readers a nuts-and-bolts "how-to": How do I take control of paperwork, arrange a hectic schedule, organize my books, clear out my closets? What are some innovative ideas for getting the most from available space? For these purposes, *Getting Organized* was and is a straightforward reference, similar to a dictionary or encyclopedia. Consult the table of contents or extensive index for the pages that deal with your problem and work from there.

The second question, more personal and more pervasive in its effect, was, "Why is my life so confused? Why do I always seem to be in the midst of clutter? Why do I have trouble seeing my feet? And why is this always happening to me?"

Getting Organized looks at some of the reasons why you lose your way, and at some of the hidden triggers that seem to block your ability to take control of your life, the basic attitudes involved, and, most important, it offers new ways to think about how to use your time, how to use your space, and how to give your life some consistent form.

Well, the 1980s have passed, and during those years, although the basic issues have not changed, we have seen enormous changes in the way people live their lives. If anything, some of these life-style changes challenge our ability to organize even more than they did thirteen years ago, because there seems to be so much more to do, so much less time to do it in, and, frequently, fewer hands to do all of the tasks that seem to be necessary. And perhaps women, in particular, have had to shoulder the biggest burden over these last years in attempting to "do it all."

So while the principles haven't changed, while the basic uses of time, space, and paper are still essentially the same as they were when *Getting Organized* was first written, the applications have changed, sometimes dramatically. The purpose of this revised *Getting Organized* is to take the principles that were so successful thirteen years ago, to look at them in new ways, and, without losing anything of the old, to apply them to the new situations that we see ourselves in today.

Doing it all. The traditional "woman's work is never done" syndrome has not died, but it has changed shape. How does a woman—or more accurately, the family—do it all, get it all in, without buying into false notions of being a superwoman?

The home office. This is particularly significant now that many people, both men and women, have opted to work at home, either part-time or full-time. An office at home is often no longer a simple corner where you pay your bills and organize your grocery list, but rather a fairly sophisticated professional situation. This office-at-home involves its own organizing patterns and brings with it some special problems.

Computer-age technology and electronic gadgetry. When your living room begins to look like an arcade, it's time to gain some mastery over high tech.

The modern family. Most mothers are working, and two-career couples are the norm. The single parent has emerged as a major factor. Suddenly you have unusual family groupings. It's not uncommon today for children to be living one week with Mom and Stepdad, the next week with Dad and Stepmom—the bottom line being that simply organizing the logistics of all this moving around among nontraditional family groupings is a new challenge.

Variations of living together. Homes are changing; the kinds of places we call our home is changing. Even married couples today have to organize more complex living and financial arrangements than in the past. Grown children are coming back home when they find that they can no longer afford their own private dwellings.

Negotiating terms of living together becomes even more delicate in the case of cohabiting couples and adult roommates. *Kate & Allie* was popular as a result of these nontraditional patterns. How do a Kate and Allie, and perhaps their children, manage to live together without falling over each other?

Mobility—moving, scaling up and scaling down. People are on the move more than they ever were before. At one time, people had one or two, perhaps three, homes in their lifetimes. Now, between shifting marriages, cohabitation, people living longer and moving into retirement communities, and various other alternatives, we find that space and the use of space are changing. We are scaling down, scaling in, scaling up. How do we organize around those changing needs?

Whichever approaches speak most strongly to you, I recommend that you read through the entire book before turning to specific organizing tasks, because familiarity with the basics of good organizing is so important.

The background I draw upon is primarily my own experience as director of the firm The Organizing Principle. We work in offices designing paperwork flow, filing systems, time management, staff deployment, and physical layout; and in homes, working with personal paperwork, kitchens, closets, and general household functions. Such a wide range of experience has made it possible for me to pinpoint the specific areas in which systems design has a place, and to recognize the basic attitudes that foster good organizing in any situation.

I would be glad to know of any planning or organizing tips from your own experience, or any suggestions on the book you may care to offer. Please write to me c/o Warner Books, 666 Fifth Avenue, New York, NY 10103. All correspondence will be received with interest and appreciation.

Organizing is fun, really—once you get the knack, it becomes almost a game. Approach the task with a light spirit; there is hardly anything more satisfying than feeling that sense of completion when you know you finally did it. You got rid of the chore. The closet is straight, you're in charge of your world.

But it's more than fun. It's essential—it's essential to take the stress out of trying to do it all, and to design life "your way." So good luck, and enjoy it.

STEPHANIE WINSTON

New York City
October 1990

Acknowledgments

I would like to thank the people whose confidence and encouragement were so important to me in establishing my business and writing this book: my parents, Miriam and Harry Winston; my sisters, Terry Pickett and Dinah Lovitch; and Ruth Stark, Margaret and Sheldon Klein, Shirley and Lou Winston, Marnie Winston-Macauley, and Joshua Winston.

Norma Fox, the best of friends, offered me the use of her offices at Human Sciences Press (thanks also to Dr. Sheldon Roen), where I wrote much of this book. Emily Fox Kales was always *there*. Ann Jackowitz was a loyal and steadfast friend, and Sanford Schmidt too.

Specific ideas used in the book were contributed by: Dinah Lovitch, gourmet cook *extraordinaire*, who helped me with the kitchen chapter; Faith MacFadden and close friends Sara Miles and Muriel Gelbart, who defined the conundrums of children and family life; and students Chris Clark, Don Goalstone, Joan Masket, Marjorie Atwood Murray, Julius Shulman, and Karen Olsen.

The organizing of *Getting Organized* was accomplished by Susan Ann Protter, literary agent and friend, and the *three* fine editors it was my privilege to work with: Carol Houck Smith, Sharon Morgan, and Chris Steinmetz. Thank you all.

The guiding light behind this revised edition of *Getting Organized* is Marnie Winston-Macauley, my cousin, friend, and colleague, who worked with me generously and brilliantly to help define and develop organizing problems and solutions for today's complicated world.

Thanks and appreciation are due my editor at Warner Books, Susan Suffes, for her keen critical eye and assistance all along the way.

S.W.

How Organized Are You?—A Quiz

1. Does it often take you more than ten minutes to unearth a particular letter, bill, report, or other paper from your files (or piles of paper on your desk)?

2. Are there papers on your desk, other than reference materials, that you haven't looked through for a week or more?

3. Has your electricity or another utility ever been turned off because you forgot to pay the bill?

4. Within the last two months, have you forgotten any scheduled appointment, anniversary, or specific date you wanted to acknowledge?

5. Do magazines and newspapers pile up unread?

6. If there were to be a tragedy, and your spouse or parent or significant other died, would you be totally lost as to what valuable papers and records existed, and where to find them?

7. Do you frequently procrastinate so long on a work assignment that it becomes an emergency or panic situation?

8. When you're involved in something at home, do you find that you're constantly interrupted either by de-

mands from family members or by the telephone? Does it seem you're at the mercy of everyone?

9. Has anything ever been misplaced in your home or office for longer than two months?

10. Do you often misplace doorkeys, glasses, gloves, handbag, briefcase, or other "regulars"?

11. Is your definition of "organized space" to fit as many objects as you can into a limited area?

12. Do things amass in corners of closets, or on the floor, because you can't decide where to put them?

13. Do you often wonder where to put the VCR? Does your family get into arguments over who should have control of the Nintendo? Has your house erupted into a confusing arcade of electronic gimmickry that you have no place for?

14. Do you feel that your storage problems would be solved if you had more space?

15. Do you want to get organized, but everything is in such a mess that you don't know where to start?

16. The garbage hasn't been taken out yet, even though it's your son's responsibility. Will you probably end up taking it out yourself?

17. When you're at work, have you sometimes felt concerned that your various family players—e.g., your kids, the babysitter, spouse—don't know when your five-year-old's dancing lessons are and how they're supposed to get him there and back home?

18. When you go shopping, do you find yourself running all over town and usually coming home only to find that you forgot something?

19. Does it drive you crazy when your spouse or companion constantly throws his/her clothes in the corner? Or is there some other organizational issue that is a thorn in your or your significant other's side?

20. If you're the noncustodial parent or have joint custody, do you find that bringing the kids becomes a major van-line procedure each weekend?

21. By the end of an average day, have you accomplished at least the most important tasks you set for yourself?

22. Do you regularly take advantage of housecleaning help, babysitters, dry cleaners, other services? (Assuming money isn't a serious impediment.)

23. Are the kitchen items you use most often in the most convenient place?

24. Is your living room arranged so that family and/or guests can speak comfortably without raising their voices? Are there places for drinks and snacks?

SCORING: Questions 1–20: one point for each "yes"
Questions 21–24: one point for each "no"

IF YOUR SCORE IS:

1–6 Systems are under control. Some of the innovative tips in this book might make things even better.

7–10 Disorganization is troublesome. The book's program could help considerably.

11–14 Life must be very difficult. Careful study and execution of the program outlined in the book is advisable.

15 Disorganized to the point of chaos. Following the book's program could change your life.

PART ONE

The Organizing Principle

1
On Getting It All Together

More than once you may have felt that someone wasn't looking when your "life management" card was dealt out. You are intelligent, you are a likable person, but how can you explain the fact that you are always running late and, all too frequently, seem to be drowning in busywork? Although the following sad tales may not apply to you in all their particulars, there is probably something here that will cause you to grimace and sigh, "Oh God, it's me."

Lisa, a twenty-eight-year-old lawyer in Far Hills, New Jersey, stumbles out of bed at 7:30 A.M., stomach churning in panic, because that important appointment is set for

8:30, and the alarm didn't go off. Lisa dashes out of the house disheveled because there was no time to dress and groom properly, and because the blouse that goes with the tweed suit is missing as usual.

Breakfast is coffee because Lisa has no time, naturally, for a real meal. But even under less harassed circumstances breakfast is a pain; who can ever find the eggs which are invariably hidden at the back of the refrigerator? And pulling the only decent frying pan out from under the pile of pots in the cabinet hardly seems worth the trouble.

As usual, Lisa misses the 8:00 bus, which she generally does about half the time, stumbles onto the next one ten minutes later, and in her disheveled state, spends her fifteen minutes on the bus attempting to riffle through her briefcase searching for the crucial document for her meeting.

Home again. Cooking a meal seems unendurable when utensils are piled into every nook and cranny of the kitchen. So once again, Lisa opens a can of tuna or orders a pizza.

Early evening might be a good time to get started on the income tax, but who knows what deductions to claim when the canceled checks have disappeared?

At last, a warm, relaxing bath to soothe away the tensions of the day. But relaxation turns to rage with the realization that all the towels are in the laundry.

And so to bed; with muscles taut, nerves jangling, and the sinking feeling that the whole thing is going to happen all over again tomorrow.

Bill Marshall is in advertising. You can count on late nights for Bill twice or three times a week. He frequently has to take clients out for drinks or dinner.

His wife, Diane, an office manager for an import-export firm, is generally able to make it home to relieve the babysitter by around 5:30. For Diane it's all go, go, go as soon as she walks in the door.

She generally comes home to find beds unmade, homework not yet done, and the children clamoring for dinner. While screaming at the children to get their homework done, she's trying to get the dinner fixings together. While the stew is cooking, she's running up to make the beds and screaming for the children to bring the laundry for folding.

Finally Diane is able to grab the kids and sit them down for stew at 7:00 P.M. Next comes another screaming session to get them undressed and into the bath, while she's doing the dishes.

At which point, Bill walks in. He's had a hard day. He goes first to his room and calls out, "Honey, the bed isn't made!" Then he comes back, pours out some white wine, sits down, and says, "Hi, sweetie. How was your day?"

Not a good question. Can this family be helped?

The Jordans have seen a major shift in their lives since their twins, Benjy and Allison, reached their fifth birthdays. Suddenly their home has been invaded by mechanically moving things they scarcely understand. They find that they are tripping over wires, that their den has been invaded by machines on top of machines that they once recognized, and worse, there have been several near collisions with various assorted and sundry disks, tapes, and other paraphernalia that seem to go with these mechanical monsters that their children have put into their homes—not to mention their own computers, VCRs, stereos, and other gear.

They're damn well tired of falling over things they can't understand and can't fit in and that are menacing them all over the place. Frank Lloyd Wright never thought of this! Certainly something has to be done.

* * *

If these stories apply to you at all, you must wonder what causes your wheels to spin in this way. The answer is complex, but there is nothing in your stars or your nature that dooms you to live out your days chafed and affronted on every side by such indignities. On the contrary, your innate capacity to organize is powerful indeed, but for a variety of complex reasons that instinctive capability was shortcircuited. The causes are primarily psychological, stemming from childhood; not to mention the constant challenge of coping with the mechanics of a highly sophisticated, complex world that our grandparents never knew.

You *are* capable, however, of setting your own life in order. Your inner drives toward order and clarity are much more powerful than the forces of chaos. Consider, for example, a major traffic circle and the experience of crossing it on foot or in a car. In your intrepid passage from one side to the other, whether as pedestrian or driver, you are spontaneously organizing a good deal of complex information: the velocity of the cars, their different angles of approach, their interrelationships with one another and with you. Managing this intricate situation signifies that you are highly successful at processing an assortment of information into a pattern that makes sense; the basic definition of organization.

Given the premise that we are all born with the inherent capacity to organize, what happened? I believe that many people get trapped in a sort of time warp in which they live out their present lives responding to forces that were in operation many years ago—as much as ten, twenty, thirty, or more years. The majority of people who are consistently (as opposed to only occasionally) troubled by the issue of order and disorder and by the logistics of managing their lives, are still, as adults, often living out guilty defiance of a childhood authority—usually a parent.

The process occurs in roughly the following way: An

authority figure teaches a very young child that there is a way things "ought" to be. There is a "right" way to do things, and a "good" person is "disciplined" and "orderly." This attitude toward life further affects the child when, as usually happens, the question of his or her own room becomes an issue. The constant refrain "Terry, clean up your room" becomes as maddening as fingernails scratching a blackboard. The child interprets this invasion of territory as an attack on his or her identity and autonomy. Sometimes this sense of assault is nothing more than imagination, but in many cases the child correctly senses a parent's need to control.

At some point defiance begins. The young person digs in his or her heels and mentally says, "I won't. I won't be orderly or disciplined." So he or she proceeds to make life chaotic in the belief that order means entrapment or loss of identity, and therefore disorder means freedom and affirmation of the self.

There is another factor that complicates this false assumption: guilt. As children or adolescents few people can defy their parents with a clear conscience. So even while one part of the personality may be affirming itself through defiance, the other part is saying, "I must be wrong, I must be bad."

The resulting burden exacts a heavy cost. A person moves from the imprisonment of someone else's rules to the imprisonment of a continuing functional disorder and, even more disheartening, to the deeper entrapment of a conflict in his or her own mind. In order to avoid this dilemma, people frequently assume conscious styles of living which seem to justify disorderliness.

One of these styles is "busy, busy, busy." Using this technique, a person becomes so frantically active with so many responsibilities, activities, problems, and excursions that there just isn't a moment to pull it all together.

There is a distinction between "busy, busy, busy" as a style and the genuine overbooking that is so much a reality of our time—the subject of Oprah Winfrey shows and "getting it all together" articles. The difference is that the first is a "look" and the second is an organizing reality. But sometimes that reality can be managed just a bit more efficiently so as to turn legitimate claims into more of a pleasure and less of a burden.

Another style, not quite so widespread, is "free spirit." The "free spirit" is usually vaguely "artistic" or "creative," and thinks of organizing as the dullest possible activity for a person engaged in higher pursuits.

The most characteristic way people cope with the emotional bind of the order-versus-disorder conflict is by developing the attitude of "compliance/defiance." Many of my clients, for example, desperately want to be "right." They yearn to have their lives organized the way they "ought to be." That is compliance—the conscious acceptance of parental standards. Accordingly, they set specific goals of an exaggerated precision that would shame a computer scientist. Then, because these goals are unrealistic and often irrelevant to any genuine practical need, the person says, "The hell with it. I can't do it and I won't." That is defiance.

Guilty defiance no longer has much effect on your parents, but it serves effectively to block *you* from true freedom—true freedom, in the context of this book, meaning a system of *real* order, intrinsic to the person that you are, that liberates rather than constricts.

The specific elements of real order include a physical environment that is easy to move around in, easy to look at, and easy to function in; a simple technique for dealing effectively with the volume of paperwork and money business that we all must confront; and the development of a satisfying response to the fact that time is life, time is often money, and time is limited. This world takes shape as you develop a sensitivity to your own needs. In fact, this entire book is based on the proposition that there is no "correct" order, no right way to do things—whether setting up a file or a workroom or planning time—unless it is correct for you.

In other words, order is not an end in itself. Order is whatever helps you to function effectively—nothing more and nothing less. *You* set the rules and the goals, however special, idiosyncratic, or individualistic they may be. Then, using this book as a guideline, you can define your particular purposes and set up the practical systems to implement them. Figuring out your goals and purposes begins in the next chapter.

2
The Organizing Principle: The Key to Straightening Things Out

All concepts of order, from the simplest system of closet arrangement to the most complex rocket technology, share one essential characteristic: an organizing principle. The idea behind the organizing principle is that any intellectual or practical system always contains a central pole, an essential priority, around which all the other components group themselves.

For example, any State Department official worth his pinstripes has learned to recognize that the shape of a conference table can sometimes make or break a country's ability to negotiate. You may remember that back in the seventies the North Vietnamese made a great fuss about the conference table at the Paris negotiations to end the

Vietnam War. Once it was recognized that questions of status were the organizing principle behind the brouhaha —that is, people at a rectangular table have different status depending on where they're sitting, but everyone is equal at a round table—then the solution of choosing a round table became obvious.

Once the organizing principle behind an existing situation, or governing a task, has been identified, you can decide whether it is the one that is right for *you*. If it is not, then you have the option of revising the principle.

One example of a distressing event that occurred because the project was governed by a skewed organizing principle is the debacle in 1990 of the Hubble telescope— a grand telescope sent above the earth's atmosphere to view the universe unobstructedly. Because the working organizing principle was "shave costs by cutting corners," important expensive tests were not carried out on the ground. Thus, when the telescope reached space, it was found that it could not do what it was supposed to do, it could not see clearly into deep space, because of mistakes that could have been detected earlier.

Had the organizing principle been, "We must explore and test for every possible error or flaw, and beg, borrow, or steal the money necessary," then the gigantic Hubble miscalculations would simply never have happened. As it is, there was terrible disappointment, embarrassment, and erosion of NASA's credibility, and it will probably end up being more expensive than if they had done it right in the first place.

The point of the organizing principle is to isolate the purpose you want to achieve and/or define a guiding pole that governs action. The whats and the hows—that is, the practical solutions—will flow fairly easily once you understand the whys.

Let's consider the organizing principle in terms of the

psychological factors discussed previously. Probably, as your life became more and more complicated over the years, you have occasionally been able to step back and say to yourself, "I am being self-destructive. I've got to stop this right away." Whereupon you went through a period of intense, determined organizing which ended a day or two later when you discovered that nothing had really changed and you were right back where you started!

At that point the feeling of helplessness, of life out of control, must have been intense and painful. But if you look at this whole pattern with the idea of finding the organizing principle, the hidden factors may begin to reveal themselves. In all likelihood you are causing yourself genuine pain in the service of a powerful theme, a powerful organizing principle: defiance of authority.

You have chosen defiance as your focus, and so long as it is in operation, you will always revert to the old pattern of defiance leading to chaos.

However, by recognizing that this outmoded, destructive organizing principle has been functioning quietly all these years, you are now free to bring it to the surface and change it—to devise a new principle more appropriate to your present life. Your organizing principle might then become: "The purpose of order in my life is my own ease and convenience—not domination by some impractical ideal." With that in mind as a basic point of reference, many changes become possible. Just as your previous actions were completely and spontaneously logical in terms of your old "defiance" motif, your newer mode of behavior will, after you accustom yourself to it, become completely logical in terms of the new "ease and convenience" theme.

And that's what this book is about. It will not only help you plan your personal business affairs or time or closets more efficiently, but it will also help you establish a permanent way of life fitted to your own desires and goals.

However, there is a considerable leap from the grand abstraction of the organizing principle to the actual solving of a problem. First you have to understand very clearly just what the problem *is*. The rest of this chapter concentrates on how to pinpoint the problems in your life and bring them to manageable, solvable proportions.

It is not uncommon for clients to approach me with the cry "Please straighten out my life." Their daily life seems overwhelming, and organizing it seems hopeless. Such people cannot see that specific, smaller difficulties must be resolved before the whole becomes manageable. Some clients, on the other hand, feel confronted by so many tiny problems that they are defeated by their very quantity.

The first step toward taking things in hand is to define just what a "problem" is. Never yet, in my experience, has a situation been so complex that it couldn't be unraveled.

To begin, provide yourself with a notebook—either looseleaf or spiral-bound—small enough to carry around with you. This notebook will become your "master list"— a single continuous list that replaces all the small slips of paper you're probably used to. Use the notebook to keep track of all errands, things to do or buy, and general notes to yourself about anything that will require action. This basic organizing technique is the first in a series of principles that will appear throughout the book highlighting the prime rules of organization.

Principle #1   **Use a single notebook for notes to yourself.**

Choose a time with no distractions and sit down with your notebook and pencil. List six elements in your life that need to be put in order. Forget about straightening out your life as a whole.

Instead, focus on things like these:

I spend so much time looking for kitchen utensils that cooking a meal takes hours. How can I make my kitchen "work" properly?

I want to start painting again, but my brushes and canvases and paints are all over the house. What do I do to get them together?

The living room is always a mess because I don't know what to do with all those magazines and newspapers I haven't read.

It seems that the rooms in my house cannot keep up fast enough with the various Nintendos, Ataris, and assorted disks that my two boys are strewing every which way. Short of moving, what do I do?

I'm always running back to the supermarket for something I forgot to put on the list. So I'm always adding lists to my lists to make sure I remember everything. Isn't there an easier, more organized way to remember all the things I need to buy?

It takes me forever to get ready in the morning and I'm always late for work. How can I streamline the "up and out" process?

Every time I'm in the middle of my paperwork, I am interrupted by somebody wanting me. I would like for once not to be jangled out of what I'm doing by some call or bell or buzzer or phone. How do I create some space for myself, to do what I need to do?

Substitute your own examples for mine, and you've completed the first step. If your mind tends to blur when you try to isolate problems, the "movie" technique may help. Take a deep breath and relax. Then close your eyes and mentally run through a typical day, letting it unroll like a movie. "I get up, brush my teeth . . ." and so on. When you come to a scene or situation that creates a problem, write it down. While you are screening your day's movie, remember that you may not be consciously aware of some problems but your mind and body are. If your stomach lurches or your muscles tighten or your head aches when you come to a particular scene, then you can be sure you have locked onto a problem.

If, for example, a twinge of tension occurs at the idea of brushing your teeth, perhaps you're always running out of toothpaste—a problem in maintaining an inventory control system for household supplies. Or, the toothpaste might be there, but the medicine chest is so jammed that a dozen other things fall into the sink every time you reach into the cabinet.

Write down each problem as you come to it, then shut your eyes again, relax, and continue. List no more than six problems, otherwise the list itself may overwhelm you!

This procedure of problem definition illustrates a fundamental rule of organizing—every life situation, no matter what it may be, can be divided into its significant parts. Stated as a principle:

Principle #2 **Divide up a complex problem into manageable segments.**

Some of the problems on your list will be fairly straightforward. A messy clothes closet, for example, is a small area with one function, and organizing it is a fairly simple procedure. But changing your morning ritual so that you're on time for work is a considerably more complex matter. It may involve changing your habits, revising your time schedule, reorganizing your bathroom or laundry system—or all of these things. Keeping Principle #2 in mind, the next step is to divide the *complex* problems on your list into more manageable units. These more complex situations usually fall into one of two categories:

1. *Physical areas: rooms.* If an entire room needs reorganizing, you must first isolate its various problem areas. Stand in the doorway of the room and, choosing any corner at random, mentally block out an area about five feet square. Cast a sharp eye over every inch of that area to inspect it for "knots." In the living room, a knot might be a sloppy desk and work area, a disorganized wall unit with books piled in disarray, or an inconvenient and unappealing furniture arrangement. Whatever jars your nerves or sensibilities is a fit subject for reworking. List these specific "knot" areas on your master problem list under the general problem of which they are a part. Block out another five-foot-square area immediately adjacent to the first and repeat the process. Follow this procedure until you have checked the entire room and have a complete list of individual elements to work on.

2. *Processes or systems.* To break down a process or a system into its manageable parts, use the same movie technique, mentally running through the particular process that's giving you trouble. Each time you feel tension about an action or function, write it down. For instance, the stumbling blocks in the "up-and-out-in-the-morning" process might include some of the following: Alarm clock rings too softly; cannot move quickly in the morning; don't have time to decide what clothes or accessories to wear; kitchen always messy so making breakfast is a chore.

There is one more very significant step that provides the bridge between defining the problem and finding the solution. On a scale of 1 to 10, rank each of the six major items on your list according to how much it irritates you. Stated as a principle:

Principle #3   **After articulating a small group of projects, rank them by number according to how aggravating they are.**

A problem that creates serious tension is a #1; one that could wait until next year is #10. Write the number next to each item on your list. This is a very important impetus to action. You may end up with two problems which are #1, two #2, one #5, and one #7. Do *not* try to arrange the problems 1, 2, 3, 4, 5, 6 in numerical order of importance. People tend to get so involved in figuring out which problem is fifth and which is sixth or whatever that they lose sight of what they're trying to accomplish. If any of your six major problems can be subdivided as discussed on page 20, rank those subdivisions in the same way.

With this step of ranking, the process of establishing order is well and truly begun. The issues have been outlined, priorities have been set, and a foundation for action has been laid. All that remains before actually tackling the problems is to set a specific and regular time for organizing work. If you can't choose a good time, play a little game with yourself. Imagine that for the next several weeks you have a fixed appointment with yourself that you note in your appointment calendar as if it were a regular medical or dental appointment. Your "appointments" could be every day for an hour, or every day for fifteen minutes, or twice a week for two hours each, or an hour a week; whatever is practical in terms of other responsibilities and your own temperament. If you know you'll start getting jittery after half an hour, don't set a two-hour appointment because it will be "good" for you or you "ought" to. Instead, be kind to yourself and give yourself appointments that you know you can keep and handle.

But remember, these are firm appointments and must be kept, except in case of emergency. Making this commitment to yourself will be one of the smartest things you ever did.

PROBLEM-SOLVING CHECKLIST

Before you begin, review this checklist which summarizes your first steps.

1. Select and list in your notebook no more than six problems at one time.
2. Break the complex problems on the list into manageable units.
3. Rank the problems and their units according to aggravation level.
4. Turn to the appropriate section or sections of this book and solve the first #1 problem on the list; do not omit any units.
5. Go to the next #1 item, then the #2's, and so on until all the problems have been solved.
6. Choose another set of problems and follow the same steps.

PART TWO

Time and Paper

3
The Basics of Managing Time

The productive use of time is ultimately a personal judgment; by your actions through the day, week, year, do you achieve the life that you want for yourself and your family? If so, your handling of time is basically sound. But if you constantly swing between periods of frantic and often useless activity and periods of inertia and procrastination, perhaps you should rethink your use of time—both in your daily life and in terms of your long-range ambitions. Before you can begin to organize your household and business systems effectively, you must learn how to use your time more efficiently and to your best advantage.

THE TWO-LIST TIME
MANAGEMENT PROGRAM

Marian told us an old, old story. "Well," she said, "I have lots of lists. I am a list person. I make up lists for everything. I have lists for the babysitter, I have lists for my decorating clients, there's my 'must do' list, my next-week list, my call list, shopping lists, my what-to-do lists, my when-to-do-it lists, an ideas list, a 'next project' list, and . . . well, I guess that about covers it. Oh, and I also keep a list of my lists. Unfortunately, I get so confused that I never know what I'm doing."

The effective use of lists is critical to any well-organized time management system. Unfortunately, Marian's approach to list-making is all too familiar. In Marian's case, at least, all her lists were kept in a nice, neat stack. Many devoted list-makers are also creative in where and how they keep their lists.

Millie's lists get scribbled on the backs of envelopes that get scrunched up at the bottom of her purse, or she writes on little-bitty scraps of paper that she tucks into her address book where either (a) they fall out or (b) she forgets all about them. To solve the problem of forgetting, she started to put her reminders to herself on a bulletin board right in front of her face as she worked at her desk, but they quickly became part of the decor. And though she saw them every day, she never saw them again, especially as she began tacking new lists on top of the old ones.

Here is some good news. Relief is on the way. A basic time management program that many people have found helpful is the (only!) Two-List Master List/Daily List system. It is a simple method that really does work. And the only equipment you need to maintain this effective daily time plan is a day-by-day appointment calendar and a spiral or looseleaf notebook that is big enough to write in comfortably but small enough to take with you wherever you go.

This is the key: In your spiral or looseleaf notebook (this is the same notebook referred to in Chapter 2, page 17), write down every single task that arises *as* it arises: an assignment from your boss; a reminder to yourself to call Phil with a question about the spring line; the commitment you made to your friend on the neighborhood recycling committee to bundle up your newspapers and bring them to the recycling center. Write it down.

Simply write the tasks in order as they come up, making no attempt to "organize" them or set priorities or anything of that kind. This is simply a *Master List*, a reservoir or catchment basin in which you capture everything you have to do. One exception: Some people prefer to separate business tasks from personal ones. In that case, use one of those little notebook-divider stick-on tabs to separate the personal side from the business side.

Now put the program in motion with your *Daily List*: Each morning or evening, on a separate piece of paper (some people prefer index cards, but it could be anything that's convenient) list ten things to do that day, compiled for the most part from items in your Master List notebook, "follow-ups" in the calendar, plus one or two items from your "Things to do" file folder (page 66) that require special attention, and immediate tasks that have just arisen. And it's a great idea, maybe two or three times a week, to list something on your Daily List for yourself: take a bike ride through the park, go to a museum, call three friends you haven't spoken to for a while. It's a genuinely refreshing treat.

The Daily List is your working daily action guide. It becomes your working tool for the day. The few minutes you spend each day making a Daily List will repay you

COMPOSING THE DAILY LIST

Elaine teaches fitness classes from her home three times a week. Starting as an informal cottage industry, her business has grown and emerged into a rather formal structure, which includes not only fitness classes for adults but 3:30 classes for children as well.

Elaine's Daily List on a particular October day reads:

Task	From what source
Get Halloween costume for daughter Jennifer.	Calendar. Elaine had marked this reminder in her calendar over a month ago.
Revise and update client list.	Master List
Get in touch with athletic equipment supplier to see about refurbishing floor mats.	Master List
Draft outline for new fitness manual.	One entry on Elaine's Master List reads "produce new fitness manual." However, that's not a single task. That is a complex task of many parts. So what she has entered on her Daily List is a single manageable task that will forward the larger project.
Call Brent's mother to see why Brent didn't show up for class yesterday.	Immediate task that just cropped up.

Task	From what source
Repair and/or rerecord the music tape that broke yesterday, used for the intermediate class.	Immediate task
Alphabetize cards for people on mailing list.	Master List
Return new dress to the store because alteration wasn't done properly.	Immediate task that just cropped up when she received the delivery.

many times over. Accomplish as many To Do's on the list each day as your schedule permits, and roll any remaining tasks over onto tomorrow's list. (However, if three tasks are left, that doesn't mean making tomorrow's list thirteen items long, but rather adding seven new jobs to make ten.)*

Most To Do's should be specific and limited. The "Blackwell report," for example, may be too broad a prospect for one day; instead enter some of its components— "introduction" and "section on transportation"—as separate items on the list. Similarly, divide "clean the basement" into "tool corner," "pile of old furniture," and so forth. On the other hand, some To Do items might stand for a group of routine jobs: "errands," "phone calls," "routine correspondence."

In a nice older book, the *I Hate to Housekeep Book*, Peg Bracken offers an entertaining suggestion: Play Time-Planner's Russian Roulette. On individual slips of paper, list some of the unpleasant jobs you've been putting off—

---

*Readers interested in more detailed discussions of time management in a business context might wish to take a look at *The Organized Executive* by the same author.

"reorganize the first five file folders in the cabinet," "bring address book up to date," "reorganize the medicine cabinet"—and, to make the game sporting, include some pleasurable activities—"go home early," "read a novel for an hour," "go bike riding"—in a three-to-one ratio of pain to pleasure. Put the slips in an empty can, and on an off-day, draw one. Even if you draw a grim job, gambler's honor will get you started and there's always hope for next time.

As a general rule, however, the Daily List is the axis around which your day revolves. First, decide which chores might be more profitably delegated to other people—family, if at home, or colleagues.

The program just described here is strictly low-tech. Can computers or electronic gadgetry play a role? They certainly are not necessary. The Two-List program can be managed perfectly well with primitive paper and pen. But for readers who enjoy electronic tools, certain advantages can be had with small, hand-held computers such as the Sharp Wizard and the Casio Boss.

The Sharp Wizard, to use the example with which the author is more familiar, enables you to create a Master List simply by typing in tasks at will. Where the real advantage comes in is that you can code each entry and then call them up as a group. Say, for example, that you enter "Call Phil about spring line." And then at other times you enter various other calls. Okay, now you're at the airport and have a half hour before boarding your flight. Simply type in the word "call," and all entries in which you have used that term will come up on a single list, so you can easily make short shrift of many of those calls in the half hour.

It is easy to code the Master List any way you wish. Another idea is to *date* each task as you enter it, using the final date by which it should be accomplished. Then on

June 12, say, you type in "6/17" to call up all the tasks for which that is the final date.

As for the Daily List, you can transfer an entry from the Master List to the Daily List—that is, one listed by calendar date—at the touch of a button, and then type in any other items as desired.

Some people prefer to use the "calendar pages" on the Wizard as an actual appointment calendar, but the screen viewing area seems too small for that to be really practical. A regular calendar or agenda for appointments makes more sense to this observer. But the "pages" are perfectly well sized for a Daily List.

The PC time management program one hears most about is "Sidekick." Many people use it and enjoy it, but quite a few find it overly complicated for what is essentially a simple process and they eventually revert to pen and paper.

Setting Priorities

The next key step of the Two-List Time Management Program is to set priorities—that is, to rank each item on the Daily List in terms of its importance. But this is priority-setting with a twist. Rather than a straight 1 to 10 listing, I recommend marking each item on your list either #1 for high priority, #2 for medium priority, or #3 for least urgent.

A task qualifies for #1 in one of three ways. The first kind of #1 is the obvious time-pressured urgent task. For example, sending out notices about the Christmas program becomes an urgent, #1 task soon after Thanksgiving.

But there's another kind of #1 task that people tend not to think of in that way, and that is a task that makes heavy demands on your creativity, ability to reason, or ability to plan. Say, for example, that you need to develop a fresh new advertising campaign to win a new client. Thinking through your basic approach qualifies as a #1 task—whether there are pressing time constraints or not —because the demands of the task require that you be at your freshest and sharpest.

Stressful tasks can also qualify as #1 because they make great demands on you, although in a different way. Say, for example, that you carpool a group of children regularly, and one of the children is seriously disruptive—yelling, unruly, hurts the other children. You've tried all the psychology and understanding you can muster, but now you're going to have to tell the child's mother that you won't pick up her child anymore. For most people that would be pretty darn stressful, which makes it a #1 task.

Think of a #2 task as your basic work. It's the warp and woof of your daily life that makes genuine demands on you because it's what you do; it's your job in life, whatever that might be.

For a teacher, preparing daily lesson plans would be a #2 job; for a fitness instructor, working out new music backing for her programs. The basic #2 task of a working lawyer would be to prepare briefs; of a free-lance writer, to draft proposals to different editors.

To a chef, preparing a complex dish, but one that he knows well, would qualify as a #2 task, whereas inventing a new recipe would be a #1, because it requires that his powers be at their highest.

Many people find the routine office clerical jobs easy and sometimes even relaxing. This kind of busywork qualifies as #3 on the priority scale, with tasks such as filing, alphabetizing, typing, and keeping a phone log up to date.

However, one person's busywork is another person's poison. When you factor in the stress element, one person's

ELAINE'S PRIORITIES

The next step Elaine must take after writing up her Daily List is to establish priorities according to the #1, #2, #3 system. Taking the same list as before, this is how she worked it out:

Task	Priority
Get Halloween costume for Jennifer.	Because it's now mid-October, this is a #2 task—that is, medium. However, if it were October 29, the task would become a #1 because it would be urgent.
Revise and update client list.	#2, because it's a medium important task making medium demands.
Get in touch with equipment supplier about floor mats.	#2, because it's a basic, medium-range task.
Draft outline for new fitness manual.	#1. Although there is no particular time pressure on this task, Elaine believes the fitness manual could open up whole new vistas for her business. So it's a long-term task with a potentially great payoff, and she must be at her sharpest when she sits down to think this through.
Call Brent's mother to see why Brent didn't show up for class.	#2, because it's a basic, medium-range task.

Task	Priority
Repair and/or rerecord the broken music tape used for the intermediate class.	#1, because it's urgent. Elaine can't conduct class without it.
Alphabetize cards for people on mailing list.	#3. Busywork.
Return new dress because alteration wasn't done properly.	#1, because it's stressful. She knows she'll get into a hassle with the store because the garment has already been altered, and she hates confrontations. But it must be done.

You'll have noticed that of the eight tasks on Elaine's list, five of them are #2 and #3, with only three #1's. Of the #1's, one is high priority because it is urgent—that is, there is heavy time pressure—and the other is high priority because it makes heavy demands on Elaine's "sharpness." She has to be at her best.

This is about the proper proportion. Overloading your Daily List with #1's, so that you become too tired, stressed out, or busy to accomplish them, is a prescription for failure.

priority levels may be very different from someone else's. For example, say that your daughter, who is in the tenth grade, asks you to check her paper for grammar before she turns it in. To someone who is comfortable with language and grammar, this is an easy, relaxing #3 task. Another parent, however, may feel insecure in these areas to the degree that the request causes stress that may bring the task to the #2, or even #1, level.

Scheduling Your Daily List

To make your Daily List work *for* you, schedule your tasks in terms of the practical factor, the biological factor, and the deadline factor.

The Practical Factor

Tasks such as report writing that require concentration should obviously be scheduled for hours when peace and quiet are available. Time of day and weather may also be factors. Ironing might be scheduled for the early morning, before the heat of the day. For the same reason, early morning may be the only comfortable time you have for gardening. Certain tasks require special equipment only available between certain hours; for example, there might be a backup on computer time.

First, then, mark on your calender the Daily List tasks that can only be performed at specific hours.

The Biological Factor

The concept of biological rhythm—the tendency, in its common definition, to be a "morning person" or a "night person"—is a fascinating and still relatively unexplored aspect of human experience. Every individual, during the course of a day, goes through a regular cycle of energy and acuity. Most people operate on "high" the first few hours of the morning, then dip in energy until a late afternoon low when energy ups again into early evening's "second high." Another drop between ten and eleven leads to bed.

Then there are the "night people" who have trouble adjusting to the nine-to-five world. They generally start with morning torpor, perk up around noon and through the late afternoon, and decline after dinner until about ten or eleven, when energy rises again, making it hard to go to bed at a reasonable hour.

It can make a big difference to your general productivity to schedule your Daily List tasks as much as possible around the highs and lows of your own rhythms. That is, do your #1 tasks in your personal #1 time—what time management specialist Alan Lakein called "prime time." If you are trying to gain the organizing advantage, you want to go *with* your strength, not against it. A professional tennis player, for example, could not master a tricky new stroke although he practiced it every afternoon at 3:00. One evening the player saw a TV documentary about biorhythm and decided to reschedule his practice session to his "higher" hour of 9:00 A.M. He mastered the new stroke on the second day and, as in all good tales, went on to win the tournament. He noted, "It was a strange sensation. At the 3:00 P.M. practices my body felt clumsy, and my judgment and depth perception seemed off. But the first day we started working at 9:00 A.M. I had a sense of confidence, and the second day I made it."

Our friend Elaine, the fitness instructor, takes advantage of her own tempos similarly. She finds that in terms of her own biological clock it is optimal for her to do the kind of #1 priority task that involves quiet and personal thinking at 9:30 at night. This is the time when she feels relaxed enough, yet focused and enthusiastic enough, to do a task like planning her fitness manual.

You can check your own biorhythm by briskly exercising for five minutes in the morning and again in late afternoon. If you feel exhausted in the morning and invigorated in the afternoon, you may be a night person; if it's the other way around, you're probably a morning person. Check your mental faculties as well. Work half of a challenging crossword puzzle in the morning and try the other half in the afternoon. Can you detect a difference in acuity?

When you know your individual pattern, draw up a rough plan and note your highs and lows. The pattern below is fairly typical.

9:00 A.M. to noon	High gear
Noon to 4:00 P.M.	Fairly alert
4:00 P.M. to 6:00 P.M.	Low gear
6:00 P.M. to 10:00 P.M.	Fairly alert
After 10:00 P.M.	Resting

To the extent that you can, structure your Daily List according to your energy levels, with #1 tasks like top-priority projects, projects requiring intense concentration or original thinking, and tasks that are unpleasant or stressful being reserved for your "high" time.

Stressful or unpleasant tasks are allocated to your prime-time period because that is when both emotional resilience and mental powers are strongest.

Routine jobs that you dislike qualify as "high" too. If starting dinner at 4:00 P.M. is a burden, organize dinner and set the table in the morning. The organizing projects suggested throughout this book should also be accomplished during "high" hours because they involve a change of habit, which can create stress.

Reserve "fairly alert" time for #2 tasks: meetings, ordinary correspondence, phoning, and so forth. During your very low time, do #3 tasks, such as planning for the next day, signing letters, or doing some professional reading. Try to relax a bit too. Chat with your colleagues, close your eyes for fifteen minutes, do several yoga exercises.

During these periods, try to avoid situations—or people—that irritate you.

If you *must* attend the anxiety-producing staff meeting that is invariably called during your low time of 4:00 P.M., give yourself a boost with a high-energy snack—a few spoonfuls of cottage cheese or some nuts and a glass of orange juice—about fifteen minutes before the meeting. Blood sugar levels, a factor in mood and energy, can be raised by a protein snack.

The Deadline Factor and Other Scheduling Tips

Knowing when to stop a project is as important as knowing when to start one. Everyone has different task toleration levels. One person can productively concentrate on a single project for four hours while another gets woozy and sloppy after an hour. And of course, different projects make different types of demands. Your personal responses are the key: When the sentence you've read three times makes no sense, when your muscles are aching—quit. The more effort you put into a project beyond the quitting point, the less value you are going to show for it. It is hard to judge the quality of your work when you are tired, so you may not even realize until the next day that your efforts were unproductive.

Because overwork leads to diminishing returns, crash programs are generally unsatisfactory, which is why careful planning that allows you to pace yourself—to drop what you are doing for a time and return later with renewed energy—is so important.

Some people, on the other hand, who require pressure to work at top capacity really prefer to start a report due at 3:00 P.M. at 2:30. If that suits you, fine, *as long as* the documentation or information needed for the report is at hand. Scrambling for information at the last minute only causes panic.

Some people like to schedule their days very closely, from hour to hour. That's fine as long as you allow yourself flexibility. Reserve at least an hour a day for unexpected events and keep some time just for yourself.

Many time management experts advise that you try to drop the low-priority, unimportant (#3) projects altogether, or postpone them into the indefinite future. But putting a project on the Daily List means it's on your mind, and ignoring it completely will create tension, which is even more nonproductive. I suggest that you reserve two or three hours a week, either in a block or divided up, strictly for #3 projects. Divide the tasks into small segments; clean out only one shelf of the medicine chest, answer only the ten oldest letters.

The Two-List Time Plan Summary

1. Each evening or early morning list approximately ten items to accomplish that day. This is your Daily List. Compose the list from items in your Master List, entries in your calendar, important projects in your "Things to do" file folder (page 66), and tasks that come up during the day.
2. Rank each item on the list #1, #2, or #3, depending on its importance or stress level.
3. Enter the Daily List tasks in your calendar so that they correspond, to the extent practicable, with your biological rhythms.
4. Cross each item off the list as you complete it, and transfer unfinished items to the next day's list.

THE EFFICIENCY ADVANTAGE

It's fun sometimes to figure out the fastest, most efficient, most timesaving way to do something. For example, in New York City, where many large office buildings have block-through lobbies, many steps can be saved by going from here to there by walking through lobbies rather than around the buildings on the street. (And it's nice in cold weather, when you can walk considerable distances via lobbies, going outside only to cross the street.)

Make better use of your hours and get the most from your time by taking advantage of a bouquet of efficiency techniques, tips, and tricks. Here follows a collection of some timesaving, time-enhancing approaches and techniques that have stood the test of time and seem to offer particularly exceptional time advantages.

Barter

If a job is inconvenient, distasteful, or unmanageable for you, you might consider bartering. Ask a friend or relative or colleague to take on a task in exchange for a service from you. Bartering can be a one-shot deal or it can be a systematic arrangement that you work out with somebody else.

An example of the one-shot deal is Marcie, who lives in a third-floor walk-up, sans doorman or elevator, who needed the not-so-terrible-looking hunk down the hall to help her up the stairs with her new stereo. He, on the other hand, was absolutely helpless at hanging his curtains. The only valances he knew about had to do with high school chemistry.

So they worked out a very equitable (and social, we

might add) exchange, with Marcie being his curtain-hanging advisor in exchange for his lugging up the stereo.

Eleanor and her cousin Harriet worked out a systematic barter arrangement. Eleanor hated bill paying and all the paperwork of handling money. Harriet, an accountant, took care of all Eleanor's money busywork, and in exchange Eleanor did Harriet's marketing twice a week when she did her own shopping.

Such a barter system is excellent for roommates, one of whom might always cook while the other one always cleans up.

Cooperative Arrangements

Cooperative arrangements are a boon above all to parents and people who care for children, because children tend to herd, and like most herds, they need a shepherd—to events like Little League, dancing class, gym, swim lessons, and certainly school. Babysitting too. So frequently co-opping is an effective way to keep a lifetime of chauffeuring under control.

For example, Ellen is a schoolteacher, so she was always able to bring a carload of kids with her to her school, which happened to be in her neighborhood. However, she frequently had to stay late for meetings and conferences after school, so she couldn't bring the kids home. It was convenient for Lydia, who was at home during the day, to pick the kids up every day at 3:30. In other words, Ellen and Lydia found, not identical, but conveniently dovetailing time frames.

Joanna and David, a married couple, alternated days rather than times. Since David had Thursdays off, he took care of all Thursday pickups and deliveries of Rebecca and Jimmy and their friends, including dancing school and

Little League, while Joanna handled Tuesdays. The remaining three weekdays were free, with the kids' comings and goings taken care of in co-opping arrangements with friends and neighbors.

Make Use of Services

Rely on the professionals. Journalist Jane O'Reilly once wrote in *New York* magazine, "I once spent a week getting a vaccination certificate stamped. I wondered, does Elizabeth Taylor have to do this? No, and neither did I. The travel agent will get the tickets and see to the certificate, free of extra charge." In fact, there are a lot of people who would like to help you out—usually, however, for a price. If you work, pay the premium to engage home repair people before 9:00 A.M. or in the evening. Exercise professionals and hairstylists make house or office calls. Answering services will take phone messages for you. Messenger services deliver packages. One working mother opened a charge account with a taxi company to pick up and deliver laundry and packages, and take her children to their various appointments.

Take advantage of pickup and delivery services offered by neighborhood merchants—the drugstore, dry cleaner, butcher, and fish market—or, if possible, hire a teenager or college student on the block for errands: do some marketing, pick up the shoes that were repaired, etc. Designate a spot for all items needing repair or cleaning. When you go out on a round of errands, check your Daily List and notebook to make sure that nothing is left out, and try to consolidate all your errands into one trip.

If you can afford it, a one-day-a-week cleaning person can be a boon. Draw up a list of regular assignments for your helper, and specify which products are to be used for what purpose. Within the first few sessions establish the standards of cleanliness you expect. An alternative that comes highly recommended is the professional cleaning service—a team of people who come in on a contract basis once or twice a week to clean the whole house. They can also be hired as needed for specific tasks you loathe. Check the Yellow Pages under "Cleaning Services" or "House Cleaning." Only patronize firms that are bonded and insured.

Double Up on Tasks

Many jobs that don't require your full concentration can be handled simultaneously. Listen to taped reports while driving to work, or dictate letters while stuck in traffic. Sort and sign routine papers while returning routine phone calls. Flip through trade magazines or your junk-mail folder when you're on the phone with a long-winded caller. Exercise while watching TV. Do mending while chatting or helping the kids with homework.

Make Use of Bits of Time

Plan small projects during waiting periods. Outline a report or pay bills while sitting in the doctor's office; polish silver while clothes are in the dryer; pick out a birthday card between appointments; make up the bed while waiting for the water to boil; make out your shopping list while riding on the bus. Most small chores can be accomplished in bits and pieces of time, as the following lists indicate:

What you can do in five minutes or less:

Make an appointment.
Make out a shopping list.

Correct a letter in the computer.
Make out a small-party guest list.
Dictate a short letter or write a note.
Set your VCR.
Update tomorrow's schedule on your family calendar.
File your nails.
Water the plants.

What you can do in ten minutes:

Pick out a birthday card.
Sort through the daily mail.
Order tickets for a concert or ball game.
Repot a plant.
Hand-wash some clothes.
Boot up your computer.
Scan a magazine article.
Dust the living room.
Clean up the top of your desk.
Do some isometrics or stretching exercises.

What you can do in thirty minutes:

Skim a report and mark parts for later study.
Go through backed-up journals, magazines, and news-
    papers.
Work on a crafts project.
Write thank-you notes.
Put last summer's photos in album.
Aerobic exercise.
Balance your checkbook.

One of the most helpful techniques I've found for myself to take care of those pesky little tasks that drive you nuts is what I call the "fifteener." I came to it this way:

One day I looked around and got very irritated at all the little "loose end" tasks that were still floating around and never getting done. For example, two weeks previously during a bout of kitchen reorganizing, I had piled some things on top of the refrigerator and now, two weeks later, they were still there. There were also some shoes to polish and a broken teapot handle to glue; some clothes that had come from the dry cleaner a week ago were still hanging on a hook and hadn't yet been put into the closet, etc.

I had been faithfully entering these jobs in my Master List, but then passing them right by.

I decided to set myself fifteen minutes on the kitchen timer, and do whatever I could in that period of time and then stop. I was amazed at how many of those jobs I was able to cross off my list. So I decided to employ the technique systematically. I rewrote all those little ditsy tasks that were outstanding (of which there was quite a slew at that point) on one of my grocery list sheets that are kept in the kitchen, and set myself two "fifteeners" a day. That was easy enough, as a break from other tasks, and I worked steadily down the list.

For shoe polishing and brass polishing and the like, to protect my clothes, I threw on an old chef's apron that covered me up completely. That way I couldn't evade these chores by the old "I'll get my clothes dirty" ploy.

The sweetest moment came about a week after I started the "fifteener" method when I went in to check the list and get started, and there wasn't anything left to do.

New tasks keep on acomin', of course, so I mark them on my fifteener list, and one fifteener a day usually keeps things pretty well up to snuff, with a temporary increase to two a day if the list builds up.

Plan Ahead

Set out clothes and breakfast utensils the night before. Check beforehand that you have all the necessary information to write a certain report. Make up a packing list for a trip a week or so in advance.

Consolidate

Return all phone calls during a specific time period rather than responding to each one. Combine errands: When you're out grocery shopping, also pick up the shoes and take in the broken lamp. Also consolidate movement: For instance, pull up the sheets, blanket, and spread on one side of the bed before crossing to the other. Keep file folders you use most often at your fingertips. Use rolling carts or mobile caddies whenever possible.

Laborsaving Technology

Use laborsaving devices or appliances as much as possible. Take advantage of easy-care materials, no-iron fabrics, "no-show" carpets.

Planning: Short- and Long-range

If you are working on a complex project, it is extremely important to pace yourself over the weeks or months that it takes. Consider, for instance, that you have been assigned overall responsibility in March for the December sales conference, an elaborate affair at a Florida resort hotel. The first thing to do—your #1 To Do the day the assignment is given—is to rough out the entire project. List all its main elements from start to finish—arranging a hotel, speakers, an agenda, audio-visual presentations—and list starting dates and deadlines for each component. Be *very* generous in your time estimates; double your first guess of how long each component will take.

List on a single sheet the starting and deadline dates for each component. They can, of course, overlap; you don't necessarily have to finish one aspect before going on to another. Then enter each starting and deadline date on your daily calendar. When you reach that page, you can then put that job or its subelements on your Daily List and follow up in the usual way.

Planning a less complex long-range job is easier, but the principle is the same. If, for example, you prepare your own taxes, select a deadline (preferably not too near the legal April 15 deadline), and list the components: Buy a current tax guide, pick up supplemental forms if necessary, assemble documentation, do the actual calculations, fill out the form and send it in. Enter each component in your daily calendar at an appropriate date, and on that date enter it on the Daily List.

Long-term planning should be determined by your goals and aspirations, whether they're specific ("I want to learn carpentry") or general ("I want to make a lot of money"). I don't intend to explore the question of defining your goals, but since the way you spend your time is ultimately a function of long-range goals, it's important to consider it, if only briefly.

The designer Milton Glaser challenged his students at the School of Visual Arts with a provocative assignment: Design a perfect day for yourself five years from now. Not a fantasy day, but a real day that you would like to see yourself living in five years, one that is fully satisfying in terms of work, relationships with family and friends, and physical environment. The day can be an extension of your present life if that is essentially satisfactory, or a complete turnabout.

List your goals as that day reveals them. If you envision yourself in the country, put that down. If you see yourself speaking French in a cosmopolitan setting, list that. These are major goals.

Then identify the information you will need to decide whether to pursue these goals seriously. Those interested in country life might research farming, rural social life, and job opportunities. The French-speaking sophisticate might look into French classes, jobs available in travel, translation, and diplomacy, and the qualifications that are required.

Once you've decided you're seriously interested in a particular goal, transfer your goal list to the Master List. Begin the next day's Daily List with a concrete action to get things started; for example, registering for a class. It may also be time to drop some activities that are not leading toward your goal.

At least two or three times a week thereafter add a concrete, goal-directed item to your Daily List. Feel free to drop or revise your goals at any time if they seem unrealistic or incompatible with your chosen life-style.

EFFICIENCY SABOTEURS: PROCRASTINATION, PERFECTIONISM, AND IRRITATIONS

There are two kinds of saboteurs that can rear their ugly heads, ruin your day, and perhaps damage your ability to function effectively. The difference between them is that one is caused by others, and the other is caused by you.

The outside saboteurs are those forces that threaten to interrupt you or throw you off course. The question of how to handle interuptions from others will be discussed on pages 94-101. But the question on the table right now is how to neutralize those sly *interior* villains of procrastination, perfectionism, and preventable irritations.

Procrastination

Putting off or delaying work is, to a large degree, caused by setting impossibly high standards. Knowing that the task simply cannot be done, you then attempt to ignore the work or put it off indefinitely. And justifying your inability to act by self-accusation—the "I'm just a lazy bum" syndrome—only locks you more firmly into a pattern of procrastination. You are, in effect, *instructing* yourself not to act!

How do you know if you're a procrastinator? If you "can't get started." If you find that you spend a lot more time in the morning puttering and muttering than doing. If projects that you're working on are habitually late. Or, you may finish the project, but only by dint of a panic-stricken, frantic, last-ditch, last-gasp effort. That's procrastination.

No matter how excellent the scheme or plan, procrastinating can screw it up and give you the unhappy sense that your life is out of control. But there are ways to transmit new instructions to yourself that supersede the old delaying tactics.

You may be a victim of the clear-the-boards self-blocking technique: "I'll clean up the workroom as soon as I . . ." The only answer is to force yourself, by an act of will, to put on blinders concerning other possible projects and take two *baby steps*. In the case of the workroom, lift one tool from the shelf, decide how to handle it, then lift another tool. When you've gone that far you will usually find the impetus to continue. If baby steps don't get you started, try again tomorrow. If you drop the job, *really* drop it, don't let it clutter your mind or your overwrought guilt mechanism.

Time management specialist Alan Lakein suggested punching holes into overwhelming projects by executing instant tasks that can be done in five minutes or less: drawing up a short outline of a report; making a phone call to get preliminary information.

Another effective method for punching holes in large tasks is to apply the *"Well, as long as I . . ."* technique: "Well, as long as I've got this file open I'll organize it." "As long as I've got the refrigerator open I'll wipe out one shelf." By the time you officially assign yourself the project, you may find that it's practically done.

These techniques are two examples of the basic remedy to procrastination: Break large tasks up into small pieces or parcels. In my experience, by far the greater number of instances of procrastination can be laid at the door of feeling stymied by a task that seems overwhelming. For example, many is the person who, inspired by the worthwhile ambition to reorganize the closets, pulls a whole closet's contents out onto the floor, says "Feh!" and pushes the whole mess back in again, worse off than before he started.

At The Organizing Principle we understand that laudable tendency to large ambitions which sometimes, however, require boiling down into more manageable specifics. The "task bites" or "parcels" that are specific to each topic, such as organizing paperwork, closets, home efficiency, are discussed in the chapters on those topics. In this section we will offer some "procrastination principles" that apply to numerous situations.

One way to break up a larger task is by *chunking*. To chunk a task, write it down on your Master List, and then list directly under the main head the task's pieces or "chunks." Elaine, the fitness instructor, entered the task "prepare fitness manual" in her Master List. Then, still in the Master List, she listed as subtasks: "draft initial outline," "review old class records to come up with interesting anecdotes," "talk to writer friend about possible collaboration," etc.

Martin Ellison applied the chunking concept to a different kind of project. Martin was a hobbyist carpenter, and he had recently taken an advanced carpentry and cabinetry course which equipped him (he hoped) to build a whole wall unit for his home which would include shelves, cabinets, drawers, and a pull-out bar. This was quite an elaborate project, which rather intimidated him by its magnitude. So he sat down one evening and brainstormed with himself as to every single aspect of this task, from measuring out the dimensions of the space and sketching a rough design to finally screwing the pulls onto the drawers. He didn't try to think of the tasks in sequence, but just as they occurred to him.

Once he had a pretty complete task list, *then* he put them in order, listed materials and tools he would need for each part of the project, and finally entered the whole thing on three pages of his Master List. Then, just as Elaine entered her specific tasks on her Daily List, Martin tried to do at least one or two specific tasks each day in the evening. On weekends he tried to reserve several hours for the project, making quite a dent in his list.

The project took four months, including final sanding and polishing and installation. And at the end of that time, Martin and his family had the enjoyment of a very handsome piece that enhanced their home, and gave Martin a special sense of pride.

Another technique that helps turn overwhelming projects into manageable tasks is the *six of one, half a dozen of the other* method. This method simply means that you process or handle a certain number of elements of the larger task each day, or on some other regular basis. If you're reorganizing a file system, you might say, "I'll go through and sort out three old files a day." If you've recently married and have many thank-you notes to send, it would be helpful and manageable to write five or seven a day.

Other similar types of divisions are geographical ("I'll review the client lists in Wisconsin first, then Minnesota, and then Nebraska") or sequential ("last year, this year, next year").

Arbitrarily *setting a fixed period of time* to tackle a large project is an extremely effective way of wrestling what might be an overwhelming task to the ground. *New York Times* health editor Jane Brody completed a 500-page book working from 5:00 to 6:30 on weekday mornings. One entrepreneur produced documentation for a bank loan on alternate Sunday mornings between 6:00 and 8:00—her only "free" time.

Because tasks that you tend to procrastinate on are most likely fairly knotty and/or stressful jobs, don't forget to rank them as #1 tasks that you accomplish in #1 time.

If resistance to a particular task is overpowering, consider whether it is possible to drop it altogether. Can you hire someone else to do it? Or delegate it? Or exchange it for a service to someone else? In addition, for an extra little zing, promise yourself a reward when you finish a job; a small reward for a small segment—a snack, a fifteen-minute yoga break, or a walk around the block—and a big reward for major accomplishments: a movie, a new pair of shoes, or even a day at the races.

Don't hesitate to avail yourself of the "barter" or "use services" or "delegate" options. Avoid the martyr stance of "I must do this job," and move instead to the effectiveness stance of "I must find a way to get this job done," which opens up a wealth of other options. If that is not realistic, it is worth taking some time to consider what the block might *mean*: Are you angry at your boss? Does the familiar chaos around you offer a kind of security? Do you dislike your job? Until you've solved the underlying problem, Lakein offers an interesting way to deal with the immediate inertia: Sit quietly with eyes closed and say to yourself, "Well, I'm not going to do it, but this is what I would do if I were going to do it." Fantasize yourself going through the motions, and very often energy will start to rise.

Perfectionism

Perfectionism is a significant factor in procrastination: overorganization, overcleanliness, overconscientiousness. The supply closet, when you get around to organizing it someday, will be a model of perfection. Pencils will be laid out in parallel lines. Each box of paper will be separately labeled and at right angles to the pencils. It's exhausting to contemplate and it's not what organizing is about.

Perfectionism Quiz

To determine whether you might be imposing standards that have more to do with an ideal of perfection than functional efficiency, ask yourself these questions:

1. Does the mere thought of the job you are planning make you groan with exhaustion because it seems overwhelming?
2. Are you most likely to put the pencils or pens all in one place on a part of the desk that looks neat, rather than the part of the desk next to the telephone where you would be more likely to use them?
3. Answer this statement "yes" or "no": I'm an all-or-

nothing person. If I can't do it exactly right, if I can't fulfill exactly the dream or image I have, then I'd rather not do it at all.

4. I want to reorganize my closets and finish by lining the shelving with scalloped edging. But in the meantime, because I can't find the time for such a big job, I have to leave the closets in chaos.

5. If I had to choose a roommate, I would feel more comfortable living with Felix, the neat one in *The Odd Couple*, rather than Oscar.

6. Do you think of alphabetizing your spices as perfectionistic rather than functional?

7. Do you think of having a specific location in the refrigerator for specific foods—for example, the cheese box is always on the second shelf in front on the right—as perfectionistic rather than functional?

If you answered questions 1–5 with a "yes" or "true," you probably are subject to some perfectionist tendencies. You might have answered 6 and 7 with a "yes" too. But those two questions are really intended to highlight the real differences between perfectionism and function.

Sure, it sounds a bit persnickety to alphabetize your spices. But those pesky little bottles can get lost very quickly, and keeping spices in alphabetical order makes good sense. It is, in a word, functional. Whereas, to draw a contrast, organizing your spices by red tops and green tops is nonfunctional because it fulfills no practical purpose.

And keeping the cheese in one place is functional too. If you see a blank spot in the refrigerator where you know the cheese usually is, that tells you immediately that you need cheese. Just ask your more casual spouse who poohpoohs this kind of arrangement to do the shopping and arranging for a few weeks, and he/she will soon find him/

herself overrun with cans of peas ("Oh, I didn't know we had that!"), meanwhile having run out of lima beans.

This whole book is oriented toward cutting down to size the exaggerated demands of the urge to perfectionism, and substituting in its place a realistic, manageable, and wholly functional organization.

Perhaps the single most effective technique for gaining mastery over destructive, and sometimes immobilizing, perfectionism is to apply two questions: the "payoff" and the "blocking" questions. The payoff question is:

> Is the amount of time I'm putting into a project (or more likely, *thinking* about putting into it) worth it in terms of what the final payoff might be? Is it worth it?

And second, even if there is a final payoff that makes the more elaborate or "perfect" solution worthwhile, the blocking question is:

> While waiting for the opportunity to accomplish the perfect or ideal goal, am I blocking the accomplishment of a more modest but workable solution, and causing discomfort or confusion to persist unnecessarily?

Small Insults:
Protecting Yourself from Irritation

Eliminating or ameliorating the many regular irritations, the small insults, that affect your life can provide important results. For example, an unpleasant daily route to work through an industrial wasteland may prove depressing. Waiting in line is anathema to many people. Take a few minutes to analyze the irritants that stud your day, and then revise your schedule or your environment in whatever ways possible to at least soften their effect.

One client, a young journalist, consulted me because she was having trouble meeting deadlines. Her working system was good and didn't seem to account for the difficulties. But when she happened to mention how much she hated her trip to work on two subways and a bus, I suggested that the travel ordeal might be making her tense, and proposed an alternate route that eliminated one subway. The change took ten minutes longer, but was much more pleasant. Two weeks later the deadline problem was in hand. My client had not realized how much her entire attitude toward her work had been affected by her arduous commute.

"I do it this way because that's how I've always done it" is not written in stone. Make sure to examine and reexamine old habits and old priorities and see if they are still workable for you.

Flexible thinking and analysis of alternatives is the key: If lines are a problem, plan bank visits to avoid the lunchtime crowd, or catch the early evening showing of a popular movie. One woman who was frazzled by rush-hour crowds renegotiated her office hours to avoid traveling with crowds.

The task of examining and discarding bypassed notions applies to the big questions as well as to the small. For example, shibboleths like "Anything I want done right I have to do myself" must be looked at carefully and sometimes discarded.

Physical decor or environment can have a strong psychological effect on your mood and work habits. Don't just resign yourself to the office you were assigned; adapt it to your pleasure: Hang a few pictures, paint the walls, or recover the chair. Do as much as your employer will allow to make your working environment comfortable for *you*. The office is "home" for so many hours that it is well worth the time and money to make it as pleasant as possible. And you may find yourself working more efficiently in an atmosphere that *you* have designed to your taste.

4

Conquering the Paper Tiger: What to Do with Paper, How to File It, When to Throw It Away

From my experience, paper—letters, bills, communications and information of infinite variety—is the single greatest human irritant. And yet, there are only three things that can be done with a piece of paper: It can be thrown away; something can be *done* about it, such as writing a letter or making a phone call; or it can be temporarily put away. This holds true for a private individual conducting a modest amount of personal business or for IBM; IBM just has more paper to handle.

The difficulties of handling paper arise when one must choose which papers have value and which do not. It is not uncommon to feel that one's life is somehow bound up with keeping papers and files, and the idea of throwing anything out can be quite frightening.

I remember one client, an elderly woman whose small New York apartment was massed with the paper accumulations of a lifetime. She wanted desperately to clear out this stifling undergrowth, and yet when I came to her home she was trembling and close to tears. "I just know," she said, "that you're going to take my past away. My life, my history, is in these papers."

I explained to her that what I try to do is help people choose what has value for them; and sentimental or historical value has just as much meaning as financial value. I would never force this woman to throw away anything; I would simply help her to make those value/nonvalue distinctions in order to make her life more orderly.

As we worked, my client realized that much of the material stacked up in her apartment had no meaning to her. We kept the papers that really did contain her life history; other musty documents that she was saving because somehow, someday, one of them might "come in handy," we threw out. By the end of that day she had learned how to discriminate between valuable and valueless papers, and thus was able to throw many away with a clear conscience.

Other people may not have accumulated great masses of paper, but they have never learned how to *use* paper as a means of carrying on the business of life. That is another purpose of this chapter: to teach you how to let paper assume its true function as a cue and a trigger for action, not as a smothering weight in your life.

In order to learn this lesson, let's trace the fortunes of an imaginary day's mail. We will follow this batch of mail through all the stages of its life, until, by the end of the chapter, you will be able to face any mass of paper, big or small, with the confidence that you know how to integrate it into your life.

FOLLOWING THE PAPER TRAIL:
TRACING THE DAY'S MAIL

You have just picked up the daily mail; before glancing at it, immediately take the mail to your office area. Your schedule may be such that you can't work on it now, which is fine; in that case, just drop it off on your desk. Do *not* sit down on the living room couch and start opening letters. Opening mail elsewhere than your designated "office" adds an extra physical action and an extra thought process. Once you are surrounded with the torn envelopes and the contents of the mail, you will have to gather it all up again and take it to your desk for sorting and action. Or, more likely, you will *not* take it back to the desk and sort it. Rather, everything will look such a mess that your stomach will begin to tighten and you will push that day's mail—and perhaps several other days'—out of sight.

By taking the mail to your desk, you are "intersecting" with the system designed precisely to deal with that kind of activity. In fact, this "intersection" idea applies to many different contexts. This particular variation of it can be stated:

Principle #4 **Always carry out actions in a location that intersects with the system designed to deal with those actions.**

Stage One: Sorting It Out

Now you are sitting comfortably at your desk with a stack of mail before you.

There are seventeen pieces:

1. Electric bill
2. Department store bill
3. Personal letter to you
4. Personal letter to your spouse
5. Letter from your lawyer asking you and your spouse to set up an appointment to discuss some property you have just bought
6. The deed to your new property
7. Notice of sale at local camera store
8. Invitation to a surprise party for your neighbor next week
9. Flyer from your congressperson telling you how well he/she is doing in Washington, D.C.
10. Local repertory theater schedule for this coming season
11. Letter from local Boys Club asking you to contribute time toward putting together the annual fund-raising fair
12. Notice from the doctor that it is time for your child's annual polio booster
13. Magazine subscription renewal notice
14. L. L. Bean Catalog
15. Brochure from Learning Annex
16. Two magazines
17. Newspaper

These miscellaneous bits of paper all fall into one of the three broad categories outlined at the beginning of the chapter: those to be thrown away; those to be acted upon; and those filed for reference. You will need the following "places" in order to sort your paperwork:

A wastebasket
File folders marked:
    Things to do

To file
Your spouse's name (if you have one)
Financial

The two last categories are special but necessary subdivisions of the "things to do" category. You can use pretty baskets or boxes instead of file folders, but I've found that the folders are the most practical. They can be put away out of sight in your file drawer, or you can leave them out on the desk in one of those standup organizers.

Let's begin by tracking through the pile piece by piece:

1. Electric bill. This goes into your financial folder. All documents related to money should be placed in the financial folder for handling all at one time. This includes bills, bank statements, canceled checks, investment notices, etc.

2. Department store bill. Also put into the financial folder.

3. Personal letter to you. After you have read it, assuming you plan to reply, slip it into your "Things to do" folder.

4. Personal letter to your spouse. Put into the folder marked with your spouse's name.

5–6. Letter from lawyer and deed. This is actually two items. The letter requires discussion with your spouse so it goes into the spouse folder. The deed is slipped into the "To file" folder or basket.

7. Notice of sale at local camera store. Many people have a terrible time deciding what to do with miscellaneous pieces of paper like this one. Because there may be some ambiguity involved, let's go through the alternatives pretty thoroughly. The question to ask yourself is, "Do I care?" Does someone else in the household care? Consider these possibilities:

    a. Your spouse is a camera buff. Then, the spouse folder seems like a good place.

    b. *You* are a camera buff and there are some supplies you have been meaning to buy. Put the notice in the "Things to do" folder.

    c. You do photographic work, but don't need anything now. If the name and address of the store is valuable information to you, put the notice in the "To file" folder.

    d. You don't do photography, have never done photography, don't think you ever will do photography, but someday you just might want to know about this store. Then the notice goes out. Yes, out. This information has no current meaning for you; to save it is to clutter up your life uselessly. If you ever do need a camera store, go to the Yellow Pages or get suggestions from friends.

        Remember that saving things for a rainy day, or because they might come in handy sometime, is self-destructive. Fear is the driving force that causes people to cling to things that have no value to them. Learn to master that fear by making decisions about what has real value for you and what doesn't. Then you will be well on your way to getting organized!

8. Invitation to surprise party next week. Is this something to be discussed with your spouse? If so, the spouse folder is where it goes. If you yourself make the social decisions, then slip the invitation into your "Things to do" folder.

9. Flyer from your congressperson. Do you care? Again, this is the important question. If you are actively involved in politics, then you might indeed want to read it and even save it to follow an issue you are partic-

ularly concerned about. If you want to keep it, the information goes in "To file." But if it is of no special interest, then out it goes.

10. Local repertory theater schedule. Again, does this information have value to you? If so, you might want to make plans with your spouse. In that case, the schedule goes into the spouse folder. Or perhaps you will buy some tickets just for yourself, or yourself and some friends. Then, put it into "Things to do." If there is no genuine interest—out!

11. Boys Club letter. If this is a personal letter that you have to deal with in some way, it is a "Thing to do." But if it is a form letter, you can throw it out if you're not interested.

12. Polio booster. A "Thing to do."

13. Magazine subscription renewal. If you are not going to renew, throw it out. If you are, the notice is a "Thing to do."

14. L. L. Bean catalog. Flip through it quickly to see if there's anything you might want to buy. Don't make a decision now, but if something catches your eye, tear the page out, together with the order form and envelope, staple them together, and put them in the financial folder. Throw the rest of the catalog away. That way, after you've paid your bills, you'll see how your funds stand, and can order your purchases then.

15. Learning Annex brochure. Flip through quickly and book any courses you know you want to take. Are there some maybes? Tear those pages out and mark the outside date in your calendar by when a decision has to be made. Put the clipped pages in your "Things to do" file (see page 66) and throw the rest of the brochure away.

16. Two magazines. Keep all your unread magazines in one place and make sure they are read and thrown

away regularly. If you find that a particular magazine is accumulating unread, then stop the subscription.

17. Newspaper. Basically the newspaper should go into the "Things to do" file because it should be read quickly. People respond to their daily newspaper in different ways. Most read it and get rid of it, but some hold on to their newspapers. I've worked with many a client whose stacks of newspapers blocked out light and air. This is one instance where you must be extremely firm about throwing out. Get rid of every newspaper right up to yesterday's if you haven't read it, and add "no time to read the newspaper" to your list of "life problems" to be solved!

Be sure and recycle the papers whenever possible!

There is also the question of clippings. Newspapers provide much useful information about stores, services, travel, restaurants, health information, etc. By all means clip anything interesting, and put your clippings in "To file."

Once you get the hang of the sorting process, it won't take even half as long to do as it takes to read about it. Here is a straightforward summary of what we have just done. You can consult it every time you work at your desk, until the steps become automatic:

Sorting Checklist

1. Divide the mail according to what has interest and value to you and what does not.
2. Throw away the "no interest" pile.
3. Divide what you're saving into reference piles and action piles. Put the reference pile into the "To file" box or folder.
4. The "action" material can be divided still further.

Things having to do with money—bills, banks, financial statements—go into the financial folder, which is handled once a month. There is a special folder for things to discuss with your spouse; otherwise, all action materials go into the "Things to do" folder.

Stage Two: "Things to Do" and Follow-up

Once everything has been sorted out and set into its appropriate folder, you are ready to begin actual work.

If your spouse is available, I suggest dealing with that folder first, so those items can be integrated into your main "Things to do." If that is not possible, be sure to go over the folder with him or her before your next "office hours" session.* Then the items that require more work—ordering theater tickets, for example—can be slipped into the "Things to do" file for the next "office hours" session, and the rest can be thrown away or put into the "To file" folder.

Now take out your "Things to do" folder. Make those phone calls, write those letters, do whatever is called for. To make it clear how this works and how to tie it in with the other elements of your paperwork system, let's deal with a few of the items from the morning mail that landed in the "Things to do" folder.

Personal letter to you
Camera store notice
Surprise-party invitation

---

*Set a regular time for personal and family "office hours" that fits into your existing schedule. Two hours a week is sufficient for most people, either in one sitting or divided up. Don't try to catch up on backed-up organizing work in this time period; this is for current business. Go through the older materials in the time period you chose for organizing (Chapter 2, page 21).

Repertory theater schedule
Polio booster notice

After you have answered the personal letter you may want to save it, in which case the letter goes into "To file." Otherwise throw it out. As for the camera store notice, make a note to yourself in your notebook (which is always with you, of course!) to go to the camera store during your next shopping trip. Then if the notice itself contains some information you want or need, tuck it in the notebook or stick it up on your bulletin board.

The invitation to the party requires two actions: an RSVP and, assuming you plan to go, marking it down in your appointment calendar. Similarly with the theater schedule: Send for your tickets and mark the dates on the calendar. For the polio booster notice, call your doctor and make an appointment for your child to get his or her shot, mark it on your calendar, and then put the notice in "To file."

There is one other area we haven't mentioned yet. What do you do when you plan to *initiate* a project? Suppose, for instance, you start thinking about getting a cost estimate for turning the garage into a family room. Right then and there, jot the idea down in your notebook. Thus, your office hours will also include, besides responding to mail that comes in, checking your notebook for self-initiated projects requiring your attention. When you decide to get in touch with the contractor about an estimate, write, don't phone. Phone requests are lost very easily because not everyone is as organized as you are going to be! Keep a duplicate of the letter itself and put it into a new file folder labeled "Pending" or pin it on the bulletin board. Then—*this is really important in order to keep your system flowing*—mark on your appointment calendar a date by which you might reasonably expect a reply. If, for example, you mail the letter on Monday the 18th, and estimate that the contractor needs a week and a half to think the thing over, mark "contractor?" on your calendar for Wednesday the 27th. This cryptic question will indicate that you should follow up if you haven't heard anything by that day.

If the contractor does get in touch, make notes of any discussion on the copy of the letter, mark any appointments you make on the calendar, and put the letter in "To file."

"Things to Do" Checklist

1. Go through each piece of paper in the "Things to do" pile and respond to it in some way—write a letter, make a phone call, whatever is appropriate.
2. "Track" each piece of paper, after you have worked on it, into its proper channel: wastebasket, "Pending," or "To file."
3. If there is to be any follow up, mark that in your calendar.
4. Check your notebook for projects that you want to set in motion, and do whatever has to be done.
5. Check the appointment calendar for any notices scheduled for that day, and follow up.

After a while this rhythm will come so naturally to you, you'll wonder how you ever had trouble with it before.

Stage Three: The Fine Art of Filing and Finding Again

Once you've taken care of "Things to do," all that's left is to file whatever remains in the "To file" folder. The idea of filing frightens some people; they feel they will never be able to find anything again. Don't let such fears get the better of you. Keep in mind that we are simply dealing with pieces of paper that are going to be put away precisely in order that they *can* be found again.

The process is simple. Examine each piece of paper, establish its reason for being in the file (which gives the clue for categorizing it), and then physically place the paper in one or another labeled file folder. The trick is, of course, to file things under the right labels so that you can find them again. Let's follow this procedure with that imaginary pile of mail that ended up in the "To file" folder:

1. Personal letter. Personal letters are usually saved because the writer's correspondence has emotional value for you. How do you categorize this piece of paper? It is a *personal letter*. The first clue to setting up a file folder is to determine the *broadest* category that a piece of paper can belong to. Nine times out of ten, that broad category is perfectly sufficient to label any file folder. In this case, take out a file folder and label it "Letters" or "Personal letters." Then slip the letter into the folder, and that's it.

Let's say, though, that you have stacks and stacks of personal mail to keep—much too much to fit into one folder. Then you might want to subdivide the letters into more than one category. One alternative is to do it by date: "Letters '91," "Letters '92," "Letters '93." Or you might label folders with the individual names of the persons who sent the letters. Now we get into a slightly confusing area, the kind of point that throws people off. Should these folders be labeled "Letters, Susan," or "Susan, Letters," or what? If the *person* is the relevant subject, then the folder should be labeled "Susan," or "Michael," rather than "Letters, Susan" or "Letters, Michael." If Susan and Michael are so important that there's a whole folder's worth of letters from each of them, there will probably be other materials about Susan or Michael that will go into the same folder. In other words, if you ask the question "What is the file about?" and the answer is the *person*, not "letters," then the name should go on the label.

2. Property deed from the lawyer. This could be confusing. Should the deed be filed under the name of the lawyer? Or, supposing this specific property is located in a little town called Eastgate, perhaps it should be filed under "Eastgate"? Again, what is this piece of paper about in its *broadest* terms? The answer is "property." Unless you have a great many holdings indeed, the chances are that any correspondence or documents about all of your property will fit into one single folder.

Don't forget the accompanying letter sent by the lawyer. Right now it is out to be discussed with your spouse, but when the letter is ready to be filed, I would suggest slipping it into the same folder as the deed. This brings to mind another tip for filing: Papers connected to each other are filed with each other.

But why not use the name of the lawyer or law firm? If they are your regular attorneys you may already have a correspondence file headed with the name of the firm. In that case, shouldn't this property material go into that folder, on the principle of unifying materials as much as possible? Good thinking, but on the whole I recommend that you set up a "property" folder. You will probably, over time, accumulate material concerning this piece of property from sources other than the lawyer—tax assessments, contractors doing improvements, etc.—so the focus of the file is the property, not the lawyer. However, the argument in favor of filing the deed under the lawyer's name is a good one and could give rise to legitimate debate. I suggest that you use a device known as a "cross-reference" to draw your attention from one file to another. Thus, in this particular case, write a little note saying, "Material concerning property in 'Property' file," and slip the note into the file headed by the attorney's name.

3. Camera store notice. In this case, "Photography" is the most obvious and broadest answer to the question "What is this piece of paper about?" That heading makes the most sense, *so long as there are other materials on photography* to keep it company. The other materials might include a "how-to" article on taking pictures in dim light, or a clipping discussing the relative merits of different types of cameras, but no item should ever repose alone in a file. The point is to devise *broad categories*.

If there are no other file materials concerned with photography, choose the next broad category it might fit into. It is also a store, which gives us the broader, useful heading of "Stores" or "Shopping"—whichever term is more comfortable for you.

4. Flyer from congressperson. If your interest in politics is vital enough to warrant saving the flyer, the obvious choice for a file heading would be "Politics." Or if you plan to save the flyer for its discussion of a specific issue on which you are collecting other material, such as "Environment" or "Foreign Policy," then the flyer fits most comfortably into the folder headed by the name of the issue.

5. Notice about polio booster. Here the choices are pretty obvious: One option is the broad heading "Medical," while the other one seems to be the name of the child. In this instance, there are two equally clear-cut answers to the question "What is it about?" The notice is as much about "medical" as it is about the child. Simply choose the alternative which triggers an association for you, and then stick to it consistently over time.

Thus, if you choose "Medical," the entire family's medical history would be kept in that folder; that would be the subject. If you prefer to keep the medical information in an individual folder for each member of the family, it would be placed in the same folder with other papers having to do with that individual, including letters. It doesn't matter, as long as you follow a consistent path one way or the other.

6. Newspaper clippings. As a tip to lessen your reading load, pick out the specific magazine or newspaper articles you want to read from the table of contents rather than by flipping through the whole issue, which invariably means you will end up reading the entire issue. For the sake of discussion, let's suppose you have cut out five articles to be filed for reference. Here's how to file them, always remembering that central question, "What is the piece about for me?"

a. An article on how much Vitamin C to take if you feel a cold coming on. The umbrella term here is "Health" and that is what the file should be headed. If you are in the habit of cutting out articles like this, make a separate folder for this subject. Otherwise put the clipping in your medical folder dealing with other medical matters.

b. An article giving tips on hotels in Tahiti, where you've always wanted to go. Why not "Travel"?

c. A piece on craft schools. This subject is a little ambiguous and will need some thinking through. If you have various other materials on the broad subject of crafts, then this seems like the obvious heading. But if you're in a general self-improvement mood and are cutting out lists of classes in a variety of different areas, then maybe "Schools," "Instruction," "Classes," or some related term that evokes an association from you is the answer. Or maybe "Self-improvement," if that term covers a variety of different items for you.

A client of mine came up with a fine idea for problems of this kind. We had been going through her files, and eventually collected a little batch of items that we couldn't decide what to do with—things like a list of craft schools, instructions on making a lamp out of an old bottle, a few books she planned to read one day. There weren't enough items to make individual files, but we still had to make some decision— and *not* "Miscellaneous," please! Any file labeled "Miscellaneous" is going to prove a horror. My client mused for a moment and then said, "How about 'Aspirations'? These are all my aspirations for the future." It was perfect for her, and it might be perfect for you.

d. Review of a newly opened nightclub. How about "Entertainment"?

e. An article on where to find the best selection of sweaters. Put this item in a "Stores" or "Shopping" folder, the same one that contains the camera store notice. If you find that folder is becoming too bulky with items on clothing, you might want to take those items out and set them up in a separate folder called "Clothing" or "Fashion." Similarly, if you are a woman, you might find that quite a few of your shopping items have to do with cosmetics, hairdressers, etc., and in that case you might want to make a separate "Beauty" folder, or include beauty items in "Fashion." Sit quietly for a moment and let yourself respond to the association your mind makes spontaneously. Follow it through and you'll be fine.

One final tip about your personal filing system: It is usually a good idea to file every folder in strict alphabetical order by its heading, and avoid any subgroupings that may occur to you. One client, for example, proposed to collect all the folders concerned with the members of her family —Susan, Mary, Tom—and group them in one "Family" section. I advised against that plan, and recommended that "Susan" just be filed under "S," "Mary" under "M," and so on. This kind of overarching category is not usually a good idea because, in order to find the file again, you have to remember both the major heading *and* the subheading.

File Reorganization Checklist

Here is a filing checklist which can be used to develop a system from scratch; to revise an existing system that isn't working well; or to maintain effective files on a day-to-day basis.

1. Gather together all materials to be filed so that they are all in one location.
2. Have a wastebasket or box for trash handy, along with file folders, labels, and pen.
3. Pick up the item on the top of the pile (or the first paper in the first folder if you are revising an existing file) and decide whether this item has value for you. If it does not, throw it away. If it does, go on to the next step.
4. If the piece of paper is worth retaining, ask yourself the question "What is this about *for me*?" and choose a folder heading for it.
5. Now label the file folder and slip the piece of paper in. Here are some of the most typical headings for a home file:

Computer Information
Decoration
Entertainment
Excursions (for example, things to do with the kids, weekend jaunts)
Fashion
Financial

Health
Household
Insurance
Investment Documents
Legal Documents
Letters *or* Correspondence
Medical
Property
Receipts for Major Purchases
Restaurants
School & Camp
Services (household services, such as plumbers, electricians)
Taxes
Travel
Warranties & Guarantees (for appliances, television sets)

6. Pick up the next piece of paper and go through the same procedure, the only variation being that this new piece of paper might well fit into an already existing file, rather than one with a new heading. Consolidate as much as possible.
7. When your mind begins to blur, stop filing for that day.
8. Assemble your pile of file folders and put them in strict alphabetical order.
9. Put your alphabetized folders into your file drawer, prop them upright with the sliding support in the drawer, close it, and you are finished for this session.
10. Finally, to maintain your file once it is established, each time you consult a file folder, riffle through it quickly to pick out and throw away the dead wood.

The Desk Check

At the end of your office hours, or at the end of the work day, assure that papers won't go out of control again and make ready for tomorrow by carrying out the three-point desk check:

1. Are all "To do" papers in the "To do" file?
2. Are all "To file" papers in the "To file" box?
3. Any papers left out on the desk are as yet untracked. Track them before you leave. Any paper you're unsure of means that some decision has to be made—even if the decision is only whether or not to throw it away. Making a decision is an act, and therefore the paper is a "To do."

SETTING UP A PAPERWORK SYSTEM FROM SCRATCH

You now have a good background in all of the basic ways to handle the flow of paper in your life. What about those poor souls who have to start from scratch, whose lives are currently so disorganized that they have nothing but a bare desk surface and some basic supplies? First, gather together all your paperwork from its various locations throughout the house. Ferret out those piles of magazines, canceled checks, clippings, and documents from closets, drawers, the kitchen table, and wherever they can be found. What-ever and wherever your paper may be, pull it *all* together and collect it at your desk or in your work area.

Don't panic if your papers fill a carton or two or five. These cartons may look as if they will take months to go through, but they won't. The longest home office job I *ever* had took only three days!

Once the material is collected, make up the basic file

folders we've discussed—Things to do, To file, Spouse, Financial, and Pending. Then start out with the top of the pile, just as we did with the "daily mail" example, and take care of each item. One word of caution: Don't work too long at one sitting on this job. Your mind will become fuzzy. Just make sure that you keep those regular appointments with yourself; those parts of the day that you have promised to devote to getting your life together. You will be surprised at how quickly the papers move out of their cartons and into the wastebasket or their new homes. In no time at all you will bring order and clarity out of chaos.

TWO FILING PROBLEMS: FILE OVERFLOW AND LONG-TERM FILES

File Overflow

If you've got more file cabinets than your space can comfortably hold, not to mention allowing for growth, any one of four approaches might bring the problem under control.

Divide and conquer. Divide your files into three categories: "deep storage," occasional use, and current use. Pack up the "deep storage" folders—materials with legal or historical or nostalgia value (see pages 78–80)—and store them in an old file cabinet or in storage boxes assigned to the garage or attic. Tape a list of what's inside to the side of the cabinet or box against the possibility that you'll need the materials again.

Files that you consult maybe once or twice a week, or at any rate, often enough that they shouldn't be too far away, are "occasional use" files. File them in accessible cabinets kept outside the office area.

Current or "fingertip" files—files you consult frequently or need at once when you need them—are what's left. These files should go in your immediate office area.

With luck, dividing your files up according to immediacy of use will open up your office file space considerably.

Double-use files. Fortunately, file cabinets—especially two-drawer cabinets—can be configured in lots of ways, thus giving you lots of space-saving file options. Create a desk by setting a slab over two two-drawer filing cabinets, leaving leg space in between them. With enough wall space, three filing cabinets might fit in. Also, two-drawer cabinets will often fit underneath the slab-on-supports desk style.

Banks of file cabinets might be placed right up against the front of your desk, giving you an extra surface for equipment or other uses, or they can be lined up behind you in place of a credenza.

Stand-alone files. A rack of hanging files (Pendaflex) can stand on a shelf or atop a file cabinet by itself, or even on the floor. Frankly, file racks hanging about give an office a cluttered look, but if file space is at a premium, hanging-file racks can increase your options.

File reorganization. In my experience, a thoroughgoing file reorganization often reduces a filing system by one third or more. See page 74 for an approach to a file reorganization.

Long-term Files and Storing Valuable Papers

While each of Jesse's nursery finger paintings was your family's crown jewels, some of the luster has diminished as you find yourself drowning in a sea of kiddie art a scant year later. *Do* you keep Jesse's drawings? If so, for how long, and where and how do you keep them? If truth be told, memorabilia—cards, letters, invitations, photos, finger paintings, personal souvenirs of all kinds—can sometimes be a precious burden.

The same questions arise in regard to valuable papers

that you might want or need to keep for legal or historical purposes.

There's only one criterion for whether or not to keep a piece of *memorabilia*. Is it precious to you and your family? One way to help you select what to keep is to ask yourself, "If the house were on fire and I ran out and left this behind, how much would I regret losing it?" Whether it be play programs, your high school prom corsage, old Christmas cards and letters . . . if you want them, then keep them! The key is simply to make a definite decision based on a strong preference.

On the other hand, you do not want to drown in the stuff. One ardent collector of personal memorabilia maintains a sort of halfway house in two egg-crate cartons set up against the family room wall. Everyone drops in anything they think someone might want to keep. Then, at Christmas break and end of term, the chief collector and her children sort through everything, toss a good deal that doesn't seem essential anymore, and bundle the rest up in folders or manila envelopes labeled "Jesse—Nursery School" and the date, "Birthday Cards," etc. (It's helpful to label the side of the packet as well.) The folders are then deposited into the "family archives"—two beat-up file cabinets that live in the garage.

One woman, Marjorie, who didn't want old memories around anymore, but couldn't bring herself to actually toss them out, packed up her old papers in boxes and stored them in a kindly friend's basement for six months. She arranged with her friend that in six months either she would take the boxes back or her friend would throw them out.

When the six months were up, Marjorie decided she had survived without the boxes, bit the bullet, and asked her friend to throw the boxes out without her looking at them again.

Legal/historical files divide into two categories: those that are active and in force, and those that are primarily of historical or archival interest.

Archival documents include the following:

1. *House and property.*   Save your deed and anything pertaining to title, building plans, and records of any significant repairs, remodeling, or add-ons. Also include inspection reports. These records can affect taxes, insurance claims, refinancing, and the resale value of your home.

   Is it worthwhile to keep records on property you no longer own? Maybe. You never can tell.

2. *Insurance.*   Keep policies currently in force in the safe-deposit box at the bank. Many people like to keep old policies for informational purposes, though it's probably not necessary.

3. *Banking and financial materials.*   Questions rarely arise relating to old bank passbooks, old investment transactions, old mortgages, and the like, but it's not a bad idea to keep those old papers anyway. Such documents give you a picture of your financial history, which is often interesting and illuminating.

A fireproof safe or file cabinet in your garage, basement, or attic would be a prudent choice for these historical materials. Protect them against dampness and mildew.

Tip: Make a list of your "archival" files and indicate where they are kept. File the list in the "Household" folder of your general filing system.

Addendum: Addresses and Special Dates

Two questions that people ask me over and over are: How do you keep track of the stores or services you may someday

YOUR VITAL DOCUMENTS CHECKLIST

Store all legal documents, securities, insurance policies, and so forth—any papers whose loss would create great hardship—in a safe-deposit box or fireproof safe. A key question in determining what to save: If there were a fire, which documents would you most hate to lose? List these documents and their whereabouts, keep one copy of the list for yourself, send one copy to a trusted relative or friend, and send one to your lawyer. This list should include:

Bank account information. Include account names, numbers, signers, banks, and any bank officers you deal with.

Credit card information. Keep a list of credit card account numbers and also list any outstanding loans.

Insurance policies. For each policy, list type (fire, liability, etc.), insurer, agent or contact, number and date, key provisions (optional but wise), and expiration or renewal date, if any.

Inventory. Insurance specialists recommend that you make up a complete inventory of valuable articles in your home such as furniture, jewelry, and antiques. Note the date and place of purchase, and the purchase price. It is wise to photograph any particularly valuable articles and attach them to the inventory list.

Legal documents. Examples are incorporation or partnership instruments, certifications, licenses, leases, and deeds and titles.

Safe-deposit box. The following types of documents should generally be kept in your safe-deposit box: *Personal data*—birth certificates, marriage licenses, divorce papers, adoption papers, passports, nuptial and prenuptial agreements, naturalization papers. Important note: Do not put the original of your will in the safe-deposit box. *Financial and legal data*—ownership deeds for car, boat, antiques, jewelry, other valuables, negotiable securities, stocks and bonds, insurance policies, home deed and mortgage documents, leases and rental agreements, IRA documentation, Keogh Plan documentation.

Tax returns and supporting materials. Keep IRS returns

for six years, then discard or store indefinitely, as you wish. Keep backup materials (canceled checks, bills, receipts, etc.) easily accessible for three years, then store for another three years, after which they can usually be discarded. Confirm with your lawyer or accountant.

Warranties and bills of purchase for major items such as appliances, expensive camera or computer equipment, jewelry, antiques, etc.

Consulting professionals. List names and addresses of attorneys, accountants, brokers, insurance agents, bankers, and so forth.

Will. Leave the original with your lawyer and keep a copy at home. Don't put the original in a safe-deposit box.

need, and how do you remember birthdays and special anniversaries from year to year?

The solution to the first problem is to set up your personal classified phone directory. Suppose you collect antiques. List "Antique Dealers" all together under "A" rather than under the names of the firms. Similarly, "Furniture Restorers" would go together under "F." It's generally a good idea to use a different address book for your personal "Yellow Pages" rather than combining them with your personal address book. One client, instead of using an address book, bought a handsome rotary file with plastic pockets—actually intended for photographs—and slipped the firms' business cards into the pockets. If you always think of a firm by its name, then list it that way with a cross-reference to its function. You might, for instance, enter "Acme Cleaners" under "A," and then enter under "C," "Cleaners—see Acme."

To remind yourself of birthdays and anniversaries, make up a master list. Then enter each individual date on your calendar, and staple the list itself to the last page of the calendar. Make a note to yourself in late December to "transfer birthday list and dates" to next year's calendar. This can be carried over from year to year.

PART THREE

An Organizing Guide to Working at Home

5

Timespace:
Negotiating
Quality Time

Marsha was a computer programmer who became a full-time homemaker for a few years when her children were very small, but she kept her skills updated, and once both children were in school she decided to start a business as a part-time computer programmer working out of her home.

Within two weeks she was driving herself and everyone else nuts. She would get up at 6:30 in the morning, scrub the kids clean, get them ready for school, pack the lunches, drive the kids to school, come back, make up some beds and clear the kitchen, and sit down to her computer at 10:00 A.M. At which time, invariably, her mother would call for a morning chat.

These chats had once been a joy for Marsha, but now they were much more of an obligation and a little bit of a nuisance. Marsha's mother had started picking up on the annoyance cues in Marsha's voice, had begun making some comments of her own, and things were getting a little tense.

By 10:30, Marsha had begun to sweat because she was beginning to feel that she was falling behind.

At 12:00, one of the children came home for the day. Marsha, at this point—hardly having accomplished an hour of work—made Kevin's lunch, chatted about the day with him, and played a game for a half hour or so.

By now, it was about 2:00 and Marsha could work another hour until 3:00, when Janie came home. Then it was pretty much the same routine, including milk and cookies. At that point, Marsha started dinner.

Joe, Marsha's husband, arrived home about 6:30 and demanded his time to talk about his day. Then it was dinner, and now the children needed to be bathed and tucked into bed.

So it was now 8:00 or 8:30, which didn't exactly leave time for things like the wash, dusting, cleaning, watering the plants, and all the other things that had to be done. Meanwhile Joe had begun to notice that some dishes have stayed longer in the sink than they should have, and the dust was piling up. The last straw was Joe's innocent query, "Hey, Marsha, why didn't you take my blue suit to the cleaner's? You know, you always do that. What happened?" Explosion and nervous-breakdown time—because Marsha herself was feeling guilty about her inability to be Supermom and, as the phrase goes, "to have it all."

Thus, Marsha's decision to work for what really amounted to no more than a few hours a day wound up becoming a gargantuan issue involving a huge number of fights and irritations and tensions.

This sounds like an impossible situation. But it's not. This situation can be solved.

The key to solving the problem of working at home is *selective control*: to refocus and harness the time you can control, and institute defensive measures to minimize the impact of the demands that you can't control.

Men and women are increasingly opting to work from the home. The explosion in the availability of relatively inexpensive technology—computers and other machines such as fax machines and home copiers—that can be used in the home, and the ability to hook up with long-distance computer networks, now make it not only affordable but reasonable to work from the home. Alvin Toffler, in his book *The Third Wave*, predicts the return of workers to the "electronic cottage"—that is, to the home. These are the new cottage industries of the nineties and beyond.

Home-based enterprises are particularly advantageous for families with small children, giving them opportunities for flexible time arrangements, time with the children, and just generally providing greater stability for the family unit. Interestingly enough, it can also be financially advantageous. A friend of mine, Gretta, who is a social worker who now maintains a private therapy practice out of her home, did a financial breakdown and determined that her part-time private practice at home nets her basically the same amount of money per week as her full-time job did.

This pleasantly surprising result came about, first, from reduced costs and savings in expenditures. Child-care costs were reduced, suddenly there were no tolls and commuting costs, she used her automobile less, her clothes were more relaxed so wardrobe expenditures were reduced, there were few lunches out, etc. The second big area of savings resulted from the very substantial tax write-offs available to a self-employed person working from home. Gretta found that something like one-third of her gross revenues was deductible.

There are some excellent books on how to run a business from your home, so *Getting Organized* won't duplicate those efforts. Our mandate is to cast an eye on some of the special challenges, problems, and pitfalls of working from home in terms of comfortably integrating a serious money-making enterprise with the claims and demands of home and family.

In this chapter we'll talk, first, about attitudes, which are so key to a time management program that works, and then about time management itself. Then we'll take a look at the forces that pull against your program—interruptions and self-distraction.

The problems will be laid out, they will be tied in to organizing issues, and a way to solutions will be pointed out.

TAKING YOUR WORK SERIOUSLY

When you work in an outside office, the whole environment conspires to aid you and enhance you in doing your task. Whereas when you work at home, your whole environment conspires against you. Not only are there numerous claims on your time but, no less important, your own attitudes and expectations about the legitimacy of claiming your work time in the face of often legitimate demands from family and friends are often uncertain. It is hard to get other people—and sometimes to get yourself—to take your work seriously.

No matter how much money people who work at home make—and some people make quite a lot, $80,000 to $100,000 and more—their aura of seriousness seems to decline in direct proportion to the decline in totage mileage racked up by their briefcase. In fact, there is a place and a block of time which is your workday. And the fact that your work place happens to be in your home doesn't change or remove or diminish or in any way alter the seriousness of the intention, which is to accomplish whatever work it is—therapy, public relations, writing, or any other kind of business. So this requires a very firm notion in your mind, and in other people's minds, that working at home is as serious as working outside of the house.

Gretta, the social worker/therapist, used to say she felt like Rodney Dangerfield—"I don't get no respect!" At the end of a hard day, her husband, Tom, would come home and say, "Why isn't the house clean? Why aren't the beds made? Why isn't dinner ready?"

Things took a nasty turn toward escalation when she began to counter, "I'll start mopping the kitchen floor when you start sweeping the floor of your office before you leave at night."

Neither Gretta nor Tom was right, of course. Tom was not treating either Gretta's profession or her income with the respect they deserved, and Gretta was not taking seriously Tom's desire (and Tom was the primary income producer by a significant margin) to come home to a clean and comfortable house.

Gretta and Tom were able to resolve the problems and restore an even keel to their family life by implementing the techniques described on pages 281–83. The point to be made here is that central to the implementation of the practical time and space techniques discussed in this chapter is taking a productive stance toward your work. Like any other person who works for a living or contributes to a living, your right to private work time and space is legitimate. Thus a guilty stance ("I'm a terrible person") is inappropriate. At the same time these claims must be reconciled with the also legitimate claims of family and others. So a defiant stance ("The hell with you!") isn't appropriate either.

In order to establish that your work at home is a reality, as much in your own eyes as in the eyes of others, three cues are very helpful in clarifying and underlining that reality. You have to say in your own mind, "The clock is on now, the meter is running. I'm now officially working."

One technique that many people have found useful to let yourself know that you really are at work, and to differentiate work time from private time, is to *dress the part*. Many people can't believe they're really at work if they hang out in the clothes they rolled out of bed in, or just throw on any old pair of jeans. It's not necessary to dress as if you were going to a downtown office, but psychologically it seems to be very important to be fully dressed and well groomed . . . not, for a woman, high-heeled shoes, but pressed pants, a fresh shirt, perhaps a scarf.

Another important differentiation to establish is location. *Physically set out your workspace.* Choosing and implementing an office location in your home will be discussed on page 110. But what matters from the point of view of attitude is that there *is* a location which is somehow separate from the rest of the house, even if that separation is defined only by a small bookcase or screen or plant.

Third, both for practical and differentiation purposes, *do not use the family telephone* for your business. You may not want to order a business telephone, since the deposit is very high, but at least get another residential line. Margaret is a lawyer who works two days a week out of her home. She decided that a phone of her own was definitely in the cards the day she was talking to a client when her six-year-old picked up the upstairs extension and said, "Mommy, I can't find the paints we bought for my art project." This did not win her brownie points with her client.

DESIGNING YOUR TIMESPACE: AN ORGANIZING SYSTEM

Novelist Virginia Woolf referred to the joy—and indeed, the necessity—of having a room or space of one's own. That delight is no less precious than it once was, but our time has seen the rise of a relatively new quest—for time of one's own. There is no indication that we are willing to cut back on any part of the heavy work loads, exercise programs, career and family obligations with which we have packed every minute of the eighties and nineties.

So designing your own timespace, both for business purposes and to include some private quiet time, is one of your key challenges.

Let's go back and visit our old chum Elaine, the fitness instructor, who, after various fits and starts, established a "time style" that works for her in two ways: She has the time she needs to establish her business and get done what needs to get done during the course of the working day, and her time is generously available to her family, so that what needs to get done within the home gets done in a timely way.

Establishing a Productive Time Style

Elaine is married to Murray, the manager of a large auto-parts store in the city. They have two children—Jennifer, ten, and Jason, twelve. The kids are old enough to pretty much take care of themselves now, but young enough that Elaine continues to be a very active mom.

First thing off the plate, the reality of potential conflict between Elaine's work responsibilities and her home responsibilities had to be dealt with. Where Elaine had been going wrong was in declaring unilaterally that her work hours were 9:00 to 5:00, which was causing a lot of family conflict. The children were feeling neglected, the house had become slipshod, and in general everyone was feeling pretty low.

So Elaine called a family conference. She and Murray and the kids sat down and, over cocoa and marshmallows, hashed out for a couple of hours what Elaine wanted to do, and what Murray and the kids felt bad about. What they decided upon as a family was that Elaine would work Monday to Friday from 9:00 to 3:00. But, so as not to miss out on the lucrative after-school children's market, she would give children's classes from 3:00 to 5:00 on Tuesday and Thursday and from 9:00 to 11:00 on Saturday morning.

Okay, so that was the first hurdle conquered: that of office hours. The next phase was to resolve the more complex question of how the household was to be organized and run. Fortunately, Elaine would be able to hire some help, but she was not so well off as to be able to purchase services at will, so all of her creativity and resourcefulness were called into play. This is the procedure Elaine followed:

1. *Listing tasks.* Elaine listed every single family and household task she could think of, from making up beds to watering the plants to getting the kids to their various appointments and classes. An approach to that task is outlined in Chapter 16.
2. *Laborsaving options.* She considered each appliance in her home to make sure that it was the most laborsaving model available—self-defrosting refrigerator, self-

cleaning oven, etc. The more tasks the machines could do, then the fewer Elaine and the family had to worry about.

3. *Making tasks more efficient.* Next, Elaine reviewed each task on her list, applying to each one the following questions: *Can the task be reduced in level of effort or frequency, or even eliminated?* Elaine had been changing the sheets twice a week. From now on, it would be once a week. *Can the task be made simpler or more efficient?* Instead of watering plants every day, Elaine purchased "travel bulbs," which feed plants water for three weeks. Then twice a week she would mist them. Many useful efficiency techniques are discussed in Chapter 16, most in relation to cooking and food preparation. And of course, *simply being organized* is probably the single greatest efficiency technique of all.

4. *"Can somebody else do it?"* The next step was to apply to each task the host of LSEDO ("let somebody else do it") techniques.

Barter. Elaine worked out a deal with her friend Margery in which Margery would take two classes a week in exchange for handling many time-eating errands for Elaine.

Co-opping. Elaine worked out pickup arrangements for her kids on her late Tuesday and Thursday workdays, and the other days she made the rounds for her own kids and their friends. That necessitated an unexpected adjustment in her work hours on the other days, which had to end at 2:30 in order to get to school in time. Elaine compensated by starting her classes a half hour earlier.

Hiring services. By calling up the local high school and community college, Elaine was able to find a whole battery of young people, whom she called "elves," to do a whole host of services for her, both home and business, at bargain rates. They did typing, checked things at the library, made pickups and deliveries, did some basic marketing, and in general liberated Elaine in countless ways. A couple of the kids were also willing to do heavy cleaning jobs such as floor mopping and cleaning out the basement.

It was advantageous to have several elves "in play" at one time, so as not to be dependent on any one person, who would not be able to work during exams or vacations.

Elaine also felt the time had come to graduate to a regular cleaning person twice a week, rather than doing most cleaning herself as in the past. Her income from her business had gone well beyond the pin money stage, and she felt this was appropriate.

Family delegation. After her thorough review of the household task list, Elaine and Murray called a second family meeting to discuss how remaining tasks could be divided up among the family members. Family delegation, which is essentially a process of negotiation, is discussed in Chapter 16.

Well—Elaine was set up. The system was good, and it all worked out pretty well. There's just one more piece of the puzzle: Once a system is in place, you must protect it from invaders.

PROTECTING YOUR TIMESPACE: INTERRUPTIONS AND DISTRACTIONS

Interruptions are one of the most intractable time management problems because they are, to some extent, uncontrollable.

If ringing telephones are your problem, an answering machine can be a boon. Choose a machine, however, that allows you a *very* short message. Many callers hang up during the thirty- or-forty-five-second message periods set by some brands. In lieu of a machine, ask friends to call only at certain times.

An answering machine can also be a means of fitting some uninterrupted time into your schedule if you are one of the many people who simply cannot, or do not know how to, extricate themselves from a telephone conversation.

Another technique for cutting down on phone interruptions at home is to take advantage of the time spent in your car as phone time. Cellular phones—that is, car phones—have become a boon to both the busy homemaker and businessperson. If you are on the road a lot, whether for business or chauffeuring your kids, and your life demands a lot of telephone time, save some of those phone calls to make while you're out and about. A writer friend of mine, for example, sometimes conducts interviews strictly by car phone. One particular interview she remembers was with a busy psychologist who could only fit the interview in while she went from her office to her masseuse. So they set up the time for the call, and in this case, the car became the office.

This is happening increasingly nowadays. You can also listen to language or instructional tapes on your car tape deck to make the most of drive time.

Once you're on the phone, there are many ways to utilize time during extended phone conversations, especially if you have a shoulder attachment or speakerphone that frees your hands for taking notes, cooking, or simple housecleaning. It makes sense, in fact, to reserve some small chores—sewing buttons, writing checks, filing nails —specifically for times when you're on the phone. Cordless phones permit you to range anywhere inside or outside the house. Otherwise, keep extensions in the kitchen and work areas, and see that cords are long enough for mobility.

Getting off the phone is sometimes a challenge with talkative friends and colleagues. A few stock lines are helpful: "Excuse me, I have a client coming in five minutes." This is a nice one: "I must make a phone call before the phones go down in London." Or "tango them to the door" by recapping your points: "Jim, I'm delighted to have had this conversation with you. And before we end the conversation, let me just recap the points we discussed, 1, 2, 3, goodbye."

One person I know, who *hates* to get caught in extended conversations, makes as many phone calls as he can from public phones when he's out and about. People tend to get very brisk when they hear street noises and the clankings of public phones and "twenty-five cents for the next five minutes, pleeeeze." He said it worked so well that he was tempted to have a pay phone installed in his office, but then visitors would learn his secret.

Mastering telephone conversations with persistent salespeople who wish to sell you Florida swampland or your friendly cable TV representative is an art form all its own. My friend Marilyn sat there one day, toe-tapping, absolutely seething with self-loathing at her cowardice, while a salesman hit her over the head for twenty minutes about buying land in the Poconos. Somehow she couldn't bring herself, for fear of being rude or hurting the salesperson's feelings, to say, "I'm not interested now . . . goodbye."

When Marilyn finally felt she'd been polite long enough and said she wasn't interested, the salesman got angry at her for wasting his time!

There are two things to keep in mind here: First, no one has the right to impose their time allocations on you without your consent. And second, remember that these are professionals who are sometimes trained to hook you into embarrassment and intimidation. In any event, you are not making or breaking their life or career. They are trained to take rejection, and you are not hurting or insulting them personally.

Marilyn's solution, taking her cue from the salesman's accusation, which had, in point of fact, some justification, was, from then on, to break into the salesperson's spiel and say, "Look, I don't mean to be rude, but I'm sure you would appreciate the opportunity to move on quickly to your next prospect instead of wasting time with me. So thank you and goodbye." Usually they were so stunned that they simply said goodbye in return, but if they didn't, Marilyn felt she'd done her part and hung up.

Sometimes it's necessary to remove yourself physically from distraction. The reading rooms of public libraries are soothing and conducive to concentration. Some libraries are equipped with individual study cubicles and have typewriters available for use. University libraries, which you can usually use if you register for one course, almost always have work areas.

Another way to get away from it all, without leaving home, is to rearrange your time. Some people go to bed early and set the alarm for midnight in order to have a few hours of uninterrupted work.

When interruptions are unavoidable, think of your project as a magnet that draws you back when circumstances allow. Don't emulate the dieter who lapses once and then says, "Okay, I failed, so I'll start stuffing myself again." After an interruption, return to your project with renewed steadfastness.

The suggestions above apply primarily to garden-variety interruptions. Interruptions from family, friends, and loved ones create some special problems and call for some special skills to solve them.

NEGOTIATING INTERRUPTIONS
FROM FAMILY AND FRIENDS

One of the perpetual problems people have with interruptions is the inability to simply say no to or set limits on other people. Because whether it's the neighbor next door or your mother-in-law or the insurance agent who's called to try to sell you a policy, saying no is very difficult for anybody. But it's also a gentle art.

The task boils down to being able to establish your own limits, to prevent invasion in order to get a job done, while at the same time not alienating your significant others.

Three situations illustrate three approaches to managing interruptions during working hours:

Situation 1. Let's say that you're working at home and Betty, a good friend of yours, who's got a lot of problems, calls you. Her latest amour packed up and said "Bye-bye," and she's crushed. However, she's been crushed now for the last two months, you've been helping her uncrush, and now enough is enough, at least during your work time.

Your response is: "Betty, you know how concerned I am about you, and you know I would love to talk to you and give you my attention. But I'm not going to be able to do you justice now because this is my working time, between 8:00 and 3:00. And if I don't get this job done I'm cooked. So, my dear, you're first on my list when my work time is over . . . kiss, kiss . . . bye-bye."

Principle: **Acquaint your friends with your work schedule.**

Many people, including your friends and loved ones, think, "well, she's only working in her home. I can interrupt. She can go back to whatever she's doing five minutes later."

This is not true. We at The Organizing Principle respect your time and understand that it is as much your office and your working time as if you were walking into IBM every day. Those little "it's only five minutes" interruptions can be genuinely disruptive. It is therefore critical that you acquaint your friends with your schedule, and impress upon them how important it is that whenever possible, they respect your privacy during those hours.

Situation 2. Ralph ran a full-time enterprise from his home, analyzing raw market research data and turning his findings into reports that he sold to subscribers. Yet his mother, who lived nearby, felt no compunction about popping in several times a week to bring fresh tomatoes from her garden, or phoning to ask whether she could pick something up for him at the supermarket.

Ralph had already tried the straightforward approach of saying, "Mom, I love to see you at other times, but 9:00 to 5:00 are my working hours, so would you please not come around then." It didn't take. The problem is that a lot of people, and not only Ralph's mother, think being at home means you're sort of working, but not really. As long as you're at home, why don't I drop in? There's simply a lack of real understanding that what you're doing has a work value which is equal to that of somebody who is not at home.

Ralph found an effective response by "packaging" the interchange between them in his own mind as a kind of adversarial game like chess. Thus, he was free to counter with an oppositional move, which was: "Mom, I'd love to have you. But I'm working now. We have a couple of choices: You're more than welcome to go upstairs and watch television or play with Susie, or I can get back to you later, or we can make a date for tonight at 6:00."

Principle: **Offer options, and kindly ones, but do not under any circumstances capitulate.**

If things become sticky, recognize that the problem goes deeper than organization, and must be solved on the level of the relationship—that is, what are your respective assumptions about what the nature of the relationship should be, and if there are differences, how can they be resolved?

Situation 3. Interruptions from your children are to some extent unavoidable, but even young children can learn not to disturb a parent between certain hours, or when the door is shut, except for emergencies. Arrange your home so your children won't need you to take care of some of their everyday needs. For example, a four-year-old can pour himself a glass of milk if both milk and glass are within reach.

If your children continually nag you about performing various tasks for them, analyze the action to see whether it can be made child-scale so the child can do it. If your child still persists in nagging you, the problem may not only be a matter of making things child-scale; it might be that too much time is being taken away from the child. Your youngster may, in fact, be asking for more attention.

There's a nice way to make both of you happier by taking planned fifteen-minute breaks, say every two hours. This will give both of you something to look forward to and make your child less impatient for your attention while you're working.

Barbara, a community activist who is extremely tied up with meetings, phone calls, and so forth, found that these fifteen-minute breaks with her four-year-old Jamie were welcome oases for them both.

What she did was make up a list of fifteen-minute projects. Then at the appointed time, she set off the kitchen timer to announce the beginning of "Jamie-time," and then set it for fifteen minutes. She found that it was easier for a four-year-old to grasp the concept of limited time when it is delineated by something concrete like a timer.

Barbara and Jamie used their special times together in a variety of ways. Barbara felt that fun projects you can work on together are great. Just make sure that it's a project that can give you both a sense of completion. For example, until she learned the rules, so to speak, they would start a Monopoly game, and then Jamie would be frustrated and angry at being left dangling when the timer went off. On the other hand, it was all right to do a portion of a longer project, so long as that little portion was complete in itself. "If you're doing a jigsaw puzzle," Barbara advised, "say, 'This corner is what we're going to work on right now,' making sure that whatever the project is, it's something the child can turn away from when the time is ended. That way both of you are not left dangling and frustrated."

It's also very helpful, so as not to end your time together too abruptly, to have a sort of "two-minute warning" and say, "Okay, we've got two more minutes left. Now, shall we put this piece of puzzle in, or should we put the puzzle back and just talk about the book you're reading? What is it you'd like to do for the two minutes that are left?"

FINDING YOUR OPTIMUM WORK STYLE

Pogo: "We have seen the enemy and they is us."

Oftentimes the primary culprit in having difficulty achieving your time-based goals is less the claims of the outside world than the destructive effects of a damaging personal time style. Let's take a look at two home-based professionals whose personal time styles worked against their productivity and peace of mind.

Eleanor: the self-distracted day. Every morning, Eleanor, who provides an enriched tutoring program in math and science for gifted children, sits down at her desk prepared for a good three hours of solid work reviewing her notes on the different students, updating lesson plans, checking student progress, and the like. The house is quiet—her husband is at work, the kids are at school, and she has all this time for herself until they come home for lunch at noon.

But then a friend calls, they get into a chat, and suddenly it's 9:20. Then Eleanor remembers that her husband said there was an article in this morning's paper about innovative teaching methods that might interest her, so she goes to find the paper, reads the article, reads a few other articles of interest, and then notices that Bloomingdale's white sale starts on Saturday. They need some sheets, so she calls her friend Georgia to see if she'd like to go shopping on Saturday.

By this time it's 10:00, and, what with one thing and another, if Eleanor gets in a good hour and a half of solid work, she's doing pretty well. Yet the home-based worker has to understand that he/she, like any other person, has a certain obligation to the task and that that obligation has to be met.

Self-distraction, procrastination, and the other important sabotage issue of perfectionism, which are discussed on pages 48–55, are stubborn because many times they are bound up with personality and temperament and/or they can represent the tip of the iceberg of underlying issues.

However, that isn't the whole story by any means. We identified three very practical techniques that reduced the pressure of or even dissolved these sometimes very damaging characteristics:

1. *Instituting the Basic Master List/Daily List Two-List Program* discussed in Chapter 3. This gave Eleanor's day a structure it had previously lacked. She was clear on what had to be done and when she had to do it, which enabled her to be much more attentive to the passage of time.

2. *Finding her optimum work style.* Eleanor's easy distractibility indicated that she had a mental pattern that operated best in short bursts of activity, whereas trying for long sustained efforts simply went against her nature. So we made sure she had plenty of opportunities to shift her attention during the workday. For example, say that she was scheduled to review the records of three students. She would spend fifteen or twenty minutes on one review, and then get up for five to ten minutes, engaging in some stretching exercises, or taking a little walk, or watering the plants, or making a (brief!) phone call, and the like. She would time those intervals with the kitchen timer, since she recognized her propensity to go off in another direction altogether.

   Then she was ready to sit down and go on with the review of the second student.

   We divided up her responsibilities to make sure that no single stretch of work went on for longer than fifteen or twenty minutes. The problem didn't arise during her class sessions, even though each session lasted an hour, because each one was filled with plenty of diversity, from problem-solving to exercises to homework reviews.

3. *Reward.* Eleanor loaded her life with rewards for a job well done. During a daily work session, after she'd gotten through a couple of intervals without going off on a tangent, she brewed herself a cup of her favorite

herbal tea. After completing a whole productive work session, she took some time off to read a couple of chapters in a book she was enjoying, or went to a yoga class, or in some way gave herself some private "treat" time. And after a full week of productive time, she and her husband celebrated by going to the theater.

Sarah: the day that never ends. Sarah's problem is the opposite of Eleanor's. She cannot set limits. Sarah has the kind of personality that becomes immersed in what she does. Sarah is an independent management consultant. She works many days with clients, and then comes home to do her paper work, write up client reports, etc. Other days she works full-time at home. And because there's no "natural" end to the workday, forced by leaving the office or by the demands of young children, the workday never ends. Sarah's office hours have become twenty-four hours a day. There's always something else to do, and she's always doing it, often until 11:00 or 12:00 at night.

Not only is her obsessive concentration on her work making her exhausted, but her friends are dropping away because she has no time for them, and her husband, as understanding as he has tried to be, is becoming impatient, and their marriage is beginning to suffer.

So the question of establishing some *restraints* on time—knowing how and when to stop—is a legitimate question of time management.

Interestingly enough, the solution to Sarah's problem lay in the exact same three steps that Eleanor utilized, but with a very different intention and focus.

1. *Master List/Daily List.* The gain that Sarah received from the Two-List system was to establish some limits to her activities. Although she extended her Daily List average to thirteen items rather than the more typical ten or fewer, having a Daily List established closure

for her. Finishing her list meant that she could stop for the day.

2. *Finding her optimum work style.* Obviously Sarah's personal style was to immerse herself in her work for hours at a time. She could easily concentrate for eight or nine or ten hours at a stretch, without coming up for air.

    Our first idea was to break her day up into three- or four-hour blocks, but she got irritated and annoyed by that kind of breakup of time.

    So we got the idea instead, not of breaking up her day, but of breaking up her week. That is, she had "immersion" days, when she would work straight through at her desk for as long as she liked, and then she had "up and out" days, when she would take client assignments, do library work, make phone calls, run errands, and generally catch up on all the business of life.

    She worked out an understanding with her husband that he would fend for himself for dinner on the three days a week that were her immersion days, so she could work straight through the dinner hour, while on the other days they would be together and really *with* each other.

3. *Reward.* Obviously Sarah needed no reward to work. The work was its own reward. But she did need to give herself something to look forward to on her days out.

    So Sarah planned some special treat for herself on every "up and out" day. One day she bought herself a frivolous and probably too-expensive summer straw hat, on another day she took an hour exercise class, and on a third day she took in a grand Cézanne show at the museum. She also took advantage of her days out to reestablish contact with her friends by making lunch or tea or museum dates.

6
Workspace: Creating an Office at Home

Paper handling, more than almost any other function, is dependent on a responsive physical environment—responsiveness defined as an appealing and practical location furnished with a comfortable working surface and sufficient supplies for every regular need. This office will become a permanent installation where the business of business and the business of life are transacted—readily accessible, with all supplies, implements, and files immediately at your fingertips, and where other household operations do not interfere.

Because establishment of a personal office is so basic, this chapter provides a step-by-step guide to pulling together an effective working environment.

YOUR OFFICE PROFILE:
A 12-POINT NEEDS ASSESSMENT

To achieve the office that will fulfill your expectations and needs, it is helpful to develop an "office profile" through a needs assessment. A needs assessment asks four basic questions: What am I going to do in that space? For how many hours? In what time period (day, after school, evening)? And what facilities, space, tools, privacy, concern for others' comfort do I need in order to do it?

Begin by writing a statement of basic purpose. For example, "I need teaching space and office space for the purpose of tutoring twenty hours per week. The main time period will be after school into early evening, and also Saturday mornings."

Now head a sheet of paper with three columns: *Now, 6 months, 1 year*. Keep this sheet with you as you work through the needs assessment. As a project, purchase, or task occurs to you, enter it into the appropriate column.

A project or purchase goes in the "Now" column if you can't do business without that tool or amenity. The "6 months" and "1 year" columns would consist of expansion projects or projects postponed till later. For example, a typing service obviously needs one computer right away. But if you dream of hiring additional typists, you might plan for two computers in six months, and aspire to having three or four machines within a year.

So a "needs assessment" not only creates a working task list (which can be gradually handled through your Master List if you like, or dealt with all at once in a blitz) but helps define priorities and lays out the direction of your business into the future.

Activities and Tools

1. *Telephone.* Do you spend a great deal of time on the phone? Is the accent note going to be the telephone? Will a simple residential phone suffice? Or should you have a multiple line, special services and features such as call waiting, call forwarding, single-digit dialing, automatic redial, or conference calling? What kind of answering machine should you have?

2. *Typing.* Do you generate a substantial volume of typed material? If so, is your tool of choice a computer, or would an electronic typewriter suit your purposes? See page 128 for a discussion of this question.

3. *Fax, copier.* Do you own these devices now, or do you anticipate purchasing them in the fairly near future? See page 129.

Storage and Infrastructure

4. *Files.* How many file drawers do you use now? Expand that by one third to allow for growth. Your file count might be sharply reduced if you reorganize your files, but for now, put the expanded file drawer total on your list.

5. *Stocks and storage.* Will you need a closet or some other cabinet to store stocks of paper and other supplies? If you teach exercise classes, where do you plan to keep the mats? Do you provide supplies for students that will need shelf storage space?

6. *Infrastructure.* How many electrical outlets will you need and where should they be placed? Can your residential system support your electricity load? Should

you check with an electrician? The same questions might arise in regard to the telephone if you use a complex telephone system.

Are any special adjustments required? For example, converting a little-used basement into an office might require better heat, lighting, or ventilation. Or if exercise classes were going to be held in the basement, you might want to install a sturdier banister or lay down more resilient flooring over the concrete floor.

Employees, Clients, Students, or Patients

7. *If people work for you:*   Where will they sit? What tools (telephone, computer, or typewriter) and supplies will they need access to? If you don't want to buy a second computer now, will you need to relinquish the computer during their work hours? In that event, how will you spend your time?
8. *If clients, students, or patients visit you:*   Where will they sit? If you tutor, do you need a work table? Do you use audio-visual tools? How will they be set up for use, where will they be stored? If you teach exercise classes, how much open space will you need? And where will the class rest at breaks? What are the logistics if participants need to change clothes?
9. *Traffic patterns.*   Will employees, clients, students, or patients need a reception area? Do you want people passing through your living room? Past the baby's room? Where will they hang their things, or leave umbrellas or wet boots?

Family and Household

10. *Access.* If you have children, can you hear them if they need you? Can you hear the doorbell and can you easily reach the front door if someone comes?
11. *Privacy.* Privacy can be achieved either through space or through time. That is, a psychotherapist who requires absolute privacy during office hours either needs to have a private room and perhaps someone to mind the children, or needs to confine his/her practice to hours when no one is at home. (Some therapists even like to have a separate entrance so patients don't encounter family members.)

    Most other occupations don't require such stringent privacy, but you may need freedom from household distraction. In which case, either defining a private space or working when other family members are absent are the two ways to get it.
12. *Comfort of others.* Is the hippity-hop of exercisers bouncing up and down to a merengue beat going to disturb others? If so, resilient flooring may be in order. Will a constantly ringing phone or clacking faxes get on the household's nerves? In such cases, sound muffling may be necessary.

This needs assessment will serve as a kind of navigational chart through the shoals of planning your office.

CHOOSING THE LOCATION

Using your needs assessment results to establish some general parameters, the next thing to do is to select the place for your office. In an ideal world, you could commandeer an entire room, but even if that is not practicable, it *is* possible to choose a corner of your house or apartment that can belong to you alone.

At this point, don't take measurements or rigorously analyze the space. This is the "draft version" in finally settling on your space. Just be aware of the broad requirements. If your needs assessment indicates, for example, that you need easy access to the front door because there will be frequent messengers and deliveries, then you can't put yourself down in the basement.

Never select an area that you don't like in the mistaken idea that it is "practical." A client of mine went through an experience that illustrates why. A free-lance writer who works in his home, my client, John Davidson, needed extensive home office equipment and files. The day I came to call he proudly showed me a room he had fitted up as a "real" office: executive desk, computer, fax, copier, filing cabinets, the works. It was very impressive. The problem, however, was that after putting so much money and equipment into the office, he didn't spend any time there.

First, it was removed from the main action of the household. Although privacy was essential, John felt lonely without hearing his wife and four children in the background. It was important for him to feel part of his family, not isolated from it, and this elegant office was situated where no one else in the household had occasion to go. The other reason the office felt uncomfortable was that Davidson could not see outside. The room was built in such a way that he couldn't be refreshed by the sight of trees, grass, and children playing. John had been sneaking upstairs to an empty room right in the center of the house, with a big window which looked out over the lawn and a wooded area. He could glance out at will while he sat and worked with an old electric typewriter at a rickety desk.

What happened, of course, was that little piles of paper sprouted throughout the house as he carried them from one location to the other or dropped them somewhere en route. Not to mention the fact that paper clips, stapler, stamps, and other necessary supplies were never in the right place. His work habits were driving him crazy, and he had hired me to organize him back into his "real" office so that he could start to use it properly.

I convinced John that this approach was the *wrong* one, that his beautiful, expensive office would never be the right place for him to work because he hated it. Instead of reorganizing the old office, I helped him move everything into the room he really felt comfortable in. The moral of this story is that ultimately, the most practical location is the one that is agreeable to your spirit!

Few of us, however, have homes which provide so many alternatives. So the trick is to balance external realities—space, other people in the household, the amount of money available—against internal realities like those Mr. Davidson had to deal with: his need to be among his family, and his wish to see out the window. In order to reach some kind of workable decision as to location, ask yourself the following questions:

1. Do you prefer a sunny room or a shaded one, and do you prefer to work in the morning or in the afternoon? These two questions are related because different rooms receive varying amounts of light at different times of the day.
2. Do you like being near windows or do they distract you?
3. Do you need isolation, or is it better for you to be near people?

Answering these three questions will immediately narrow your alternatives considerably. Now walk around your home and make a list of all the places which suit your preferences; for example, "windowed corner of living room," "unused breakfast nook."

Next, consider which of your alternatives makes you feel best. By this, I mean does the thought of working in a particular area make you feel internally "clear" and comfortable? Or is there a sense of internal tension, a nervous feeling? Number each alternative according to how "right" it feels to you. A really good feeling is #1, #2 is satisfactory, and #3 is just tolerable. Anything below a #3 should be forgotten immediately.

It would be ideal, of course, to settle immediately on your #1 choice, but *now* the concerns of convenience and practicality intrude themselves. To deal with them, here is a second set of questions to ask about each alternative:

1. Off the top of your head, without measuring, do you have the impression that there is enough space for a desk, files, and equipment?
2. Is the general area structurally sound? If floors are sagging and walls are peeling, it doesn't sound like a very good prospect.
3. Is there a convenient electrical outlet and telephone jack?
4. Will this area be unobstructed during the times you want to use it, or will it get in the way of other household functions? Can these other functions be shifted to another time or place?

To help make the relationships clear, draw a rough chart in your notebook—similar to Figure 1—that lists the alternatives, with numbers to indicate their order of preference, and how well each of these questions rates with each alternative.

For instance, the breakfast nook has plenty of space, so that square would be marked "1." Structural soundness

Alternatives (listed in order of preference)	Space	Sound-ness	Elec/phone	House-hold
1. Windowed corner of living room	X	1	1	3
2. Breakfast nook	1	2	X	3
3. Bedroom alcove	2	1	X	1
4. Storage room	1	1	1	1

Figure 1 Home office—Accessibility Chart

is adequate but not perfect, which would make that category about a "2." There is no electrical outlet or phone jack, so mark an "X" there. The "rest of the household" factor could be a problem. The nook isn't used to eat in, but the children have a tendency to run through the area as they go in and out of the house. They would have to be taught not to bother you when you are working, and to leave your supplies alone. So mark this square "3."

The storage room, on the other hand, fits every particular with a "1." So that's the answer, yes? No. According to the numbers on the chart, the storage room is last in preference. To choose it would involve yourself in Davidson's Dilemma. Instead, let's begin with the *favorite* alternative, and see how it intersects with the questions of convenience.

The favorite location is the windowed corner of the

living room, but the space situation there is poor, so, sadly, that alternative gets crossed off. The next preference is the breakfast nook, and it will work. It's not perfect, you may have to do a little patching up and put in some additional outlets, but it will do. It is in the breakfast nook that preference and practicality *intersect*, to provide a point where you can work while feeling good about it. This is an important rule to remember in choosing locations, or in designing any plan of action.

Principle #5 **When you have several alternatives to choose from, select one which intersects at a point between your instinctive preference and the most "practical" alternative.**

CREATING AN OFFICE AND OFFICE STYLES

A photographer needs a darkroom, perhaps a studio setting, photo storage, and facilities for record-keeping and making appointments. A fitness instructor needs a room big enough to hold classes and a simple desk or work area. Other, more conventional businesses fundamentally require, in terms of space, only a desk to work at and a chair.

Choosing a workspace, deciding the basic facilities you need, and fitting it out are key to a productive enterprise.

How much money can you allocate to this project? The amount you spend will depend on how much you already have on hand in the way of furniture and supplies versus how much you have to buy and how improvisatory you wish to be. It's a good idea to set a dollar limit and keep expense records.

The next challenge is to figure out how to get maximum use out of the space. Establish your parameters by measuring the lay of the land.

Getting the Lay of the Land

1. Measure the length and width of the entire office area and mark the dimensions in your notebook.
2. Measure all your equipment horizontally (side to side and front to back) and vertically. Equipment includes computer (keyboard, monitor, central processing unit [CPU] where the disk drives are located), printer, typewriter, fax, copier, telephone, and any other machinery. Also measure special facilities that your profession requires such as, for a graphic artist, a drawing desk or board and a surface to lay out mechanicals.

   Does your needs assessment indicate that a computer or any other gear you do not yet own will turn up in the fairly near future? In that case, approximate those measurements too.
3. Measure your file cabinets, top to bottom, side to side, and front to back. Assuming an increase of one-third more drawers, as suggested in the needs assessment, translate the number of additional drawers into different file cabinet configurations. For example, if one-third more drawers equals four drawers, then note that those four drawers can be divided into two two-drawer cabinets, or into one four-drawer upright cabinet, or into a four-drawer lateral file, or two two-drawer laterals. Note the additional dimensions.

   Check computer-disk storage similarly. What are the dimensions of the disk storage units you have on hand? What would they be if one-third more units were added?

Planning Office Layout

With space, equipment, and file measurements in hand, consider your placement options. There are four basic ways to set up an office: in a *straight line,* as an *ell, back to back,* or in a *corridor.*

Straight-Line Style

Is the dominant architectural feature of your space a long wall? If so, then probably the straight-line setup, which basically consists of either one or two slabs, depending on the length of the wall, set on supports or on top of two two-drawer filing cabinets, would probably be your solution of choice. (Stores like Conran's are your best bet for this kind of equipment.)

Compare your wall measurement with your equipment measurements to judge whether there is a rough fit: If all your equipment is laid out in a line (usually the computer monitor is set atop the disk drive), leaving a few inches in between each piece; and if two or three square

feet of open working space are added, with some room left over for desk supplies like tape, stapler, pens and pencils, a vertical desk file rack, a few reference books, and maybe an in-out box, are you within two or three feet of your wall length?

Also, does the allotted floor space accommodate your file cabinets? Don't forget space for a swivel chair with wheels that can slide in a trice from one end of your long table to the other.

If equipment and file dimensions fall somewhere in the ballpark of available space, go directly to page 122, "Fitting Too Much Stuff into Too Little Space," to work out how to fit what you have into the space available. But if the space discrepancy is too large—more than four feet or so—you may need to settle for a different space or consider one of the three other office styles.

Ell Style

The ell style is a traditional office style in which an extension or table is placed at right angles to a desk as shown on page 119. You sit in the angle.

An ell can go on either side of the desk, or it's even possible, if space permits, to have two extensions—one on the left and one on the right side of the desk. The extensions can be slabs on supports, or else cover two two-drawer file cabinets with a slab. Make sure to allow for legroom.

The double-ell setup is particularly useful if your needs assessment indicates that working space for employees is required. One of the ells can be pressed into service as an employee working surface. It's a rather cramped but doable solution in a small space.

Usually the desk is used primarily for workspace, while computer and other equipment are placed on the ell. Will

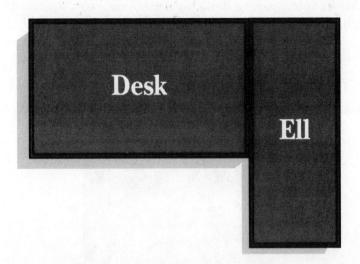

you be taking notes or orders on the phone? In that case, phone position is important. For right-handers, it makes sense to keep the phone to your left so you can hold the receiver with your left hand, thus keeping your right hand free to write.

In the ell setup, your chair is a particularly important piece of equipment because you must be able to turn readily from side to side. In general, a good chair is a valuable and underappreciated item. Any tendency to back trouble makes an ergonomically sound swivel chair a worthwhile investment.

Back-to-Back Style

Sometimes the only office space you have available is an open vestibule or hall that doesn't have much in the way of walls. The back-to-back style can turn an otherwise unusable too-open space into viable office space by fitting two desks or improvised desks together to create a single working block, like this:

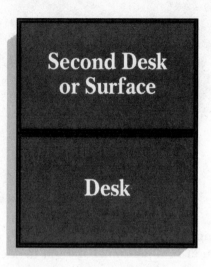

Both desks can be real desks, or they can be file cabinets with slabs over them, or a slab on supports, or a desk-height lateral file cabinet or a table, or one desk and one something else, or any combination.

Usually working space, typewriter/computer, and most-frequently-used files will go on one desk, where you will spend the larger part of your time, and the rest of the equipment and files will be at the other desk.

The back-to-back setup is not optimum for two reasons: First, you will need to move fairly frequently from one desk to the other, which could get irritating. On the other hand, some people like the exercise. In any event, I recommend purchasing two chairs, one per desk, rather than trying to scoot from one side to the other. The second problem has to do with electrical wiring. To prevent equipment cables and wires from dangerously and inconveniently festooning your floor, engage an electrician to divert them to less visible and less dangerous places.

Corridor Style

The corridor-style office arrangement, which is frequently used in executive offices, works well in a space that is a fairly large squarish or rectangular block. This style mandates a desk in front of you and a table, credenza, or second desk in back, like so:

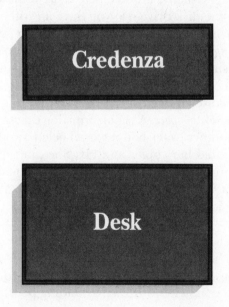

You sit in the "corridor" in between. This arrangement permits you to turn readily between the working desk in front and your "equipment center" in back.

Fitting Too Much Stuff into
Too Little Space

Okay, you've decided which office-style option makes the best fit with the shape and dimension of your selected office space, you've carefully compared your equipment and file measurements with your space measurements, and, guess what—there isn't enough room. It won't all fit.

Sometimes miracles of accommodation and efficiency can be achieved by creative space management. If your stuff seems too much and your space too small, check out these approaches to expanding your space options:

Stacking. Usually, as noted before, a computer monitor is set atop the disk drive. Do you have any other pieces of equipment or gear that can be stacked on top of each other?

Shelving and storage. Take advantage of wall space by installing shelves or cabinets. They are great for holding smaller pieces of equipment and for storage—particularly for paperwork supplies.

"Underneath" space. A client (applying the stacking principle in another way) bought a wheeled two-level open cabinet to hold her copier and fax. She put the copier on one shelf, the fax on the other, and keeps the cabinet underneath a slab desk, wheeling it out for use. A miscellany of storage ideas:

1. Use an extra bookcase shelf for portable typewriter, some files, baskets of supplies.
2. Decorative objects make good storage containers. A ceramic mug looks attractive holding pencils and pens.
3. Paper, pencils, and supplies can be kept in stackable plastic or vinyl storage cubes kept under the desk. Or use storage bins on runners which, in effect, make drawers.
4. Expand on the classic in/out box with stackable plastic boxes that can be added on indefinitely. There is a

small style for stationery and papers, and a larger one—actually meant to be a vegetable bin—for stacks of magazines and newspapers.

5. Wall organizers—molded plastic pieces that hang on the wall—are helpful for pads, pens, calendar, and other current supplies.

THE SMALL-SCALE OFFICE FOR HOME AND PERSONAL BUSINESS

It is as necessary to establish a comfortable and efficient workspace for making out grocery lists, paying bills, and writing personal notes as it is to set up a business office. The only difference is that an office for personal business is smaller in scale and thus requires less elaborate appointments.

A desk, of course, doesn't really have to be a desk. All you really need is a surface to write on. You would be surprised at some of the arrangements people come up with. One client, for example, is a theatrical agent who works out of her apartment, or, more precisely, her bed. So far as she is concerned, staying in bed until at least noon is more or less an article of faith, but that doesn't mean she doesn't work! She and I designed together a lap-desk arrangement that she could manipulate easily, write on, and store the basic supplies she needed. It was designed to meet a very special situation. Your own desk should be just as carefully suited to your needs.

Look around your home to see if there is a suitable desk or table which would fit into the dimensions of the work area. If you find a table, it should be sturdy, high enough to write on comfortably, and large enough to hold various implements on its surface. Also, if you choose a table, as opposed to a fully fitted desk, space must be allocated for a filing cabinet, and possibly for a typewriter table.

If you can't find a desk or table in your home, buy a desk. It is an investment you won't regret. There are so many different kinds of desks available that you should have no trouble finding one which has the practical characteristics of office models, but is still attractive in your home. Here are the specifications to keep in mind:

1. *Writing surface.* Like the ideal table, your desk should be sturdy and comfortable to use, with a writing surface that doesn't wobble.

2. *Place for supplies.* A modern office desk is usually fitted with a special drawer for stationery, carbon paper, and the like, with stationery sections inserted at approximately a 45° angle. This is ideal, but you can do without the specially constructed drawer if there is at least one large drawer in which paper and envelopes can be kept in folders. There should also be a shallow drawer with compartments for paper clips, rubber bands, and odds and ends.

3. *Files and records.* A home office seldom has need for more than one file drawer, or sometimes two. If your desk has at least one drawer big enough to contain "letter size" (11¾" × 9½") file folders, all your files will probably be comfortably accommodated.

Other Furniture and Equipment

A desk with lots of accoutrements is perfect, but if your basic piece of equipment is a table, a partially outfitted desk, or a slab over two filing cabinets, then you may need various supplementary items to store everything:

1. *Place for stationery,* carbons, yellow pads, envelopes, etc. I use a portable metal stationery rack, of the kind available in office supply stores. It has several small

open drawers, and can hold different kinds of paper supplies.

2. *File cabinet.*   A two-drawer file cabinet, preferably of "letter size" width, should take care of most storage requirements. You can stand it in a closet if you don't want it visible, but file cabinets are now made in pretty colors to fit home decorating schemes.

3. *Tray with compartments for small articles* like pens, paper clips, and rubber bands. Any office supply store has these trays in a variety of materials and colors.

4. *Chair.*   Don't choose a chair already in use somewhere else in the house. Your work area should have its own chair—one that is comfortable. Swivel chairs are particularly useful because you can turn from one position in your work area to another without getting up.

7
Computers and Other Tools of Your Trade

In my travels through many kinds of business offices, many is the forlorn computer I've seen, unused and unloved, whose owner bought it only because he/she felt that one is just not in the swim without a computer these days. Yet either the owner really didn't need a computer at all, or perhaps he/she didn't know how to use it.

This is a brief journey down computer lane, sketching some circumstances under which a computer could be a valuable tool. The discussion is obviously not intended for people who work with computers professionally, or for people who use specialized functions such as spreadsheets or data base management. They need no advice from me. Rather, the hope is to offer some guidance to those who are traumatized by computer confusion, basically in connection with word processing.

COMPUTERS, FAX MACHINES, AND COPIERS

Word processing is typing by another name. What distinguishes "processing," however, from simple typing is that typed words can be acted upon, or "processed." Either one by one or in bulk, they can be modified, deleted, moved, transferred to another document, reproduced, or just about anything else you can think of—all at the press of a few keys.

There are four elements that bear on whether or not the computer's ability to process words becomes a truly valuable tool.

Volume is one key factor. The difference between word-processing reams of typescript on a computer and typing on a typewriter is remarkable. In my own experience, both the original *Getting Organized* and my second book, *The Organized Executive*, were typed on a typewriter, while this revised edition of *Getting Organized* and a new book about senior executive organizing strategies are on a word processor. It has truly been a liberation. Retyping and cutting and pasting have become a thing of the past.

The second factor to consider is that of *easy correction*. Of course, paper volume and ease of correction are related, but the opening salvo of word processing into general practice came about, not so much because of volume, but because lawyers needed perfect text without erasures. Law firms were at the cutting edge of word processing because of the punctiliousness of legal documents. Before, if a typist made an error or if a lawyer made a change, the whole page had to be retyped. So you can imagine the liberation that easy correction brought.

The third element is that of *reproduction*. If you send lots of "originals," or if the same letter or document is going out to many different people, then the computer is your dish.

Mix and match is also an important factor to consider. You can combine pieces of existing documents in new ways, while adding in new material as well. Say, for example, that you tutor students preparing for the SATs. You make up a basic lesson plan and then combine for each student the relevant portions of the basic plan and type in fresh material as needed.

Advice on what computer to buy is beyond the scope of this book. I suggest going to two or three computer stores and asking the advice of knowledgeable salespeople. Also check with knowledgeable friends, and do some reading. In addition, here are two general tips:

First, do not buy a computer more advanced than the uses to which you intend to put it. Word processing, for example, doesn't require a machine capable of lightning-fast mathematical calculations. And second, don't purchase a bargain or discounted or used computer unless you *really* know what you are doing. Chances are that, like most computer users, you will need all the service and support a top dealership and company can provide.

Many people, however, conduct effective business lives without any computer at all. Many senior corporate executives don't use computers, and for that matter wouldn't be caught dead with one. So don't think you need a computer just because they are out there.

Many small-business folk find that the machine of choice is the "electronic typewriter" or "memory typewriter," rather than a personal computer.

An electronic typewriter is a typewriter, not a computer. You roll in a sheet of paper just like in the olden days. However, it has a number of computerized functions, such as underlining, centering, and margin set, that are activated at the touch of a couple of keys.

In addition, a "memory typewriter" has a certain number of pages of memory for repeating documents. For example, usually in batches of ten or fifteen, I sent over one hundred letters to executives requesting interviews for a new book.

Really extensive reworking on an electronic typewriter is, frankly, more trouble than it's worth, but the typewriter makes normal typo-type corrections a breeze.

Though I myself use a computer for book manuscripts, for me the memory typewriter has just the right relationship of high tech to low for ordinary day-to-day paperwork.

How about a fax machine? The fax is a bit of a fad. People in the creative professions whose clients or colleagues are waiting eagerly for their copywriting or graphic designs would probably be sorely bereft without them. They are also invaluable for businesses in areas where messenger or express delivery services are not readily available. Otherwise, mail or messenger or overnight delivery service would probably do as well. However, if you like to fax and people like to fax to you, then why not?

Whether a home copier is useful depends on the volume and nature of the copying you do. If you regularly copy hundreds of pages, then surely you wouldn't want to purchase an advanced copier, but would continue to patronize the copy shop. If, however, most days generate five or ten or twenty pages that should be copied, and it's a pain in the neck to run those odds and ends down to the copy shop, then your own small copier would probably be quite a convenience.

SUPPLIES CHECKLIST

This section is basically a checklist outlining the kinds of things you need to make your work area function properly. Wherever possible I suggest that you buy items in quantity—enough for current use plus extra for backup stocks. For example, a full box of five hundred sheets of white paper, a full box of copyset carbon paper, and two boxes of pens will last for a good long time. Backup stock can be kept in a closet, or some place away from the work area if your storage space is limited. As you reach the bottom of your supplies, note the items in your notebook and pick up new stocks when convenient.

Address book or Rolodex.

Appointment calendar. This item is a very important part of the personal business system. Ideally, the calendar should be small enough to carry around with your notebook, as well as for use at your desk. If you look hard enough in stationery and office supply stores, perhaps you can find a combination notebook and calendar that isn't too bulky to carry around in your briefcase or handbag. In any case, the "date" squares should be large enough to list appointments comfortably.

Bulletin board. If it fits into your work area, a bulletin board is a good place to collect notes and reminders to yourself. A few squares of stick-on cork, available in any hardware store, will do very nicely. Attach notes with push pins.

Carbon paper, if you use a typewriter. I recommend that you make a copy of any business letter you write. The most convenient kind is "copyset" carbon paper—the backup paper is attached to the carbon, which is torn off and thrown away after use.

Computer disks and storage containers.

Computer paper and supplies.

Copier paper and supplies.

Desk lamp.

Dictionary.

Fax paper and supplies.

File folders. Letter-size folders are easier to handle than the wider legal size. In either case I suggest "third cut" folders, in which the stick-up tabs are staggered so they don't block each other from view.

File folder labels.

Hanging files (Pendaflex). Many people prefer them, but they are not essential and take up much more space than manila files.

Letter opener.

Marking pens. It is useful to have on hand a few marking pens in different colors.

Paper clips, regular size and oversized. A small box of each.

Pencil sharpener. If you are a serious pencil user, I suggest a handsome electric desk model sharpener.

Pencils and pens.

Postage scale (a small one). For oversized mail.

Prop, to hold a document during retyping.

Rubber bands. Buy a small box of mixed sizes.

Rubber stamp and ink pad. This item is optional, but it is a nice idea. To eliminate the need for letterhead stationery, which is expensive, any office supply store can make up a stamp with your name and address.

Ruler.

Scissors.

Scratch paper. Buy some lined yellow pads for drafting letters and writing down thoughts.

Scotch tape and dispenser.

Stamps. Aside from regular stamps, keep the appropriate postage on hand for special mailings if you do them regularly.

Stapler, staples, staple remover.

Stationery and envelopes. For most purposes 8½″ × 11″ plain white paper (with rag content for a better quality) and matching business-size (#10) envelopes are fine. Buy smaller notepaper also, for personal use. If you use letterhead stationery, get some plain white paper anyway for second sheets and general purposes. Also buy some oversized manila envelopes if you have occasion to mail out thick documents, magazines, etc. Jiffy bags, which are padded to protect fragile packages, can be useful as well.

Telephone. Install an extension right at your desk, or consider a cordless phone.

Waste basket.

White-out fluid.

PART FOUR

Money

8
The Master Plan

"I don't know where the money goes. I make a fair income, I don't buy custom-made suits or take the Concorde to Paris, so why am I always just this side of the poverty line?" This is the Song of the Plaintive Consumer. Spontaneous extravagance, however, is generally not the problem. More to the point are the nagging day-to-day questions you can't answer: "Where is my money going?" "Why can other people on my financial level afford more rewarding vacations?" "How can I use my money to provide a generally more satisfying life?"

The answer is choice: setting priorities, consciously allocating resources for defined purposes. Unfortunately, setting financial priorities is extremely difficult. The normal difficulties in choosing between *any* alternatives are compounded by the alluring and endless options of our consumer society.

Fulfilling choices can be made, however. If you are frequently troubled by money questions, this chapter provides a framework for designing a financial master plan that will offer you or your family the greatest satisfaction. Working through the "Financial Planning Guide" that follows is an interesting and useful exercise that helps you live more comfortably within your income by forcing you to decide what's important to you. Your choices may seem strange or idiosyncratic to someone else, but acknowledging and respecting these personal values is at the heart of a truly workable financial plan.

In figuring your financial master plan, it will be helpful to have a pocket calculator designed for simple mathematical functions. A more complicated one won't be necessary.

FINANCIAL PLANNING GUIDE

Write down the household's *yearly* income—either net income ("take-home pay") if it comes from wages or salary only, or gross income if there are sources other than salary. On the same sheet of paper list your various expenses:

1. *Fixed expenses.* Money paid in fixed amounts. These expenses include:

   Debt repayments (bank loans, installment purchases)
   Insurance premiums
   Rent or mortgage payments
   Taxes (This applies only if your taxes are not withheld, or if you pay non-income taxes such as property taxes.)

2. *Flexible expenses.* Expenses over which you have more control. Food, for instance, is necessary, but there is

considerable leeway as to expenditure. This is also true of utilities. The most common flexible expenses include:

Automobile
Charitable contributions
Clothing
Entertainment
Food
Household (furniture, appliances, repairs, etc.)
Investments
Personal allowances
Savings
Schooling
Travel
Utilities

These aren't all the possible categories. A few other possibilities are: books and records, gifts, medical and dental (not covered by insurance), hobby or sports equipment. Keep the categories fairly broad. Thus, for example, include cosmetics under "clothing," and household supplies —detergent, cleansing powders, paper towels—under "food."

As an example, let's follow the master plan of a "typical" American family, John and Mary Michael, and their little boy Jimmy. John, an assistant bank manager, grosses $45,000 per year, and Mary, an assistant buyer in a department store, earns $22,500. Their combined "take-home" income after withholding is about $50,000.*

---

*John and Mary are both wage earners whose income taxes are withheld, so they don't have to put money aside for that. People who pay taxes directly should obtain the tax figures from their quarterly estimate and add 5% more for inflation.

Fixed Expenses

First, John and Mary list the amounts paid out per year on their fixed expenses. These figures are listed below. They subtract $13,030 from $50,000—deducting the fixed expenses from their take-home total—leaving a balance of $36,970 for flexible expenses.

Debts—$278 per month for the car ($15,000 at 11% over 5 years)	$ 3,330 per year
Insurance premiums—life, home, fire, etc. (Health insurance is paid by their employers)	$ 3,000 per year
Mortgage—$308 per month ($100,000 at 11% over 30 years)	$ 3,700 per year
Taxes—a property tax of $3,000 per year	$ 3,000 per year
Total fixed expenses	$13,030 per year

Flexible Expenses

Stage 1: Making Estimates

Now the fun begins. From the list of flexible expenses, John and Mary choose the categories they feel strongly about— the categories that rank #1 in *importance to them*. They put a "#1" next to each of these categories, and figure out, in rough accord with their actual income limitation, how much money they would like to spend on these items. Rough accord is necessary; you can't put down $12,000 for household expenditures when disposable income is $15,000. But you can let your imagination roam a little.

Going down the list alphabetically, Mary claims clothing as a #1 expense for her. She enjoys clothes, and her job as a buyer demands that she present a good appearance. $2,500 seems a fair figure for her clothing budget. John, on the other hand, isn't interested in clothes; one suit per year plus various accessories is sufficient, so his clothes allocation is $1,500. Jimmy is seven years old and growing rapidly, so John and Mary agree that $600 is about right for his clothes. Their total clothes budget is $4,600.

Schooling is next. Jimmy is exceptionally intelligent, and teachers have recommended that he be sent to a private school for gifted children. John and Mary agree that Jimmy should have this opportunity, so they claim the $7,000 yearly tuition as a #1 expense.

John claims occasional travel as a #1 item for himself. He finds that a change of scene relieves the tensions of his busy job. The Michael family had in the past taken one family vacation per year in the car, and then John would average two short trips on his own. They agree to allot $5,000 for total family travel.

The #2 choices are considered next; that is, the categories that the family would *like* to spend money on, but do not feel as intensely about. For John and Mary, the first #2 choice is charitable contributions, so they agree to allocate $1,500 for that category. Entertainment is the next #2 category. Not only do John and Mary enjoy going out and entertaining, but John feels that party giving is an important source of business contacts. They figure that two good-sized parties per year, costing about $600 each (and partly tax deductible), plus frequent guests for drinks, adds up to about $1,500. In addition, they both enjoy movies, theater, and ballet. An entertainment total of $3,000 is allotted.

Household expenses are next on the #2 list. Although the Michaels anticipate no purchase of major appliances in the coming year, Mary thinks the living room could use some brightening and John is eager to fix up his workroom.

They agree to keep these costs within $4,800. Adding on another $1,200 for repairs and unexpected expenses leaves a "household" total of $6,000.

For John, personal allowance is a #2 category. He feels uncomfortable carrying less than $100, so his personal allowance is set at $125 per week, giving a year's total of $6,500. Mary feels less strongly about a personal allowance, so she tables that item until they reach category #3.

Finally John and Mary face the remaining categories, all of which are #3 in rank. These categories may be crucial; everyone has to eat, and for many people an automobile is almost as essential. But the determining factor is how much you *care*, beyond actual need.

The first #3 item on the Michaels' list is "automobile." For John and Mary a car is simply a means of transportation. Their car is not new—it needed about $300 worth of servicing in the past year—but they feel it is sufficient for John's daily commute of twenty-five miles. A $1,095 allotment for gas and servicing (car insurance is covered under "premiums" in the fixed expenses list) seems sufficient.

Food doesn't present too much of a problem since the Michaels like simple meals, so they decide to keep within their present range of $150 per week for the family, which totals $7,800 a year.

They decide to lump investments together with savings. (In a more elaborate financial planning setup, savings and investments might be considered separately, since they have somewhat different purposes.) John and Mary feel fairly secure—there is adequate insurance, they are each enrolled in pension plans at their jobs, and they have several thousand dollars in the bank. They realize that in a few years they will have to start saving intensively for Jimmy's college tuition and their own future, but they can coast along for now at their present savings rate of $150 per month, or $1,800 per year.

Mary's personal allowance, which had been bypassed before, is set at $75 per week, from which she buys lunch at the low-cost employee dining room where she works, and contributes $15 per week to a car pool. The yearly sum adds up to $3,900.

And last, utilities—the item least "interesting" to them—average $200 per month (including telephone, electricity, gas, water), totaling $2,400.

Their flexible expenses are listed below.

#3	Automobile		$ 1,095
#2	Charitable contributions		1,500
#1	Clothing		4,600
#2	Entertainment		3,000
#3	Food		7,800
#2	Household expenses (furniture, appliances, etc.)		6,000
#3	Savings/investments		1,800
#2	Personal allowance (John)		6,500
#3	Personal allowance (Mary)		3,900
#1	Jimmy's schooling		7,000
#1	Travel		5,000
#3	Utilities		2,400
		Total	$50,595

"Lord, that's awful," John said to Mary, stunned, "since our disposable income is only $36,970; a difference of $13,625."

Mary was more sanguine. "It's important though. Now we know, first, the financial level we're aspiring to, and second, it makes us evaluate the things that are really important. Let's try and work with this to bring it into line with our actual income, while still leaving money available for the things that matter most to us."

Stage 2: Cutting Costs

The Michaels' next step is to go through the #3 categories, and wherever possible, subtract a solid third from each allocation—and *then* decide how to make that cut tolerable. A one-third cut is hefty, but it makes sense as a substantial but not impossible reduction. Occasionally the estimate does have to be revised back upward, but surprisingly often the cut is manageable.

Automobile. They begin by reducing their original estimate of $1,095 by one-third to $730. The $1,095 was based on the idea that John commutes twenty-five miles each day, using approximately seven gallons of gas per week, which, at $1.30 per gallon, totals about $475 per year. They estimated an additional $338 for general family driving (five gallons per week). The remaining $282 was for servicing. John now decides to join his colleagues in a round-robin car pool; he will drive the car every third week, reducing his commutation bill to $317. Since the car won't be driven as often, $52 can be shaved from the servicing allotment, leaving a $230 balance. In addition, they decided to cut down considerably on family driving. The family enjoys fishing and they went almost every nice weekend to a lake sixty miles away. They agreed to start going to another lake fifteen miles away, and only go to the more distant lake as a treat every two months. That, combined with more careful weekend family driving, would permit the cut to $730.

Food. Lowering the food allocation from $7,800 to $5,200—a cut of $2,600—seems a very big reduction indeed. Dividing the reduction by week results in a more manageable $50 reduction, leaving a total weekly food expenditure of $100. Surely, the Michaels think, that is possible. They agree to explore a variety of avenues: buying less expensive foods; buying and freezing supermarket specials in large quantities; canning and preserving at home; investigating creative economies like buying in bulk directly from wholesale sources; joining a food co-op; and/or growing some portion of food in a home garden. These economies can save quite a lot of money, but they are time-consuming. They virtually eliminate convenience foods and the quick steak for dinner, so one benefit must be weighed against the other. (See Chapter 16, page 291, for streamlined methods of meal planning and food preparation.)

Savings/investments. John and Mary agree that saving less than $120 per month is a mistake, so they decide to reduce savings to $1,440 rather than all the way down to $1,200.

Personal allowance (Mary). Cutting Mary's weekly pocket money from $75 to $50, a flat one-third reduction, seems too stringent, so she and John decide on $65, making that yearly allocation $3,380.

Utilities. The original utilities estimate of $2,400 was based on their present rate of $125 per month—for electricity, gas, water, and a large average telephone bill of $75. John and Mary both use electricity carefully, and they agreed to be even more observant of power-saving tips. Such small economies might reduce the electric bill to $100 per month.

The real problem, however, is the $75 phone bill. Mary makes long-distance calls totaling $40 each month to her sister, Louise. But when John suggests curtailing the calls or writing letters, Mary gets upset. The calls turn out to be a higher priority than anticipated. They consider asking Louise to share the cost, but since she calls Mary about as often, her bill is probably about the same. So they agree to leave the long-distance calls intact, and lower the remaining $35 per month by timing local calls to five minutes each, reducing the monthly bill to $60. So the utility allotment drops to only $1,920 instead of the hoped-for $1,600, but there was a hidden priority that had to be taken into account.

John and Mary follow the same procedures for the #2 choices, this time, however, subtracting only one-quarter instead of one-third, since these are more important categories which demand more leeway.

Charitable contributions. Mary decides that since she spends time working for her favorite charities and contributes clothes and appliances to the charity thrift shops (for a tax deduction as well!), they can cut back on the cash contributions for the time being. The charity allotment is reduced from $1,500 to $1,125.

Entertainment. The one-quarter cut from $3,000 reduces the entertainment allotment by $750, to $2,250. John and Mary had originally planned on two parties during the year, but decide that one party will be sufficient. They will save the rest by getting cheaper theater seats and cutting back a little.

Household expenses. In order to reduce the household allocation by one-quarter, from $6,000 to $4,500, the Michaels cut the household "reserve" fund from $1,200 to $1,000. They decide to do some of the work themselves, and Mary will arrange for a seamstress friend to make slipcovers in exchange for Mary's fashion counseling. They will postpone buying the less important living room items until next year.

Personal allowance (John). John admits that he might not need $125 pocket money per week, so a compromise sum of $100 is agreed upon, reducing that allotment to $5,200.

For the #1 categories, it's best to be creative and flexible rather than set a firm reduction figure.

Clothing. John feels he can reduce his clothing allotment from $1,500 to $1,100. Jimmy's is also reduced from $600 to $450. How many pairs of blue jeans and sneakers can one little boy wear? Mary is more of a problem since this is a high priority for her. She lowers her clothes budget to $2,000 by careful wardrobe planning plus creative shopping: In addition to shopping at a discount in the department store where she works, she will explore unconventional outlets like resale shops, discount houses, and manufacturers' outlets. The Michaels' clothing allotment is now reduced to $3,550.

Jimmy's schooling. This is a fixed tuition fee of $7,000, but John and Mary reserve the option to try for a scholarship or a loan.

Travel. Touring in the car is a relatively inexpensive form of family travel, but John enjoys an occasional short trip alone. If the family goes backpacking and canoeing—costing no more than $1,500—John can take one lavish three-day trip for $1,500, and another $750 excursion, thus cutting travel from $5,000 to $3,750.

The first round of budget cuts over, the Michaels draw up a new list.

Automobile	$	730
Charitable contributions		1,125
Clothing		3,550
Entertainment		2,250
Food		5,200
Household expenses (furniture, appliances, etc.)		4,500
Savings/investments		1,440
Personal allowance (John)		5,200
Personal allowance (Mary)		3,380
Jimmy's schooling		7,000
Travel		3,750
Utilities		1,920
	Total	$40,045

They are now only $3,075 over the flexible income total of $36,970—a lot more manageable than the original $13,625 discrepancy, but necessitating another round of cutting.

Stage 3: To the Bone

Automobile. No reduction is possible in this category.

Charitable contributions. Reluctantly the Michaels lower their charity allocation to a rock-bottom $900.

Clothing. Mary's $2,000 allocation still seems too high. She can manage with $1,500. Both John and Jimmy make small reductions, bringing the total clothing budget down to $2,750.

Entertainment. John and Mary agree to hold firm at $2,250.

Food. Their reduction to $5,200 seems the bare minimum.

Household expenses. A reduction to $4,000.

Savings/investments. No reduction possible.

Personal allowances. John and Mary agree to a $1,000 reduction in their combined allowances.

Jimmy's schooling. No reduction possible.

Travel. This item, because it means so much to John to go away a couple of times a year, takes some discussion. Since travel means very little to Mary, the Michaels decide to forgo a family vacation this year; Jimmy can attend a summer day camp that costs $500. John, however, will still take his two trips, one for $1,500 and one for $750. This leaves a travel allotment of $2,750.

Utilities. No further reductions.

The Michaels' list now reflects their latest cuts. Their budget of $36,520 is now $450 less than their disposable

Automobile	$	730
Charitable contributions		900
Clothing		2,750
Entertainment		2,250
Food		5,200
Household expenses (furniture, appliances, etc.)		4,000
Savings/investments		1,440
Personal allowances (John and Mary)		7,580
Jimmy's schooling		7,000
Travel		2,750
Utilities		1,920
	Total	$36,520

income limit of $36,970! John and Mary also decide to try for a scholarship for Jimmy's school. Any easing up on that allocation will be transferred into savings.

As you design your own plan, keep in mind that John's and Mary's decisions and compromises might not be right for you. You might not even approve of them! John may seem self-indulgent insisting on those private trips, but he has been flexible in every other area precisely so that he may have relative mobility on this, to him, important point.

No matter how illogical your priority may seem to someone else, you have a right to it—as long as you're prepared to compromise or even be severely restricted in other areas to compensate for relative freedom in a priority.

With that in mind, here is a brief summary of the financial planning procedure.

SUMMARY OF THE FINANCIAL PLANNING GUIDE

1. Note the household's yearly income—either net ("take-home pay") if all income derives from wages or salary, or gross if from other sources.
2. List all your expenses under two major headings: "fixed expenses" and "flexible expenses."
3. Add up the amounts paid out yearly under the "fixed expenses" category, and subtract from the yearly income. This leaves a balance to be allocated among the flexible expenses.
4. Go down the "flexible" list and select the categories that the various members of the household feel most strongly about. Mark these #1, and figure out, in rough accord with your actual income limitation, how much money you would like to allocate to each of these.
5. Select the #2 categories and figure out money allocations for these categories.
6. Do the same with #3 categories.
7. Add up all the "flexible expenses." If they total a sum no more than the disposable income as noted in step 3, congratulations. You are living within your income. If the total sum is more than your disposable income, go on to the next step.
8. Consider each #3 category in turn as follows:
    a. Subtract one-third of the present allocation. If, for example, a #3 allocation is $900, revise it down to $600.
    b. Consider how that item might be pared down to fit within the reduced limit. See pages 142–44 to familiarize yourself with some of the kinds of thinking involved.
9. Consider each #2 item in turn as follows:
    a. Subtract one-quarter of the present allocation. If,

for example, a #2 allocation is $1,000, revise it down to $750.

b. Consider how that item might be pared down to fit within the reduced limit. See pages 144–45 for pointers.

10. Consider each #1 item as follows: Don't make an absolute cut; rather, consider how your needs might be met within a less expansive financial framework. See pages 144–45 for some of the ideas involved.

11. Add up and total the revised #1, #2, and #3 figures. If you are now within your disposable income range (the balance arrived at in step 3), excellent. Your work is done. If not:

12. Go through the list again, paring down as much as you can—*but* never lose sight of your priorities. Try to keep your #1 selections as generous as you can because they are most important to you. See pages 146–47 for some approaches to this process. Keep at this until expenses have been brought into line with income.

By now you have established a basic financial planning framework that will function effectively for a long time. I recommend that you adjust it yearly—probably at tax time, while your financial situation is still fresh in your mind— to take into consideration increase or decrease in income, completion of installment debts, a change in priorities. As the needs of living change, so does the budget.

9
The Mechanics of Money

Many people are intimidated by the mechanics of handling money. One of my clients was always mislaying her bills, never knew the amount of her bank balance, and lived with the threat that her electricity might be turned off at any moment. Finally she concocted a system born of desperation: She sent off $100 every so often to the electric company in the hope that this amount would cover her bill. We devised an easier and more reliable system for her, and you can do the same for yourself. A few hours one day per month will generally be sufficient to take care of all money transactions.

WHO MINDS THE BILLS?

There was a time in the not-so-distant past when it appeared that men were as genetically suited to handling the purse strings as they were to taking out the garbage. And women were as genetically suited to spending the money as they were to teasing their hair. Fortunately, times have changed in a way that allows us to swing in and out of the roles that are congruent with our varying skills and abilities.

One person in a couple should serve as "controller" for the family's joint revenues. Before choosing which member of the couple will be appointed controller, let's take a quick walk through the controller's tasks and responsibilities in order to determine which one of you is best suited to handle it.

First, the controller is responsible for collecting and assembling the bills and financial statements, bank statements, etc., as they come in, and is responsible for paying them and filing them in a timely way. Second, he/she has to write the checks and maintain the joint checkbook. And third, the controller reconciles the bank statement and reviews investment advices to make sure that all transactions have been properly processed.

In choosing the controller, don't confuse the ability to be a shrewd and canny investor, which is a different kind of skill, with the ability to pay bills and balance bank statements. It also doesn't matter who earns more money.

The controller is the practical money manager, but is not the financial decision-maker unless both parties agree that one of you "drives" financial decisions. In any case, major decisions regarding purchasing and debt philosophy should be made together. A good discussion between the two of you about what money means to each of you, how much indebtedness you feel comfortable with, and how in general you wish to flow in terms of your overall organization and perception of money is critical.

Regardless of who is chosen as controller, it is strongly recommended that both parties review expenditures and procedures together each month after the monthly accounts have been done. It is not really the "checker's" assignment to spot clerical errors (although any errors discovered are all to the good). The checker is really there to be briefed, which is useful for three reasons:

First, if only one person is involved with money, there is a tendency to develop a shorthand way of doing things or codes that are unintelligible to anyone but the controller. Marianne, for example, for budgeting purposes, faithfully marks each credit card expenditure with an initial: "R" for household expenses (because they live on Red Apple Lane), "E" for entertainment, "D" for tax-deductible expenses, and a few other categories. The charges are funneled into the bill-paying account from different accounts, depending on the nature of the expense. Should Marianne be mowed down by a crane, she would go to credit card heaven with her codes safely and completely never to be found again.

So it's important for the partner to be able to look over the controller's shoulder and say, "What is this?" and "Where is that?"

Second, it is human nature that a person whose activities are subject to no review begins to assume that that is in the nature of things. Thus, decisions tend to become more autocratic if the family controller has no one looking over his shoulder.

For example, Greg and Anita voted Greg to be the controller. And within six months it became virtually impossible for Anita to intrude in the financial process—or even to ask questions—because Greg's invariable answer was, "Listen, I can't explain it now, but it's under control."

However, it wasn't under control—Greg had taken on debt they couldn't manage—and they had some hairy times before things got straightened out.

The third reason why it is imperative that neither partner abdicate the financial system to the other is concern for the future. Many of my clients have been elderly women whose husbands had recently died. Though many of them were affluent, they had no more idea than a flea of where their money was, how to pay bills, how to pay taxes, or anything! So on top of the emotional distress of losing their husbands, they felt extremely helpless and disoriented.

SETTING UP THE SYSTEM

If you designed a master plan similar to the one described in Chapter 8, draw up a monthly chart in order to keep actual expenses within the plan's guidelines. Again, we'll use John and Mary Michael as the example.

1. Divide each yearly allocation by twelve months and round off. The Michaels' breakdown is shown below:

Expenses	Yearly	Monthly
Automobile	$ 730	$ 61
Charitable contributions	900	75
Clothing	2,750	230
Entertainment	2,250	188
Food	5,200	433
Household expenses (furniture, appliances, etc.)	4,000	333
Savings/investments	1,440	120
Personal allowances (John and Mary)	7,580	632
Jimmy's schooling	7,000	584
Travel	2,750	230
Utilities	1,920	160
Total	$36,520	$3,043

	Jan.	Feb.	Mar.	Apr.	May	June	July	Aug.	Sept.	Oct.	Nov.	Dec.
Car Expenses	61	122	183	244	305	366	427	488	549	610	671	732
Charity	75	150	225	300	375	450	525	600	675	750	825	900
Clothes	230	460	690	920	1150	1380	1610	1840	2070	2300	2530	2760
Entertainment	188	376	564	752	940	1128	1316	1504	1692	1880	2068	2256
Food	433	866	1299	1732	2165	2598	3031	3464	3897	4330	4763	5196
Household	333	666	999	1332	1665	1998	2331	2664	2997	3330	3663	3996
Travel	230	460	690	920	1150	1380	1610	1840	2070	2300	2530	2760
Utilities	160	320	480	640	800	960	1120	1280	1440	1600	1760	1920

Figure 2 The Michaels' Discretionary Chart of flexible expenses

2. List the categories of your *flexible* expenses on a "Discretionary Chart." *This step is only for those who are using a master plan,* and is a handy way to keep track of your flexible expenses on a month-to-month basis. Take a single month's allocation—say, for car expenses, $32 —and enter that in the top half of the January box, leaving the bottom half blank. Add $32 to the first $32, making $64 for the upper half of the February box. Another $32 for March makes $96, and on through the year. Use a pocket calculator for the arithmetic.

   Write the estimated monthly totals in red, to distinguish them from the actual expenses that will eventually be filled in on the bottom half.

   The Michaels' chart is shown in Figure 2.

3. *Whether or not you have a master plan,* draw up another chart of fixed monthly or quarterly expenses (see Figure 3). This chart consists of any item that recurs in a fixed amount on a regular basis, such as debt or installment payments, regular sums allocated to savings, rent or mortgage payments, taxes, and insurance premiums.

The asterisks in the "Taxes" and "Insurance" entries signify the months that quarterly payments are due. The IRS dates are the same for everyone. The insurance dates will depend, of course, on your own policies. Use of this chart will be discussed later in the chapter.

MONEY METHODS

I recommend a minimum of three bank accounts:

1. *Savings.* If you're married, your savings account should be a joint one. If one partner is incapacitated,

	Jan.	Feb.	Mar.	Apr.	May	June	July	Aug.	Sept.	Oct.	Nov.	Dec.
Car payments ($278)												
Mortgage ($308)												
Savings ($120)												
John's & Mary's allowances ($632)												
Taxes ($250)	*			*		*			*			
Insurance* ($250)	*			*		*				*		

*Make a separate box for each type of insurance you have—health, life, etc.

Figure 3 The Michaels' Fixed Expenses Chart

the other has immediate access to the money; if the account is in one name only, legal problems will arise.

2. *Checking.* You should have one checking account that is used only once a month for paying bills. For couples, open a joint account so either party can write the checks. Although one person will generally handle the finances, the other partner should be in a position to pay the bills if circumstances call for that.

Consider whether to opt for an interest-bearing checking account. They require a higher minimum balance than non-interest-bearing accounts, but at least your money isn't sitting there not doing anything.

Consult with your bank officer as to whether a linked "cash management" account makes sense in your particular situation.

Some large corporations make special arrangements with nearby banks to offer their employees free checking.

3. *Checking.* Each person should have his or her own personal checking account for ordinary cash expenses. Deposit your personal allowance in this account. For couples, one person should be designated food buyer, and the monthly food allotment should go into that person's account. Paying expenses by check helps you keep track of where the money is going.

The bank you choose to give your business to will, in most cases, simply be the one that's most convenient. If, however, you have some equidistant alternatives, select the bank that offers services and a friendly attitude. Services include:

ATMs (automated teller machines) linked to a national network
Bank-by-computer option

Cash-reserve or checking-plus checking. (These are in effect personal loans.)

Telephone services—to check balance, get current interest rates, etc.

Special services—safe-deposit boxes, traveler's checks, exchange of foreign currency, credit cards (some banks have a service charge, others don't), estate planning. Ask about other services.

Sometimes a small neighborhood branch may offer more advantages than a large midtown bank. Since you become acquainted with the staff, you may feel freer about asking for help in a crisis, such as an emergency overdraft. A small-branch officer is also somewhat more willing to spend time when a modest sum of money is involved to advise you in financial planning and taking advantage of special services the bank may offer. He or she may also be more helpful in granting you a personal loan.

Before dealing with any bank, check to see that it has been insured by the Federal Deposit Insurance Corporation (FDIC) or the Federal Savings & Loan Insurance Corporation (FSLIC), both of which insure your deposits up to a specified amount.

THE MONTHLY PROCEDURE

This procedure applies to everyone, whether or not you've designed a master plan. As discussed previously, choose one person in the household to regularly act as "controller"—to deposit checks in the bill-paying account and pay the bills. On or near the first of each month, balance your checkbook and pay the bills. Hold any bill that arrives later until the accounting date of the next month. If you feel the entire procedure of reconciling checkbooks and paying bills is too much for one day's work, reconcile bank statements a day or two *before* the bill-paying day; that, too, should be a regular appointment. Follow this monthly procedure:

1. Assemble equipment and supplies, which are:
   a. Financial folder with pocket. This is the financial folder discussed in Chapter 5, page 62. As bills, bank statements, bank deposit slips, investment notices, anything to do with money, come in during the month, put them in the folder. Don't try to act on them until your monthly appointment unless there is an emergency of some kind.
   b. Sales slips. Make sure you have sales slips for all charge purchases, and save them. If you charge groceries, a kitchen drawer is a good place to keep grocery slips. A dresser drawer might be used for slips involving clothing purchases. Or put the slips directly into the financial folder if that is convenient. When you begin moneywork, collect all the slips and put them with the financial folder.
   c. Discretionary Chart and chart of expenses. Keep these permanently in the financial folder.
   d. Payment booklets for bank loans and car installments. Keep them in the financial folder.
   e. Calculator.
   f. Checkbook for bill-paying account. Keep it permanently in or near the financial folder.
   g. Blank envelopes and stamps.
2. Sorting out. Divide the contents of the financial folder into five piles:
   a. Banking: statements, canceled checks, deposit slips, and any other bank notices.

b. Bills, notices of renewals (magazines, club dues, and so forth), any correspondence that will require payment by check.

c. Payment booklets for debts (bank loans, installment payments) or other fixed obligations.

d. All sales slips and cash register slips.

e. Anything else, such as investment notices.

3. Reconcile the bank statements. In honesty, there's a fair chance that life would run smoothly if you never reconciled a bank statement. But banks do make mistakes. A client once had $500,000 accidentally *credited* to his account! The bank caught that one soon enough. If you've not been reconciling up till now, the reconciling instructions on the bank statement or envelope, although adequate for someone already familiar with the task, don't give enough detail for a novice. A bank officer might be willing to start you off in the right direction. But if you're on your own, forget the past and start with the most recent statement:

a. Put the canceled checks in numerical order. There will probably be numerical gaps, representing checks that have not yet been cashed. The bank statement itself should also be in front of you.

b. Note the sum on the top check—the amount only, not the payee—and look through the statement listing until you find that sum. (Note: Most banks themselves list the checks in numerical order.) Cross the sum off the statement and go on until you've finished the pile of checks.

c. If you have a special checking account, two additional amounts will be listed on your statement: check charges plus a monthly maintenance fee. Add these, subtract the total from your checkbook balance, and cross them off the statement. Remaining amounts on the statement would be one of the following:

A penalty for a bounced check, or a special charge, such as for new checkbooks. In either case, the bank will have sent you an "advice." Cross that sum off the statement and subtract it from your checkbook balance.

A mistake caused by skipping a check as you flipped quickly through the pile. Make sure that no two checks are stuck together.

The bank may have charged someone else's check to your account. We'll get to that later.

d. Now reconcile the canceled checks against your own record in your checkbook. Beginning, for example, with #801, mark the 801 entry. Continue this way for all the canceled checks. When you come to a gap—#811 is missing—don't mark off 811 in your checkbook. The check hasn't cleared yet, and it will probably appear on next month's statement. Also mark off the subtractions you just made for service charge and any penalties.

e. Select the deposit slips that register on this month's statement and mark them off in your checkbook as you did with the checks. *Don't check off deposits not registered on the bank statement.* Put the registered deposit slips with the canceled checks.

f. Figure out your current balance by following the instructions on the form imprinted either on the reverse side of the statement or on the envelope. Here's a brief summary:

List all outstanding checks—that is, checks that have not cleared and are not checked off in your checkbook—and add them up.

Add up the deposit slips that did *not* appear on this month's statement, plus your balance on the closing day of the statement (that balance is printed on the front of the statement).

Subtract the total amount of checks outstanding from the sum you arrived at in the preceding step.

The remainder should conform to your checkbook balance. If there's a small discrepancy, up to about $10, you can generally assume that the bank's computers are accurate, and you have made an error on your check stubs. Correct your checkbook balance accordingly and don't worry about it. If there's a significant discrepancy, re-check your addition and subtraction carefully. The mistake probably lies in that area.

g. Follow-up. At this point you would ordinarily close the books until next month, but some situations require follow-up action:

If there is a significant discrepancy between your balance and the bank's, take your materials to the bank and have them work out the problem.

If there is an unresolved sum listed in the bank statement, take statement and canceled checks to the bank.

If a check hasn't cleared by the time you have received two bank statements, get in touch with the payee to see if it has been put through. In some localities, a check is no longer valid thirty days after its date.

If a deposit slip has not appeared on two statements, take slip and statements to the bank.

h. When everything is reconciled, put the statement, canceled checks, deposit slips, and advices into the statement envelope, write the month and year on the outside, and put it into a drawer or small accordion file. The deposit slips that were not covered in this month's statement should be put back in the financial folder for next month. Note: If you item-

ize income tax deductions, you might want to organize your checks at this point, or you may choose
not to. See page 168 for a discussion of handling
tax materials.*

4. Now turn to the payment of bills. Check the sales slips
for department store and credit card purchases against
the itemization on the bill, and staple the slips to the
bill stub that you keep. Write a check for each bill
(always fill in your check register—it is important for
reconciling and for taxes).

5. Collect all sales slips and bill stubs—the part that you
retain for yourself—put them into an envelope, write
the month and year on the outside, and put the envelope with the bank statement.

6. Investments in stocks and bonds generate stock transaction notices and other kinds of paper. You will get
buying and selling notices from your broker for each
transaction, plus a monthly stock summary that should
be checked so that it conforms to the individual slips.
At the end of the year there is a notice summarizing
dividends received. All these materials should be saved
for the purposes of computing dividend income and
capital gains or losses.

7. Fixed obligations. Take Figure 3 (page 156) and your
payment booklets. Write checks for all items listed
(loans, installment payments, savings deposits, personal allowances, etc.) and check the appropriate box.
If it is *not* a payment month for quarterly taxes, put a
dash in the box. If it *is* a payment month, write out
your check and mark the appropriate box. Handle
insurance payments the same way.

---

*If you itemize income tax deductions, keep canceled checks for a period of
six years. You can throw away older checks. If you don't itemize, keep checks
for one year and discard older ones.

8. Filing. The simplest way to file the bill stubs and bank statements is in an accordion folder by month. Some people who itemize income tax deductions prefer, however, to sort them into their deduction categories —charitable contributions, medical expenses, business expenses—at this time. The nondeductible bills and checks would then just be filed by month. This is all right, but I personally prefer to sort these items out in one yearly work session.

   Some people "overfile" by making separate filing sections for, say, electric company, each department store, telephone company, etc. In most cases this adds an unnecessary precision to the money-handling procedure.

9. If you don't itemize income taxes, glance through the bills from one year ago this month to see whether there is a bill for a major purchase that you might want to keep permanently; if so, file it in the regular filing system under "Household" or "Warranties" if it's an appliance, or under "Art" if it's a painting or photograph. Throw away the remainder of the bills. If you do itemize, keep last year's bills until you prepare your taxes.

10. If you use the master plan, read pages 165–67.

Summary of Financial Handling Checklist

This summary briefly restates the principles and procedures involved in carrying through a monthly moneywork enterprise.

1. Select a monthly date for handling all financial obligations.
2. Assemble equipment and supplies.
3. Sort all materials in the financial folder into five piles:

    a. Banking materials

    b. Bills to pay

    c. Payment booklets for fixed obligations

    d. All sales slips and cash register slips

    e. Anything else, such as investment notices

4. Reconcile the bank statements with your checkbooks. Put the completed statements in a desk drawer or file.

5. Write checks for the bills, put *your* portions of the bills to one side.

6. Collect all bill stubs and sales slips in an envelope, mark it with the month and year, and put it in the same drawer or file as the bank statements.

7. Check stock transaction notices.

8. Write checks for the fixed obligations (Figure 3), and check off the chart.

9. If you don't itemize income taxes, throw out the bill stubs and canceled checks from one year ago. If you do itemize hold for tax work.

10. If you use the master plan, calculate those allocations.

Incorporating the Master Plan

To put your master plan to practical use you'll need the Discretionary Chart (see page 154), your carry-around notebook, calculator, personal checkbook (not the bill-paying account), and all bills and sales slips. Proceed as follows:

1. Head a page in the notebook with each category on the Discretionary Chart.

2. Take a department store bill with sales slips attached. Say, in one case, there are three sales slips—for a skirt and sweater set, a sports jacket, and a chess set. Note the skirt and sweater sum on the "clothing" page (just the amount—no other information needed), and also the sports jacket. If there's more than one person buy-

ing clothes, add that person's initial as well. The chess set is more flexible—it might go on the "hobby" page or under "entertainment" or "gifts"; whichever category can best afford it. There will always be minor adjustments for expenses that don't fit clearly into one category. Follow the same procedure for the rest of the department store bills and the credit cards.

3. Do the same with all other bills. Mark the electric and phone bills under "utilities"; a magazine renewal might be "books" or "hobby" or "entertainment." A doctor bill would obviously be "medical," and a plumber's bill is "household."

4. Enter all remaining sales slips and cash register slips on the appropriate category page. Also check the entries in your *personal* checkbook (not the bill-paying checkbook). Cash expenses—a movie, for instance, is "entertainment"—should be marked in the book as you go along.

5. Add up the figures on each of the category pages. The same page can be used month after month until you fill it up, so long as you cross off the previous months to avoid confusion. This is just for figuring, it is not a permanent record.

6. Using your Discretionary Chart, fill in the bottom half with the actual amount spent for the month, added up from your notebook list. The top figure in each box is the sum that *should* have been spent up to that point according to the master plan allocation. The two amounts—the ideal and the actual—will not always match. Clothes buying, for example, is usually concentrated in spring and fall, so the actual expenditure through July may not come up to the "guideline" amount—but will be made up in August or September. Similarly, food buying in bulk may mean very heavy expenditures one month and light ones the next.

The allocated amounts in the Discretionary Chart are guidelines that you adjust continually. For example, if actual entertainment expenditures through June are $1,500, while the chart says $1,248, don't despair. Go easy on evenings out, and adjust entertainment expenditures on the chart by September. As long as you know what your course *is*, you can diverge from it a bit to explore interesting byways—and come back again.

7. When an installment debt is completed, or if there is an increase or decrease in income, revise the master plan to incorporate the new situation.

Money Professionals

The occasion may arise when you will need or will elect to use the services of a financial professional. A brief rundown of available services follows:

Accountant. The basic service of an accountant is to review your taxes, to fill out your tax forms yearly, and if you file quarterly estimates, to maintain those for you.

Banker. A banking relationship is important for people who borrow money regularly and/or who are involved in trusts and similar types of complex financial instruments.

Bookkeeper. Some people prefer to turn the whole bill-paying/bank reconciliation project over to a bookkeeper in lieu of doing it themselves. Your accountant is probably your best source for a recommendation.

Budget, credit, and debt counselor. If your resources don't match your expenditures and if you find that your spending has somehow gotten away from you and you're in over your head, you may need immediate help in establishing a workable budget and reestablishing credit.

The Consumer Credit Counseling Services (CCCS) is

a low-cost, nonprofit organization throughout the country that will work with you and plan with you for the future.*

Financial planner. People with substantial resources can often benefit from the advice of a financial planner whose task it is to advise you on your whole financial picture. It is usually advisable to engage a planner who is independent, and is not also trying to sell you an investment product or insurance. Make sure that the planner is a member of the Institute of Certified Financial Planners. They offer a referral service that can provide the names of several Certified Financial Planners in your area.† Get recommendations through your broker, accountant, or lawyer.

Lawyer. It may be desirable to work with a tax lawyer if your financial dealings are complex to the point that legal issues are involved. If, for example, you have set up a private corporation, if you have complicated marital arrangements, have a complex compensation plan, or are taking complex or unusually large tax deductions, then a lawyer would probably be a good idea. Also, if you suddenly come into a large sum of money through inheritance, a lawyer should be consulted.

Stockbroker. To advise you on the purchase of securities (stocks and bonds) and to execute the transactions.

ORGANIZING FOR THE IRS

Starting sometime in March, the collective panic level begins to rise as people contemplate the sheaves of receipts,

---

*For the office nearest you, contact: National Foundation for Consumer Credit, 8701 Georgia Avenue, Suite 507, Silver Spring, MD 20910. (301) 589-5600.

†The Institute of Certified Financial Planners, 10065E. Harvard Avenue, Denver, CO 80231. (303) 751-7600.

bills, canceled checks, and other financial documents that must be made sense of in order to pay taxes.

Although paying taxes is never fun, the good news is that organizing the process can be accomplished simply and with minimal anxiety.

The organizing process varies depending primarily on whether or not you itemize deductions. Before beginning the procedure, buy either one or two (you will probably need two if you are self-employed) expanding slotted folders with at least twelve sections. Half-size folders are easier to work with than the full-sized folders. Also have file folder labels on hand.

Okay, here goes.

If You Do Not Itemize Deductions

Unless they anticipate very high medical expenses, most people whose income derives from salary, perhaps supplemented by fairly modest investment income, will normally not itemize deductions.

1. *Prepare your expanding file.* Label the first five sections in your expanding file as follows: "W-2," "Investments" (or "Interest"), "IRA" if you have one, "Mortgage," and "Major Purchases."

Label the remaining slots "January" through "December." Since you've used up several slots already, you'll have to double up.

2. *Monthly procedure.* Toss your paycheck stubs into your financial folder or basket. After reconciling your bank statement each month and paying monthly bills, drop your paycheck stubs into the "W-2" section and any investment advices and transactions into the "Investment" slot.

Go through your canceled checks and drop any checks connected with your IRA and mortgage payments into the appropriate slots. (For your information, interest on the mortgage of your primary residence continues to be deductible.)

The "Major Purchases" section has to do with payments connected with the purchase of a car, major appliances, furniture, jewelry, antiques, furs, and the like. For your information, if these purchases are financed, all deductibility of interest on personal debt ended as of 1991. However, it's a good idea to maintain a "Major Purchases" category anyway, for information purposes.

Tuck the remaining checks inside the folded bank statements and drop the packet into the appropriate "month" slot.

3. *At tax time.* One evening, sometime soon after you've received your W-2 from your employer, with one eye on the ballgame, take out your expanding folder and start adding things up. Check that your paycheck stubs equal the net salary listed on the W-2, check that your investment advices are reflected correctly on the annual statement, and add up the checks in the other sections.

You might want to glance quickly again through the unfiled canceled checks just to make sure you didn't overlook something, and then throw those checks and bank statements away.

Take the bills and canceled checks connected with major purchases and file them in the "Household" file of your general filing system. This is useful information for insurance, warranty, proof of purchase, and price comparison.

Are there any tax-related documents that you will also want to file elsewhere? For example, you will probably want to have an "IRA" file in your general filing system to keep track of contributions over the years. In that case, duplicate your IRA documents and checks for the IRA file, and keep the originals with the tax documents.

Now, whether you do your own taxes or send them to

an accountant, you are ready to go—and your accountant will bless you.

4. *Record-keeping*. Once your taxes have been prepared, duplicate two copies of your filled-out tax form. File one copy in a folder labeled "Taxes" kept in your general filing system, and put the other in a manila envelope marked with the tax year, slip your receipts and the canceled checks that support your tax claims into the envelope, and toss it to the top of the highest closet. You'll only need to retrieve it again if you are audited.

If You Itemize Deductions

If you itemize, the procedure is essentially the same as for those who do not itemize. You just have more things to add up and deduct. To run through the procedure:

1. *Prepare your slotted file or files (you may need two)*. In addition to the categories mentioned previously of "W-2," "Investments," "IRA," "Mortgage," and "Major Purchases," you will normally add sections for the deductible categories listed on Schedule A of the 1040 tax form: "Medical," "Taxes," "Charity," etc.

Your deductible categories *really* blossom when you are self-employed. First prepare the categories mentioned above, with the difference that, instead of labeling a slot "W-2," label that slot "Income." Collect all bills to clients and any other proofs of what has been paid to you, plus your W-2 if you also have an employed position. Moreover, as a self-employed person you will probably also have a Keogh or SEP plan (self-employed retirement plans), which also needs its file section.

Then label sections in the expanding folder per the deductions in Schedule C (the tax schedule for self-employed persons) that apply to you. Some of the more typical are travel and entertainment, advertising and promotion expenses, legal and professional help, clerical help, postage, supplies and equipment.

As to bank statements, remember that the statements themselves probably have deductible expenses on them—bank charges, check purchases, special services, penalties. So collect them, keeping the nondeductible checks with them, in a separate location or in a couple of sections of your expanding file.

2. *Monthly procedure.* As you reconcile your bank statements and pay bills, distribute the bills, canceled checks, and bank statements into the appropriate categories.

3. *At tax time.* The process is the same as for those not itemizing deductions, but you will have more to add up. Do you have the endurance for a single job that might take a whole day? If so, save the whole adding-up project for a rainy weekend.

Otherwise, set aside three or four blocks of three hours each. Or add things up periodically during the year as it occurs to you. Or keep a running list in each category slot, and add up each new item as you file it. Or hire someone else to do it—a student, perhaps, for a few dollars an hour. There's no reason to pay accountants' rates for what is a straightforward addition job.

At any rate, you know your temperament, so you know the best solution for you.

4. *Storing your records.* As before, make two copies of your tax form, one for your "Taxes" folder in the general file and the other for your tax-storage envelope. Put all your tax records into the envelope, mark the year, and stash it far out of the way.

Tip: Each year there's an overlapping period in which you've got to start collecting and filing for the new year, but you haven't yet organized the old year's material. To avoid confusion, buy and label two sets of expanding folders and alternate them. Thus, at the beginning of the year, reclaim the empty file to start *this* year's files, while records for the preceding year stay put in their folder until you can get to them, it is hoped sometime in February.

How Long Should Tax Records Be Kept?

For most people, records of income and tax-deductible expenses should be kept for at least three years after the filing deadline. In most cases, the IRS does not audit returns more than three years old.

However, the IRS can audit returns for up to six years in cases in which taxpayers understate income in the amount of more than 25 percent of the income reported. Julian Block, a tax expert with Prentice-Hall Information Services in Paramus, New Jersey, says, "Self-employed people and executives with complex compensation agreements often face questions about whether they must report certain income in a particular year. They should hold on to records of income and deductible expenses for six years, in case they make a mistake" (*The New York Times*, March 19, 1988).

PART FIVE

The Home

10
Storage Basics: Where Things Go

We all have a tendency to accumulate clothes, games, papers, photos, toys, tools, and other objects of twentieth-century life, but when accumulation turns from minor idiosyncrasy into anarchy, the reorganization of living and storage space becomes a top priority. This chapter tackles the basics of clearing out and organizing general-use closets, cabinets, and other storage areas, and offers tips on how to create new storage places and how to be sure that you can find everything again. (Clothes closets and accessories are discussed separately in the next chapter.)

This chapter is planned so that you can work at a pace of one or two hours at a time. This is important. Set a definite regular time for closet work for the next several weeks, and write down the date in your appointment calendar. It could be an hour a day, or an hour twice a week—whatever you can spare. And, most important of all, when the hour is up, *quit!* You won't become frustrated, and the closets will get organized.

ORGANIZING CLOSETS

Stage 1: Targeting a Closet

Is there a particular category of object you've been itching to organize—toys, vases and decorative ware, carpentry tools? If so, your starting point is to pinpoint a particular cabinet or closet that would be the most convenient place to house these objects, preferably near to where they are used. For instance, is the proposed toy cabinet in or near the children's playroom? Is the photographic equipment cabinet accessible to the darkroom? Does the closet contain shelves and/or hooks of the kind you will need? You can always modify a closet, but your task will be simpler if the closet is already designed to meet your storage needs. Don't try to assemble whatever object you've chosen to organize at this early stage; just pick an appropriate location.

On the other hand, a particular *closet* may be the trouble spot. If so, *that's* your "target closet" and that's where you begin. Choose its function, if one is not already established, by asking yourself, "People pass this closet on their way to where?" A cabinet between kitchen and dining room, presently cluttered with luggage, old photographs, games, and off-season clothes, could be used for kitchen overflow and serving pieces. Similarly, a closet between bedrooms would make a natural linen closet.

Principle #6   **Store things at or near the point where they are used.**

If you feel too overwhelmed to choose a target closet, the best solution is to—literally—flip a coin or stand in the center of a room, close your eyes, and point. Decide on that closet's function. Your target closet may eventually house a variety of objects, but you are determining its primary function at this point.

Stage 2: Weeding out

Have on hand a good supply of grocery cartons. Mark one box "throwaway" and one "giveaway" and weed out the target closet. The process is to consider each item individually and ask yourself the famous three-question "to keep or not to keep" test:

1. Have I used this article in the past year? If not,
2. Does it have value to me, sentimental or monetary? If the answer is no but you're still not sure whether to keep it or not, ask the clincher:
3. Might it come in handy someday?

When the answer to the third question is yes, put the article into the "throwaway" or "giveaway" box. That phrase almost always indicates that you are hanging on to clutter.

Work on one small section at a time. *Do not* under any circumstances empty the whole target closet at once. This warning is crucial. The resulting chaos is sure to set you back or even put you off completely. Instead, concentrate today for an hour or two on the two lower left-hand shelves. Tomorrow tackle the other two left shelves, then the two right lower shelves the day after, and so forth. During the sometimes painful process of throwing things away, it helps to invite a friend or relative to keep you company and prevent you from vacillating over your decisions to keep or not to keep. If, as sometimes happens, you find a month later you want a replacement for a particular article that has been discarded, consider the money well spent in exchange for functional closets.

Place things that you intend to keep in the target closet into cartons labeled "target closet." Stack the other articles into roughly organized piles—piles of books, piles of clothes, piles of toys, etc.—or into cartons marked with the name of the category. Wrap breakables either in old sheets or towels, or in tissue wrap paper or newspaper.

Fifteen minutes before you stop closet work for the day, push the target-closet boxes back into the closet (simply to get them out of the way), and distribute as many of the remaining piles or cartons as you can near their eventual location. Slip books into any available bookshelves or pile them on the floor nearby, put papers into the office area for sorting, put clothes into another closet and toys and games in the children's room. Do not, however, try organizing *those* closets or shelves. You'll get to that later. For the objects whose eventual whereabouts is a mystery, choose an out-of-the-way corner and call it a storage catch-all.

The point of roughly organizing and tidying up before finishing the day's closet work is twofold: Your progress will become apparent, which will encourage you to complete the job; and each day's work will be completed with a sense of "wrap-up." Undoubtedly you will be living for a while with boxes or piles, but as long as they are orderly and in place, you won't be as easily discouraged.

Continue the weeding-out process day by day until the target closet is completely bare.

Stage 3: Assembling

Many of the articles destined for the target closet are probably stored in other closets, or piled in some corners of the
house. Your next task is to root them out. In order not to
disrupt the whole household, tackle the problem in this
manner: Starting in the room where the target closet is
located, pull out from other closets or storage areas in that
room any "target" articles. *Do not empty out or attempt to
organize the closet you are pulling from!* Your treasure hunt
should be limited to whatever target articles you can easily
reach. Anything deeply buried that cannot be reached
without pulling out the entire closet can stay buried until
that closet is reorganized. Proceed to all closets and storage
areas in that room, putting the target objects into cartons
and culling giveaways and throwaways as you work. At the
end of the work session, push the target cartons into the
target closet.

Work systematically from room to room until you've
covered all areas and have a clearly defined set of objects
to be stored in the target closet.

Stage 4: Setting Up the Closet and
Keeping It That Way

First consider whether the closet is structurally functional.
Does it contain enough shelves and/or hanging space to
house the articles? Might there be a need for supplemental
storage spaces outside the closet proper? If existing space
or facilities are significantly insufficient—"significantly" as
opposed to the minor supplement of a few hooks or an
additional shelf or two—turn to page 185, "If Only I Had
More Space." Execute whatever improvements in or out-

side the closet you judge necessary. Then, before stocking the closet, you might want to clean, paint, line, or otherwise spruce it up.

The basic rule in stocking a closet is to keep frequently used objects low and accessible, to store items used less often on higher shelves or out of the way, and not to stack more than three pieces that are not a set on top of each other. It also helps in maintaining a storage system to keep items used together near one another: for example, ice bucket and bar equipment, or tennis racquet, balls, togs, sneakers, and admittance card to the tennis club.

If there's no light fixture in the closet, keep a flashlight tied to a hook so no one, including you, will "borrow" it.

Two techniques will help keep your closets stream-lined: *Immediately* assign a place for anything new that you buy. If you would like to switch it around later, fine; but it is courting disaster to leave an article "around" with a view to making a decision sometime later. Second, at the beginning of each season look over each closet and cabinet to identify items unused during the past season. Following the guidelines on page 179, discard any items that have outlived their usefulness.

The Coat Closet

To illustrate how to best utilize a closet without making structural changes and with only minor supplements, let's take the coat closet of an active family with young children. The coat closet is typically one of the most chaotic closets in the house because it houses a wide variety of objects and is so heavily used.

The first goal, especially with children, is to encourage everyone to put away his or her coats, hats, scarves, and

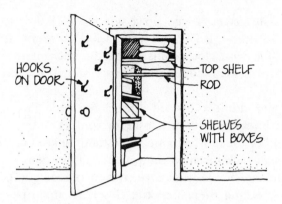

HOOKS ON DOOR

TOP SHELF

ROD

SHELVES WITH BOXES

Figure 4   Efficient use of space in a family coat closet

gloves. The solution: Make putting away so easy that a person has to go out of the way *not* to.

For scarves and hats, one family—husband, wife, and three children—installed five sturdy hooks on the back of the closet door in the pattern shown in Figure 4. The two smaller children hung scarf and hat on the lower hooks. The oldest child took the middle hook, and the two top hooks were assigned to the adults. Extra scarves and hats were stored on side shelves in special boxes made by cutting out one panel of a cardboard box—boot boxes are about the right size—to make a container whose contents are on display and easy to reach without disturbing the rest of the closet. If the closet door doesn't lend itself to hat and scarf hooks, put up a rack on the wall near the door—again, adjusted to the height of the smallest child. Alternatively, consider any convenient drawer or shelf in the vicinity: a sideboard with an empty drawer, a shelf in the nearby kitchen, a small chest of drawers near the closet.

Gloves can be stored in these drawers too, or tossed

in a small basket placed on a side shelf of the closet or nailed to the wall. For children's winter mittens, string a clothesline with clothespins along the back of the closet door. Store extra gloves in the box with extra scarves and hats.

Hang adult coats on the closet rod. Put height-adjusted hooks inside the closet for young children. A coat rack, either the old-fashioned freestanding kind or a handsome wall rack installed on a near wall, is a good supplement to the closet. It is more convenient for guests' coats than squeezing them into the closet. A single person or couple might use a coat rack for everything: coat, hat, handbag, briefcase.

An umbrella rack or stand near the door can also be useful. To hang out wet coats, lay a strip of indoor-outdoor carpeting underneath a wall rack right by the front door. Keep boots and overshoes in a handsome box or basket by the entrance, or in a box in the closet.

If the closet is still too crowded, select each person's most frequently worn coats and consign the rest to a bedroom or storage closet, or consider the suggestions on pages 187–91 for adding new closet space.

Stage 5: New Closets to Conquer

Choose a new target closet and repeat the process already described. The only difference is that in stage 4, the assembling stage, also check the storage catchall corner you established in stage 3.

When you've finished all the closets, turn your attention to any miscellaneous piles or storage catchalls and house those objects in whatever free spaces may have been opened by the main reorganizing job. Relate minor categories, if possible, to the closet's major category. For example, the toy cabinet, even allowing for toy expansion, might contain other child-related objects: clothes that are still too large to wear, extra school supplies. Or, if the toy cabinet isn't in the children's bedroom, adult games might find their home there: playing cards, poker chips, Scrabble.

Closet Organizing Summary

1. Choose a closet to work on and assign it a function.
2. Empty the closet, weeding out throwaways and giveaways, and distributing other items appropriately.
3. Work systematically from room to room, closet to closet, assembling all articles that belong in the closet you are working on. Don't try to organize or rearrange the closet you're pulling *from*. Cull giveaways and throwaways as you go along.
4. Analyze whether the target closet requires major changes. If so, execute them, following guidelines in "If Only I Had More Space."
5. Spruce up the closet and stock it.
6. Go to the next closet and continue until all the closets and miscellaneous storage piles are organized.

"IF ONLY I HAD MORE SPACE"

In our homes, about 80 percent of overcrowding is a result of disorganized space rather than insufficient space. New or expanded storage units often only create more places to be disorganized in. So always *organize* existing storage space before trying to increase or change it. Once you've done that, however, if your space is still insufficient or inappropriate for your chosen purposes, expand or modify the areas through the various techniques discussed here.

This section is a broad-based approach to storage in general. For storage techniques that apply to specific situations, see individual chapters.

Taking Advantage of What You've Got: Ways of Using Space You Haven't Thought of

The hanging and shelving techniques discussed later in this chapter may provide a solution for you, but first consider "easy storage": spaces already functional that require little or no installation work. This is a principle:

Principle #7 **The less work any project costs you in terms of installation or general aggravation, the easier it will be achieved.**

Neither furniture nor any household object has to be used as the designer intended. Extra bookshelves can house a portable sauna attachment or household supplies. Curtain the space if you'd like, or put up an attractive screen. Similarly, use decorative objects as storage containers. One client stored small household items—glue, lubricating oil, pliers—in an earthenware bowl placed just high enough so the objects remained hidden. Baskets of any size can hold a number of things. As a general rule of thumb when considering furniture and objects, *any hollow space is a potential container*. See Chapter 15, page 271, for additional furniture-as-storage ideas.

Consider also the storage potential of any space between objects. Can a folding stepladder fit in the small gap between washing machine and sink? What about a rack to hold newspapers or garbage bags? A small space between an open door and the wall behind it might accommodate a fold-up drying rack, ironing board, or folding chairs. The spaces underneath furniture are potential storage areas too. One client kept her needlepoint bag underneath the TV chair so she could do needlepoint whenever the impulse took her while watching television. In her case, the chair was skirted and hid the bag from view.

Consider making better use of corners. A decorative screen or hanging curtain might be drawn over a corner to hide caddies of cleaning supplies, games, boxes of off-season clothes, whatever seems appropriate. This is one example of the general principle of "divide and store." Any part of a room can be divided by screen or curtain to create a storage area—sometimes to attractive effect. One client whose living room was long and narrow changed its proportions, and made a new storeroom for himself, by hanging a floor-to-ceiling drape all the way across the room.

Another "easy storage" idea is to use the "organizers" that can be purchased in many variety stores. However, before you buy these, decide first how the organizer will be used; the organizers themselves won't organize you. There are a number of different kinds on the market for various purposes—vinyl storage cubes, plastic vegetable bins, wall organizers. Specific suggestions for their use will appear in later chapters.

If miscellaneous items are stored in a number of areas, you might list the locations and file the list in your "Household" folder so you can find something at a glance.

Expanding or Modifying Closet Space

First assemble the articles that require storage (see "Assembling," page 181). When you know their size and quantity, whether it's a collection of small tools and household implements or bulky items like extra bedding or luggage, you can choose intelligently between the two primary techniques for expanding or modifying storage space: shelving and hanging.

Shelves

1. Line one or more sides of a clothes closet with shelves.
2. Convert a shallow clothes closet to a cabinet by building shelves from top to bottom. This won't work well in a deep closet because the back is too hard to reach unless the shelves pull out, a much more elaborate construction project.
3. If you are *extremely* handy, consider a floor-to-ceiling revolving lazy Susan. This of course would work best in a deeper closet.
4. Convert a wide clothes closet into a dual purpose closet/cabinet by partitioning and building shelves in part of the closet.
5. Carefully measure the closet's dimensions and buy a freestanding cabinet, either open-shelved or fitted with drawers.
6. Make a storage unit from a wide, deep clothes closet by installing shelves, supported by posts, as in Figure 5.
7. Convert a cabinet into a clothes closet by removing the shelves and installing clothes racks.
8. If your closet is high and has open space in its upper reaches, install shelves for luggage and seldom-used items.

Shelf Tips

1. When possible, install adjustable shelves.
2. Store items of approximately the same height on the

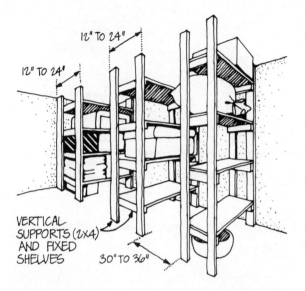

12" TO 24"

12" TO 24"

VERTICAL
SUPPORTS (2×4)
AND FIXED
SHELVES   30" TO 36"

Figure 5   Maximum use of closet storage space

same shelves. To set shelf height, measure a few typical items and allow a few inches above that.

3. Don't waste shelf space on only a few oversized items. Create intervening shelves for smaller pieces. (See Figure 6.)

It's also possible to install shelves outside the closet proper. For example, fill out a wall indentation with shelves. A five-inch indent in a little girl's bedroom wall was shelved and lined with dolls that could sit up or stand. It became both decorative and a convenient storage space. Any gap is suitable for fill-in; a two-foot gap between refrigerator and stove provides valuable storage space. New shelves can be built on *any* vertical surface; the back panel of a freestanding bookcase is just one possibility. A window can be fitted with shelves for plants.

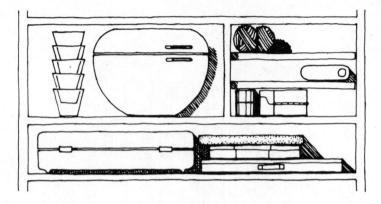

Figure 6 Storage unit with partitioned shelf space

Space near the ceiling is a relatively unexplored territory of home storage. Since most homes today have much less storage space than those built earlier, "it is important," according to decorator Milo Baughman, "to go vertically in storage pieces." Why not build your own shelf or shelves for off-season wear, luggage, etc., starting about two feet down from the ceiling? One way to retrieve small objects from these lofty reaches, aside from the obvious stepladder or stepstool, is a "pincher," the clamp device on a long stick that is used in libraries to get books down from high shelves.

Hanging Space

If you don't have much to hang, individual hooks on the side of the closet or back of the door will be adequate. To create considerable new space, however, consider grids on which numerous hooks can be shifted at will. Line all or part of a closet wall, or the back of the door, with grids. A combination of shelving and grids might be useful for some closets: Line the bottom half of the closet with shelves and the top half with grids; or shelve one wall and install grids on the other.

Grids, like shelves, can be attached to any sturdy flat space, such as the side of a cabinet or the back of a free-standing bookcase.

Flat surfaces can be exploited even more fully if you follow the art museum practice of "skying." Rather than hanging one painting per wall section, they will hang one at eye level, one higher, and sometimes one below—thus taking advantage of the whole wall area. Consider hanging pieces that you don't ordinarily think of as hangable. A bicycle, for example, can be supported on the wall with spikes.

To make an instant supergraphic, outline the bike's shape on the wall. Hanging the bike is especially convenient in a city apartment where you don't want to leave it in the building basement. Another example of an unusual hanging idea is to nail or hook a basket to the wall to hold mending supplies or small projects next to the chair where you usually sit to watch television.

The "Where Do I Put It?" Formula:
Storing Creatively

You may find that you are stuck with an object or category of objects that, organizationally speaking, doesn't clearly fit into an existing closet or storage area. Your tendency may be to put it randomly in the first space that will accommodate it. But once you've done that, you will probably repeat the pattern and your storage system will begin to unravel. Substitute the "get it out of sight, I'll think about it tomorrow" syndrome with a storage alternative based on the intersection between specific placement criteria and various storage techniques. There's actually a "Where does it go?" formula that you can apply to any storage question: point of use × access × appropriate technique = an appropriate storage choice.

Point of use. Where do you usually use this item? A vacuum cleaner, for example, is usually used—or at least started—in the living room, so in or near the living room is a more appropriate storage place than a kitchen storage closet. Sometimes a more precise answer to the point-of-use question is appropriate. If you like to sew by the window, then sewing equipment should be stored in the window vicinity.

Or, if you take the object outside with you, where can it be reached most easily? This applies not only to keys and coats but to a bicycle or shopping cart as well. For objects that might be used anywhere—household tools, for instance—choose an arbitrary storage location, but *stick with it.*

Access. How often or urgently do you use the item on a scale of 1 to 7? Everyday use makes it a 1, once a year, 7, and the rest are somewhere in between.

Appropriate technique. With point of use and access in mind as the first two elements of the equation, consider specific storage techniques that are feasible within the chosen area and appropriately accessible: very easy to reach for a 1 object, out of the way for a 7 object, or somewhere in between.

ORGANIZING YOURSELF INTO
A NEW HOME

If you're moving, take advantage of the best opportunity you'll ever have to organize all your closets at once, with only a fractional increase in the aggravation caused by the move itself. The suggestions that follow are also a streamlined way to organize your closets even if you're not moving, perhaps around the time of a paint job. But don't undertake this unless your tolerance for boxes and long-term disarray is very high.

Two or three weeks before the actual moving day, examine the contents of your present closets and list basic categories. The following list is typical:

> Clothing and accessories for each family member
> Toys and games (children's and adults)
> Athletic equipment
> Entertainment—party goods, etc.
> Coats and outerwear
> Kitchenware
> China and glass
> Linens and towels
> Miscellaneous: luggage, extra bedding, Christmas decorations
> Souvenirs and memorabilia
> Bathroom items and toiletries
> Household supplies

Survey the closets and cabinets in your new house,* note their location, and choose their function as described on page 178. Number each closet and make the following list of prospective contents:

> Closet #1: left of entrance—coat closet
> Closet #2: right side of foyer—athletic equipment
> Closet #3:built-in cabinet in living room—entertainment (playing cards, adult games, bar glasses, liquor, ice bucket)

---

*If you're moving to another city, get a plan of the new home that includes the dimensions of all closets and cabinets. The scheme won't be as precise, but planning is still feasible.

Analyze the necessary physical adaptations (see page 181), and if possible, complete them before moving in.

Before the move, accumulate dozens of closable cartons from the movers. Number each carton according to the closet for which it is destined—closet #1, #2, etc. Mark a separate set of cartons for the kitchen, since moving a kitchen has some special features (see page 243), and then start packing. As you move systematically from one closet in your present house to another, put the contents of each into the appropriate cartons, culling giveaways and throwaways as you work. Clothes can be packed in suitcases, or the movers will give you standing carton closets. Tag each suitcase or carton with a closet number. Movers also provide special cartons for pictures.

Pack a suitcase or two with necessities for the first few days, and group all the rest of the cartons (the #1 boxes together, the #2 boxes together, etc.) for the movers to pick up. When you arrive at your new home, move all the cartons to their respective closets. If you weren't able to install shelves and hanging space before, do it now. Unpack the cartons in the appropriate closet, and you're moved in.

Moving Summary

1. Accumulate a good number of closable cartons, starting several weeks in advance of the move.
2. Break down the contents of your present closets and cabinets into broad categories.
3. Go to your new home, or work from a plan, to decide which category will be stored in each closet or cabinet. Number the closets to identify them.

4. Decide as best you can the necessary physical adaptations (see page 181) and, if possible, implement them.
5. When packing, number each carton or suitcase with the appropriate closet number.
6. Complete whatever physical adaptations are necessary.
7. Unpack the cartons into the appropriate closet in your new home.

ODDS AND ENDS

Now we come to those small but important objects that are always getting misplaced: doorkeys, glasses, the magazine you're reading, and so forth. Keys are a problem for many people. When there are a lot of them—storage room, garage, bicycle locks, lockers—set up a key rack right near the door: a wooden plaque with rows of nails, each nail labeled with the appropriate key. If you tend to misplace doorkeys, put a hook right near the door or keep a small bowl on a table near the entrance. Drop the keys there as soon as you come in.

Another variant of this idea is a "front hall" basket or a corner of the foyer table reserved for the "takeouts": the lamp to be repaired, the shoes to be resoled, the overdue library books. If you overlook, or fear you might overlook, little "to do's" on your way out—are the lights out, oven off, cat not stuck in the closet—pin a checklist to the front door that you can refer to on the way out. If you have a split-level home, keep objects going upstairs or downstairs in a basket near the steps so whoever is traveling that way can take them along.

For the half-read newspaper or magazine, make a "pocket caddy" to attach to the usual reading chair: a cloth envelope out of the slipcover fabric or a compatible fabric with a long tongue fitted with snaps to attach to the chair underneath the cushion.

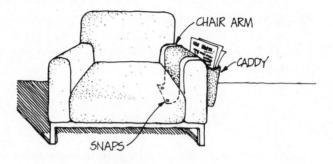

Figure 7   Chair caddy

The basic idea we are reaching for is that of convenience, which was expressed very well by Alexandra Stoddard:

> The more your organization is integrated into your every day, the more it will free your time. Have notepaper in several different locations so you can write notes spontaneously.... Have a shoebrush in a drawer next to your comfortable chair. What better time to buff a shoe than when you're relaxed? Have a clothesbrush on a hook in your front hall closet for the last dash out the door.... Everywhere you turn you should have convenience.*

---

*Style for Living: How to Make Where You Live You (Garden City, N.Y.: Doubleday, 1974).

11
Clothes and Accessories

Like Lisa, the harried heroine of Chapter 1, a person may own a variety of clothes and yet rely on a few outfits simply because closets and drawers are in such disarray that there is no time (and little incentive) to experiment with imaginative new combinations. This chapter will explore ways to organize clothing and accessories into one workable system that will encourage more creative use.

If you share your bedroom, you probably know how irritating it is to find your partner's cuff links in your drawer, or shirts in your closet. So the first step is to sit down and negotiate a firmly defined division of space that seems equitable to both. If you find yourself arguing over every inch, follow the provisional solution adopted by one couple: They arbitrarily divided the storage space in half, knowing that a good organizing job usually frees enough space to solve any problems. If overcrowding persisted after organizing, they agreed to renegotiate then.

Once space is allocated, move each person's belongings to the appropriate territory.

Principle #8 **When designing a personal system, first work out your "territory."**

Don't infringe thereafter on your partner's turf, and should he or she infringe on yours, define your lines without acrimony and maintain them firmly. *Don't* try to organize your partner's things.

Next, look at your closet. Over the years it may have become a receptacle for many things besides clothes: games, old toys, ten-year-old checkbooks. Weed out all these items, following the guidelines for stage 2 on page 179. Then go through all your closets and drawers, one at a time, pulling out the articles that you haven't worn for the past year—except for the pieces that have genuine value for you, sentimental or otherwise—to give to a charity thrift shop. Don't, however, hang on to clothing that "might come in handy someday." That phrase is an instant cue to dump.

Pull out coats and outerwear for the coat closet and transfer off-season wear (summer wear in winter, winter wear in summer) to less accessible storage areas; perhaps under the bed, packed in the underbed storage units carried by department store "closet shops," which are also handy for extra bedding. One client packed off-season clothes into infrequently used suitcases. A closet shelf too high for regular use is another possibility. Other storage suggestions are outlined on pages 185–91.

If you plan to paint your drawers and closet shelves or line them with fresh paper, this is the time to do it.

CLOTHES

First, decide which clothes to hang in closets and which to fold into drawers, and shift them accordingly. I recommend hanging as many articles as you have room for, including sweaters (on padded, shaped hangers), blouses, and shirts. Seeing clothes in a row before your eyes helps you to envision creative alternatives. If, on the other hand, drawer space is generous while closets are limited, drawers can be used in unusual ways. One client folded all her slacks into drawers but, rather than just stacking them, laid them out flat with an edge of each pair showing—like cards laid out for solitaire—making them easily visible and accessible.

To organize drawers, allocate each article according to the formula "How often do I use it?" The most frequently used items, like underwear, should be most accessible. Sweaters (unless they are hung), shirts, and sportswear are generally next; nightwear, which is changed less often, can go into the bottom drawer. Subdivide some categories—sweaters, or filmy lingerie and ordinary underwear—into their natural divisions of "frequently worn" and "less frequently worn."

If bedroom logistics permit, locate your dresser close enough to the closet so you can see both places at the same time. It's easier to create new outfits when everything is in view.

To create additional drawer space, if space or money does not permit buying a new dresser, utilize some free bookcase shelves. Curtain or screen the space if you'd like. Also consider stackable plastic or vinyl storage cubes. For more ideas about increasing shelf space, see page 188.

Arrange clothing in the closet so that articles of the same type are hanging together. Four simple categories are listed below.

For the top half of the body:	Sweaters
	Light jackets
	Blazers
	Blouses
	Shirts
For the bottom half of the body:	Slacks
	Skirts
For the whole body:	Dresses
	Men's suits
Special occasion wear:	Long dresses
	Evening wear

You'll note there is no category for "women's suits." I prefer hanging jackets with the other tops, and bottoms with the rest of the skirts. This helps liberate these articles from the "suit" restriction and allows you to consider their mix-and-match potential. If, on the other hand, you have no imagination about clothes and don't want to develop more, hang as a set the two or three outfits that you *know* go together.

Another way to arrange clothes is not only according to type but according to color as well. Marsha, for example, organizes her blouses in a range from white and very light at one end, to bright colors in the middle, and then grays and blacks at the far end. Prints and patterns are hung next to the solids.

Color coding is a strictly optional technique that works for highly visual people who find it easy to associate colors. Such people might assign reds and pinks, for example, or blues and greens, or prints and stripes, to a particular location. Another person who doesn't think according to colors and patterns would not benefit from color coding and might even get confused.

Another way to organize is by category of use. For example, I myself tend to sort out blouses as dressy or casual. Thus, dressier blouses, silk blouses, and blouses worn with suits are kept together, whereas sport tops and casual shirts are grouped separately. So color isn't much of a factor. Different strokes for different folks.

Garment bags are awkward, take up valuable space, and block clothing from view. I recommend them only for extremely fragile clothing like lace or chiffon. The closet itself protects clothing from ordinary dust, and the dry cleaner's plastic bag is good protection for clothing that is particularly lint-prone.

ACCESSORIES

Closet designers have never discovered a really good way to handle such accessories as belts, shoes, hats, handbags, scarves, gloves, and jewelry. You're bound to be disappointed if you buy lots of boxes, containers, and "organizers" in the wistful hope that they will somehow *make* you organized. They won't, without a plan behind them.

However, boxes and various containers can be helpful if you use them thoughtfully and imaginatively. The suggestions that follow present alternatives for you to mix and match according to the kind of space you have available, and the kind and quality of accessories for which you need storage.

1. If your closet is lined with shelves, get or make boxes with a flap that falls when the cover is lifted so the contents are easy to reach. See-through shoeboxes with similar flaps are also available; they can be stored on closet shelves or stacked in a corner of the room.

2. A shoebag hung on the back of the closet door or on a side wall can also hold stockings, scarves, gloves, or rolled-up belts.

3. Buy a freestanding cabinet or cupboard with shelves for hats, handbags, and shoes.

4. There are hangers specially fitted with pockets to hold handbags or shoes. Try them if you have a lot of hanging space. Check that the plastic pockets are sturdy enough not to tear easily.

5. Get a shoe rack for the closet floor. This keeps the shoes in good order and also inhibits the tendency to throw other items on the floor.

6. For scarves, gloves, handkerchiefs, underwear, stockings, and jewelry—just about any small accessory—buy a low chest, wicker or quilted, for the bottom of the closet. If you fold your pants over hangers rather than hanging them full-length, you can accommodate quite a high chest. Leave some open space to hang full-length evening wear.

7. Line the lower portion of the closet with shelves for shoes and bags.

8. Grid the sides, door, and ceiling of a closet to hang shoebags, belts, ties, hats, totes, and purses.

9. Buy pronged hangers for neckties and belts.

10. Hang belts, ties, neck chains, beads, and hats on the floor-to-ceiling poles made for hanging plants, or along the branches of a decorative coat tree.

11. For belts, attach small hooks, like those for hanging kitchen cups, along the branches of a coat tree. Hooks

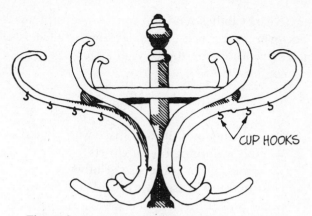

CUP HOOKS

Figure 8 Hang your accessories from a coat rack

could also work for necklaces and chains, scarves, or sweaters with a "hanging band."

12. There are special hangers for belts, ties, bags, neck chains, and necklaces.

13. Hang jewelry on nails on the closet walls or, if you have a nice sense of design, on the bedroom wall itself. A collection of bright purses and totes hung on the wall is also attractive.

14. Decorative hats might look nice piled on top of each other on a free tabletop or in a basket on the floor. Or consider using a milliner's hat rack.

KEEP IT MOVING

Once organized, a clothing system is a circulating system: new things in, old clothes out. In the fall, when you put away your summer clothes, set aside those items that weren't worn that season and give them away. The chances are very good that you will wear them even less, if ever, next year. Clothes tend not to improve with age. Glance, too, over shoes, bags, and accessories. That is all that's necessary to stay on top of your system.

Clothes-Handling Summary

1. Divide closet and drawer space with your partner.
2. Weed nonclothing out of closets.
3. Weed out old or underused clothes.
4. Distribute off-season wear and outerwear to appropriate places.
5. Execute spruce-up projects.
6. Distribute clothes into drawers or closets.
7. Organize drawers by access.
8. Organize hanging clothes by clothing types.
9. Add new closet space if necessary.
10. Organize accessories.
11. Cull clothes twice a year at the change of seasons.

GETTING MAXIMUM MILEAGE FROM CLOSET SPACE

The question on the table is, "How, when closet space is at a premium and space efficiency is the priority, can I organize my clothes so as to get maximum mileage from available space?"

Indeed, New York apartment dwellers have been known to pay exorbitant costs even by New York standards for an apartment with generous closets, even if it had little else to recommend it.

There are three ways to go about achieving a maximally efficient closet. One is to design it yourself, the second is to purchase prefabricated modular pieces that are inserted into your existing closet, and the third possibility is to commission a luxurious custom closet. Also by all means take advantage of the services of professional closet organizers. They might help you do wonders with your existing space—including solving problems like handling shoes and accessories, obviating the need for the expense and bother of closet redesign.

Your budget and your personal interest in the nuts and bolts of closet design will determine which avenue you choose.

Designing Your Own Closet

In a nutshell, designing a closet entails measuring your closet, measuring your clothes, and then figuring out how to fit more of one into less of the other, usually by the technique of creating *layers* or *decks* of hanging clothes. Taking it step by step:

1. Measure the height, width, and front-to-back depth of your closet. Some closets have extra space to the side or overhead extending past the open closet door. Note any such "hidden" space.
2. Measure your clothes:
   a. Assemble together on the rack all "half-size" clothes—that is, blouses, shirts, hangable sweaters, and jackets. Measure the longest item in that group from the top of the hanger to the bottom of the garment to determine hanging length necessary for that category. Then measure the width from side to side of that block of clothes. Don't jam them, let them hang normally. Add fourteen inches to that measure for "push back and forth" space to allow for the introduction of new clothes.
   b. Assemble "three-quarter length" clothes on the rack

and follow the same procedure. "Three-quarter" clothes are skirts, men's and women's suits, and pants folded over a hanger.

   c. Measure dresses from top to bottom and from side to side similarly. This is your full-length clothing.

   d. Do you have long evening wear? Measure that too.

3. Count up the accessories that you also intend to include in the closet:

Shoes. How many pairs?
Bags. How many, taking up how much space?
Folded shirts and sweaters. How many, of approximately what thickness?
Accessories such as hats, scarves, ties, and belts—how many?
Boxed items for storage. How many?

4. With measurements in hand, sketch your ideal closet. First, draw an outline to scale ($\frac{1}{2}'' = 1'$) of your closet. Indicate the doorway with a solid line and lightly shade any "hidden" space to the side of or up above the door.

5. Divide the width measurement of half-size clothes in half and double the height measurement. The idea is to create two horizontal rods in your closet to allow for two decks of half-size clothes. Is the closet high enough? Lightly sketch the half-size block into your closet sketch. If your closet is deep enough, install a parallel second rack on the same level to double the hanging space. Put the clothing combinations that you wear most often in the front, and clothing worn less often in the back.

6. Move next to your "three-quarter" clothes. It's unlikely that your closet is high enough to create double decks of three-quarter clothes, but you might be able to work out two decks, one for three-quarter-length clothes

and one for half-lengths. Sketch in the three-quarter block.

7. Dresses and full-length clothes can't be "decked," but the space between the dresses and the floor might be used in productive ways—for a low chest for bags, for example, or a floor shoe rack. Sketch in the full-length clothes.

8. Consider options for accessory storage. Take a look at pages 202–3 for stashing and storing techniques using shelves, hang-ups, chests, etc.

Now, in principle, you've got a closet!

Constructing the closet would be an interesting project for someone with do-it-yourself tendencies. Otherwise, hire a local carpenter to carry out your plan.

The Modular Closet

One recent phenomenon is the emergence of the "packaged" or "modular" closet: that is, prefabricated closet sections and pieces that are inserted into your existing closet space. The pieces can be configured in various ways, and it's likely that one closet line or another will have suitable pieces that can be configured to your specifications.

Contact at least two or three of these services and request their literature and fees. Clarify the following:

1. Are you purchasing the equipment alone for a do-it-yourself installation, or does the cost include advisory services and/or installation fees?

2. What services do they offer? *Advisory* means they tell you how to go about it. *Hands-on* means they do all the measuring and design a custom scheme for you. *Installation*: Do their people install the module into your

Figure 9   Double Your Closet Capacity

space? If so, do they remove the old rods? Who is responsible for fixing any wall area damaged when the old rods are removed?

3. Can you continue to use ordinary hangers, or must you buy theirs? Caution: Closet systems fitted with a fixed hanger slot for each item of clothing, so that the clothing cannot be slid along a rod, are definitely *not* recommended for many people. It can be maddening not to be able to push clothes this way and that.

Also, carefully check the sample equipment in the store:

1. Check that the pieces are smooth, that they are manufactured sturdily, and that there are no raw patches or edges. Before accepting delivery to your home, spot-check a few of the pieces to make sure they look the same way they did in the store.

2. Check for sturdiness. Pull down gently on the hanging rods. Are they sturdy? Do they "give" too much at a

gentle pressure? Do you feel confident they'll hold the weight of clothes?

3. Do drawers and bins move smoothly and easily on their runners? Bring some books with you to drop into sliding bins, making sure they move easily when weighted down. A bin that slides readily when empty may tend to become clumsy or jam when loaded.

Note: Remember that an exact-measurement system requires that you faithfully exchange in-season wear with off-season wear each season, and that you regularly give away items you're no longer wearing. No matter how efficient and well designed the modular system, it is, because of its strict space requirements, in some ways more unforgiving than a regular closet.

The Custom Closet

A true custom closet is a wonderful and expensive luxury. Constructed of fine materials to your exact requirements, the delights are many: racks that recede and come forward, sliding panels, a space for each pair of shoes, each bag, and sometimes each shirt or sweater. Sigh. But it's nice to know that the storage principles behind the custom closet are essentially the same as those we have discussed.

Closet-Expanding Tips

1. The multiple hangers that permit hanging a group of skirts, pants, or shirts do save space, but I personally find them cumbersome. If you can use them comfortably, by all means take advantage of them.

2. If there is space in the bedroom, buy a freestanding wardrobe or armoire as a second closet.

3. Buy a freestanding clothes rack such as stores use. It can be hidden with a decorative screen.

4. If you have an alcove from five to seven feet wide that you use for desk or work space, install a clothes rack or tension rod above your head for blouses, shirts, and jackets.

5. For a smaller alcove or indentation, buy two tension rods for two layers of half-length clothes, or one rod for full-length clothes. Cover the alcove with a curtain or screen.

QUESTIONS AND ANSWERS

Various specific problems crop up to puzzle many people. Here are some questions that have been posed to me:

Q: *I start throwing things around when I'm in a hurry, so the system falls apart.*

A: I've alleviated my own tendency to let clothes drop where they may (whether I'm in a hurry or not) by choosing one chair in my bedroom—a "junk chair"— on which to throw clothes or anything else that I don't feel like putting away. Putting all litter on that one chair—*not* strewing it around the room or stashing it randomly in drawers or closets—keeps things under control.

Clear off the chair at least every three days. At first, if necessary, actually write "clearing" dates in your appointment book—say, fifteen minutes twice a week—until the activity becomes a habit.

Q: *Where do I put clothes from the dry cleaner, or new clothes?*

A: Put a hook on the bedroom wall to hang dry cleaning. Put it away when you straighten out the "junk chair" and "throw tray" (see below). Put packages of new clothes on the junk chair.

Q: *Where do I put clothes for the dry cleaner?*
A: Get a handsome wicker hamper or chest, lined with fabric so it won't splinter. Keep it near the front entrance to your home. Drop items of clothing ready for dry cleaning into the wicker hamper. That's a nice, neat way of accumulating clothes. Then scoop the clothes up to take out with you, or to be ready for pickup.

Q: *I tend to leave small things like tie clasps and cuff links on the dresser. They soon become a depressing clutter.*
A: Keep a small tray, a "throw tray," on your dresser for cuff links, watch, the jewelry you wore that day, and other bits and pieces. In other words, the "junk chair" idea made small. Clear out the tray every three days or so.

Q: *My closets and drawers are organized, but I still have trouble getting myself together in the morning.*
A: That probably means you're still fuzzy when you wake up, so plan to make the morning as automatic and decisionless as possible. Lay out clothes and accessories the night before. Set the table for breakfast, take out the nonperishables you plan to eat, and set up the coffeepot. Or plan a very simple breakfast, like one of the nutrient mixes.

Q: *I have piles of jewelry, too much to keep in one box.*
A: Pick out the pieces you wear and dispose of the ones you no longer care for. Divide the remainder: Keep the cuff links, earrings, bracelets that you wear most

often in an accessible jewelry box or attractive tray. Hang necklaces and chains on nails or hooks on the wall or in the closet. Put jewelry worn less often in a box on the closet shelf.

Q: *My closet's sliding doors only open halfway, so half the closet is always blocked.*

A: Keep mix-and-match clothes of the same degree of "dress-up" on each side. Thus, streetwear tops and bottoms would hang on one side, whereas sportswear tops and bottoms—jeans and T-shirts—would be on the other.

Q: *I like to make do with two or three basic outfits when I travel. How can I streamline packing?*

A: Attach a tag to the hanger of each packable article that lists the mix-and-match possibilities for that piece, as well as matchable accessories. This helps you quickly pull out the outfits you need, and streamlines dressing for everyday too.

12

Books and Media Accessories: Records, Disks, Tapes, and Videos

Organizing books and records can actually be fun. It's an adventure to come across a book you've forgotten you owned or a memorable recording. And, of course, your enjoyment is greater when your library or music collection is well organized and easily accessible.

BOOKS

Preliminaries

Choose a starting point arbitrarily: either one bookcase if you have several, or several shelves of one unit. If some of your books are piled in various places throughout your house or apartment, assemble them all before you begin.

Next decide whether certain categories of books appropriately belong in particular locations. Hefty art books, for instance, may fit only in one area of unusually high, solid shelving. Put the books presently in the "art area" into boxes and shelve the art books. Cookbooks are handy in or near the kitchen. There may be free book space in a kitchen cabinet or on top of the refrigerator, or plan to install one or two cookbook shelves in the kitchen. Save installation work until all the books have been organized.

To organize the balance of the books, you will need a thick marking pen, a ladder for overhead shelves, grocery cartons for giveaways, and time. Reserve, if you can, two or three solid afternoons, rather than spreading the job out over a week or more. It is too easy to become discouraged (and possibly give up completely) after seeing the piles of books that are inevitably left on the floor when you take a break, so it's advisable to finish quickly. An hour-a-day schedule is possible, however, although not recommended. In that case, get at least five or six cartons in addition to the giveaways.

To start, count out thirty to forty books as the "work portion," or, if the shelves are already divided by panels, work within one panel. Begin with either the highest or lowest shelf of the bookcase on the far left. With a clear starting point you can easily keep track of the ground you've covered.

Organizing

1. Cull the work portion for books you may no longer want. Put them into a giveaway box for later pickup by a hospital, veteran's home, or charity thrift shop. They are

a tax-deductible charitable contribution so make sure you get a receipt.

2. Choose a category for the shelf you're working on. If there already is a preponderance of books on a particular subject on that shelf, choose that category if the access is appropriate. That is, an easily accessible shelf should be reserved for a frequently consulted category; categories consulted less often can be less accessible. If the access is wrong, or if there is no clear favorite, just choose a subject that corresponds to the amount of space available. The most typical home library categories include:*

Art

Biography

Current affairs

Fiction

Gardening

Health

History

"How to"

Politics

Psychology

Reference books

Religion

Self-help

Social issues

Travel

3. Remove all the books that aren't in the subject category and arrange them in piles on the floor or on tabletops by category. Lay the piles in roughly alphabetical order so that "gardening" is somewhere near "history"; then you don't have to waste time later looking for a particular pile.

4. Go over the entire bookcase, book by book, to pick out all the books in the subject category. Put them in the work portion and, if necessary, block out another work portion if space for that category still isn't adequate. When

---

*Sometimes a book can be categorized in more than one way. Biographies of Jane Austen and Thomas Hardy might go with these authors' novels or with other biographies. Just choose one category arbitrarily, and then stick with it.

you have finished one category always try to leave expansion space for several extra books.

5. In a large library, pulling *all* the books in a category might create an insurmountably huge pile. In that case, just pull enough for a work portion or so, and take note of where you stopped. When you begin work again, block out another work section, cull as in step 1, disperse the rest of the books into their piles, continue scouring the bookcase where you left off, and file the subject category. Also look through the piles of miscellaneous books assembled at the beginning. Continue moving from shelf to shelf until that category is completely assembled.

I prefer moving vertically up or down; others favor going sideways. Follow your preference, as long as you are consistent. If a category fills more than two work portions, you may want to make a block as shown in Figure 10.

6. Subdivide within a large category. The more common types of subdivision are:

Art books—by artist, period, or country
Cookbooks—by author or national cuisine
Biographies—alphabetize by name of subject
Fiction—alphabetize by last name of author. Fiction can be divided into subcategories: novels, "genre" novels (mysteries, science fiction, romance), short stories, plays, poetry.

7. Chose another category and decide its location. Access is the main determinant, but also consider its relation to the preceding category. For instance, "anthropology" might be more appropriate near "history" than "gardening." Continue with step 3 and subsequent steps. However, before scouring the bookcase and miscellaneous books for the relevant category, file the books, if any, that have already been piled on the floor in that category.

8. Continue until all the books are organized and there

are no more books in boxes or on the floor. As you near the end, if a lack of space becomes evident, buy or build another bookcase. See page 185 for space-expanding ideas.

9. If the job can be done within a couple of days, leave the book piles out when you break. Just clear enough of a path to move around in. If the job will take longer, put the books into cartons, marking which category is in which box. If there's room to fit more than one category per box, keep them in alphabetical order. Push the cartons into an out-of-the-way corner.

ONE CATEGORY
OF BOOKS IN THIS
AREA

Figure 10   Organizing your books

Finishing Touches

Look over your shelves to check that books aren't crammed together too tightly and that there's room for expansion. Shift some work portions, or even whole categories, if the shift would make a smoother flow. This is also the time to build new shelves or create space for the cookbooks or other special book categories that don't belong in the regular bookcase.

It's helpful in a large library to identify the bookshelves with labels made with hand-held, punch-out devices.

The Streamlined Plan

There is a streamlined way to organize books that I don't recommend to most people because it calls for intimidatingly large piles of books on the floor for what could be days on end. But if you are unfazed by a temporary bombed-out look, by all means consider this alternative plan.

Sketch a rough, freehand chart of all your bookshelves. Chart in hand, test each shelf for accessibility. A shelf at arm level is #1; space reached by stooping or stretching a little is #2 or #3; stretch up on tiptoe or bend all the way down for #4 or #5. Mark the chart accordingly in the style of Figure 11.

Then, starting at the lower left corner of the bookshelf, pull out all the books in the entire system, arranging them on the floor by category in roughly alphabetical order. Continue until the shelves are entirely clear. Add the miscellaneous books gathered from elsewhere in the house. Rank the categories according to your interest in them; a category of lively interest is #1, and so forth. Then file all the #1 books on #1 shelves, and so on until the library is completely reshelved and organized.

Subdivide the categories if you like according to the guidelines on page 216.

5	5	5
4	4	4
7	1	~~STEREO~~
2	2	~~EQUIPMENT~~
3	3	~~# #~~

Figure 11 Bookshelves—Accessibility Chart

Extending Book Space

If there are still more books than shelf space, buy or build new shelves or look into these expansion techniques:

Get a freestanding bookcase. Either line it up against the wall or make it a room divider. If you already have a bookcase/divider, glue or bolt the new bookcase back-to-back with the first one.

Bolt a bookcase on top of an existing bookcase. Combine handsome, vinyl stackable cubes into a wall unit or a room divider. Cubes are probably most appropriate for mixed use: books, plants, wine, etc.

Some books may be consulted so infrequently that they could be transferred to a closet shelf, or even to free space in a kitchen cabinet.

The high space in outsize shelves is largely wasted. Install an in-between shelf. Measure the space carefully, to make sure there is room for two rows of books, allowing for the shelf itself, which is probably ¾″ thick.

File paperbacks in double layers. Reserve a few of the most important books for the front row, and otherwise just organize alphabetically from front to back, by subject and then by author within the subject. Loosely pack the front row to make the back row accessible.

As a general rule, don't stack books on their sides. It seems a space saver, but it effectively removes any book but the top two from circulation.

In general, don't get locked into traditional sites for bookshelves. People frequently feel that books belong only in the library or den or bedroom, but I have seen some people use books in interesting ways.

One family with a large formal dining room warmed the cavernous space by lining the room with books. It seemed curious at first, but the books gave the room a good deal of warmth and charm, and covered some rough spaces on the walls as well. This same family, when they moved, lined their entire brick-lined living room wall with books. This created a very pleasant and homey space.

Apartment dwellers and others with limited bookshelf space can tuck books away in odd nooks, crannies, and corners. Consider lining the *top* level of the room with books that you don't often refer to. For example, a line of bookshelves placed a couple of feet down from the ceiling makes an attractive border. Hallways especially lend themselves to this treatment. People hang books from the ceiling down, lining corridors handsomely. One imaginative homeowner lined a staircase wall with books.

If your home features an empty closet, or a closet that isn't fully utilized, then build shelves on the side or use the shelves already there, to capture the book overflow. One small family in a New York apartment whose hall closet had a free wall created an entire bookcase on that wall.

Book-Organizing Summary

1. Assemble all the books you plan to organize.
2. Certain categories may belong in special locations—cookbooks in the kitchen, art books in an area of high, solid shelving. Move the books accordingly.
3. Choose a work portion (thirty to forty books, or a natural bookcase division) at the top or bottom shelf on the left.
4. Cull giveaway books from the work portion.
5. Choose a category for the work portion.
6. Remove all books from that portion except for the subject category, and arrange them by category on the floor.
7. Scour the bookcase for all subject books (unless there are great numbers—see step 5 on page 216), and fill the designated space.
8. Continue the same category in the next shelf if more space is needed, culling out and filling in, until the category is completed.
9. Subdivide, if you like, within a large category.
10. Choose a new category for the next shelf, and begin again with step 4.
11. Check for finishing touches (page 217) and, if you are still cramped, try expanding storage space (page 219).

RECORDS, TAPES, CDS, AND THE MEDIA ARCADE

America's typical home increasingly resembles a media arcade overrun with compact disks, laser disks, videotapes, computer games, Nintendo cartridges, etc. We have entered an age of gadgetry heretofore unknown. So the question is, how do we organize new gadgets into old space? If your home is not to be taken over, places must be made for these things, and they have to be organized so that you can find them when you want them.

The principles involved in organizing electronic gadgetry are not significantly different from the kinds of organizational techniques used in simpler days to catalog our records and tapes.

Basically, media "software"—the things you listen to or watch or play with—divides up into three categories: music, video, and computer games and products.

Music

The three musical items are long-playing records, cassettes, and compact disks. Records, tapes, and disks are physically too different to intermix comfortably, so organize them separately. Weed out the items that you have lost interest in and give them away.

Divide what remains into categories. In many cases, this list of basic categories is adequate:

Popular	Classical	Other
Ballads	Chamber music	Folk
Country and	Opera	Jazz
western	Orchestral music	Religious music
Dance music	Soloists	Spoken word
Mood music	(instrumental)	
Rock	Soloists (vocal)	
Show music		

Complications can arise if your emphasis is on other areas. Arranging by composer, for example—all Mozart, all Beethoven—may present a problem because many records feature works by various composers. In such cases, file the record according to the composer that's most important to you. If you'd like to categorize more than one composer, make a cross-reference card: "Schubert Fantasy in F Minor—see Beethoven, Archduke." Organize any way you wish—by composer, performer, period, instrument, whatever—so long as you are consistent in your system.

Either arrange your record, tape, or disk collection according to the one-shelf-at-a-time method recommended for books, or, if it is no larger than two hundred pieces or so, try the streamlined system discussed on page 218. Maintain the organization by physically distinguishing between the various major divisions. For example, store classical records in white vinyl cubes and pop records in yellow. Or, if you store records on bookshelves, label the shelves or insert dividers between the different categories.

One special point about tapes: Commercial tapes are rarely labeled on the side so it's difficult to identify them if they are stored upright. Label them yourself if necessary.

Long-playing records generally fit on bookshelves, or stereo cabinets often allow for LP storage. Also, the plastic crates found at stores that call themselves " 'n' things" can usually hold LPs.

For compact disk and cassette storage, individual cassette and CD units are fine for small collections of twenty or thirty items. However, once greater quantities are amassed, organizing cassettes and CDs gets troublesome because it's difficult to keep track of what is where with a quantity of individual holders. One possibility is to use a different holder for each category. So, for example, one CD box could hold classical disks, another one rock, etc., and similarly with cassette holders.

However, if your collection of CDs and/or cassettes has grown so large that these solutions no longer work, installing custom-made shelves is probably the best route to take. This is not as complicated as it may sound. Take a section of book shelving, measure the height of your cassettes and the height of your CDs, and simply have shelves installed between the existing bookshelves. You can accommodate two, or sometimes three, levels of cassettes and/or CDs.

Video

Video "software" consists of purchased videocassettes such as movies, tapes recorded off of television, home videos, and blank tapes. (The same principles also apply to laser disks.)

The first law of videocassettes is: *Label each tape immediately upon videotaping.* There are, ultimately, only three ways to find your videotape: label, label, and label. Or else you will have to replay the tapes all over again to find out what's there. Do not trust your memory at all. Just jot down on a Post-it the date and some information about the tape as soon as it comes out of the machine.

Identify videocassettes intended for your permanent library with the label that came with it or with a file folder label.

Standard VHS videocassettes can easily be stored on bookshelves. Distinguish between categories with stick-on/peel-off colored stickers. Buy three sets of stickers in different colors. Then use yellow stickers, say, to identify home videos, green for TV shows you intend to watch, and red for movies.

Organizing home videos can be a little tricky. Some people like to organize them by subject matter: "Little Eric's first birthday party," "Little Eric's first Christmas." Or all Christmases or Thanksgivings are grouped together.

It is easiest to simply label the videos chronologically,

because, in practice, people tend to put several different events on one videotape. Frequently there will be a snatch of Halloween and a little bit of birthday party. So your best bet is filing home videos chronologically with clearly dated and well-marked contents.

I would also recommend, just for safety, keeping a master list of the home videotapes which are precious to your family. It is possible, if you like, to add more detailed information than a label permits about who is on the tape and a bit more about the event. If you use a master list, number each video—1, 2, 3, 4—and list accordingly on the master list.

13
The Kitchen

The kitchen, more than any other room in your home, should be arranged and organized in the way that's most convenient for the user. Cramped space, poorly arranged utensils, and the need for constant trips between counter and oven can dampen the enthusiasm of any cook. A well-planned scheme—the one that's best for *you*—will, on the other hand, make all kitchen work more pleasant, and so much easier that maintenance will become routine.

The process begins with a budget. An expert cook may find it worthwhile to spend several thousand dollars to gut the present kitchen and design a new one from scratch. Most people, however, have neither the interest nor skills—to say nothing of the money—to take full advantage of a custom kitchen. Think, rather, of modifying your standard kitchen (which invariably has not, in my experience, been designed with comfort and efficiency in mind) to conform to your needs. You can do a lot for several hundred dollars, and ingenious modifications can be made for $200 or less. Suggestions in this chapter run the financial gamut; choose the ideas that fit your needs and budget.

DEFINING PROBLEMS

Initially, define the problems you experience in your kitchen. Almost all kitchen difficulties fall into one of three categories: work area; storage; serving and clearing. Specific instances of each are:

Work area:

1. Inadequate workspace. A client who baked had no room in her work area to set down a mixing bowl she had finished with, so she had to take it across the room to get it out of the way.
2. A poorly located work counter—one too far away from the storage cabinets and oven—creating constant and unnecessary movement.
3. A counter so awkwardly positioned that rolling dough becomes difficult.

Storage:

1. A shelf high enough to accommodate large appliances is otherwise largely wasted space.
2. Dishes stored so high that they become virtually unreachable.
3. Serving dishes and utensils piled so haphazardly that

pieces become hard to find and reach when they are needed.

Serving and clearing:

1. Too many trips between the dining area and kitchen indicates a problem in the serving and clearing process.

If you have trouble getting down to particulars, it helps to pinpoint a *process* that causes trouble—for instance, baking pies, preparing casseroles, or clearing the table. Then walk through the motions of the process, notebook in hand, and write down the specific "sticking" points as they come up.

However you arrive at your list of problems, rank them according to how troublesome they are. After you've read the instructions in the appropriate sections for solving your particular difficulties, work your way down your list, starting with the #1 problem. This chapter also covers a streamlined way to organize your kitchen when moving into a new home.

WORK AREA

In any kitchen, large or small, you should have a central work area that is generous, extremely compact, safe, comfortable, and easy to care for. According to Mimi Sheraton, former food editor of *The New York Times*, ". . . the actual work area that includes range, sink and refrigerator should be small, so that those three major pieces of equipment are each no more than a step or pivot apart." A long walk is not only exhausting but a "downright hazard if one is draining a heavy potful of boiling water that must be carried from stove to sink."

If your present kitchen fails to meet this ideal, consult with your service representative to see whether the refrigerator and/or range can be moved closer together. If not, you can to some extent compensate for poorly placed appliances by substituting miniaturized versions. For example, a toaster oven/broiler, electric frying pan, or water immersion heater kept near the sink can take the place of the less convenient range when you are preparing lunches, light meals, and snacks. You must have counter space for them, however, or be prepared to install a convenient appliance shelf.

If the main range is your only alternative, get a small wheeled cart so that you can push pots and crockery from one place to the other. If the refrigerator is off the track, an expensive but handy solution is to install a small refrigerator under the sink for milk, fruit, and a few frequently used items.

The main working counter should be large enough so that you can lay out ingredients, cut, mix, season, and prepare foods for cooking, and should be within the compact sink-range-refrigerator triangle. Counter space outside the triangle is largely wasted. To increase the efficiency of well-placed (within the triangle) counter space, keep counters as free of kitchen appliances and supplies as possible. Hang the dish drainer on the wall, and put canisters on shelves. You might want to investigate Black & Decker's line of "Spacesaver" appliances—a line of blenders, can openers, toaster ovens, and other small appliances that are installed on the bottom surface of your kitchen cabinets. Other storage tips are discussed later in this chapter.

Then, if necessary, improvise new counter spaces. Get a board, or have one cut, that is wide enough to span the sink but not so deep that it interferes with use of the faucets. A board roughly half the size of the sink is about right.

Another solution would be to fasten a hinged board to the wall which can be lowered when needed. A wheeled cart with butcherboard top or a stationary table can also provide more counter space. They can also do double duty for dishes and utensils.

Counters should be high enough to allow you to work without bending. If they are too low, get a three-inch-thick cutting board to build up counter height during extensive cutting and dicing jobs. If you are customizing, consider making the counter low enough so that you can sit while you work. In that case, your chair should be on wheels; otherwise the constant getting up and down will cause more fatigue than steady standing.

Where to put dirty dishes or utensils when counter space adjacent to the work area is insufficient is a chronic problem that causes a great deal of unnecessary movement. Rinse the dishes out if you can, or fill them with water to soak. This step is helpful even if your dishwasher purports to clean dried-out food. Put the filled bowls and pots on the stove or in the oven if those areas are free, or install a wall shelf specifically for dirty utensils. You can also use a rolling cart, or failing that, set them on newspaper in a corner on the floor.

Put dirty spoons and small implements on a little tray especially curved to hold spoons, tea bags, and other small messy items. Collect parings, bruised leaves, and scrapings on a paper towel, so as not to clutter the counter, and throw them out all at once. One client hooked a plastic flowerpot onto the wall for that purpose, and emptied it into the compost heap when it filled.

A relatively maintenance-free kitchen is, in general, one where furniture and fittings have smooth, simple shapes, and floors and cabinets demand only a swipe from damp mop or sponge.

STORAGE

Arrange to devote about an hour a day for a week or so to kitchen storage, first clearing out the deadwood, then planning and executing solutions. Go through each drawer and shelf noting unnecessary duplications (three can openers?), and apply the basic "to keep or not to keep" test to any doubtful objects:

1. Have I used this item within the past year?
2. If not, do I want to keep it anyway because it's beautiful or because it has value (sentimental or monetary)?
3. If not, might it come in handy someday?

Don't get caught by saying "maybe" to question 3. Toss the eggbeater, or whatever. You'll buy another one if you must. As always, store the excess in grocery cartons for giveaway.

Next, consider whether more kitchen storage space could be opened up by transferring some items nearer to their point of use. For example, if you generally serve dinner at the table, shift the dishes and silver as close to the eating area as possible to make table-setting less of a chore. Remove some glasses to the living room and operate your bar out of that room instead of the kitchen. This procedure not only releases kitchen space but saves a lot of trips from kitchen to living or dining area.

Charting

If the reorganization job is full-scale, chart your kitchen space to define its accessibility. Choose one of the kitchen walls to start with, open all cabinets and drawers on that wall above and below the counter, and sketch a very rough, freehand, unmeasured diagram of all the shelves, drawers,

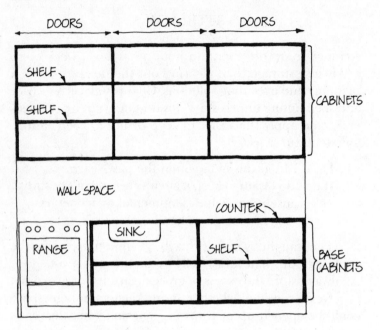

Figure 12   Kitchen—Accessibility Chart I

and surfaces. Indicate the wall itself and cabinet doors. Do this for the entire kitchen. Figure 12 is a sample.

Next, extend your hand to all the shelves, drawers, and surfaces on each wall. Space directly in front of your hand is #1; #2 space is accessible with a small stretch; #3 space is fairly accessible; and space that requires use of a stepladder is #10. The front section of a shelf may be #1 or #2, while the less accessible rear is #3 or #4. Judge these spaces according to your own comfort, not against some hypothetical ideal. A lithe person, for example, could rank a bending-down space as #2, while the same space might rank #4 or #5 for someone less agile.

Write the rank number of every shelf and surface on the diagram. The sample might now look like Figure 13.

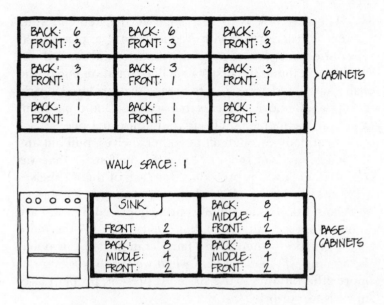

Figure 13   Kitchen—Accessibility Chart II

Getting the Most from What You've Got

Organize the spaces that already exist before considering construction possibilities. In any organizing job it's generally wise to utilize as fully as possible all existing facilities before making any major changes or additions.

Start with the cabinets. Ideally, the *top* of a kitchen cabinet should rise six feet from the floor, not too far above eye level for people of average height, and shelves should be on ball bearings so they can be pulled out. Would that it were so. In actuality, kitchen cabinets are usually rigid and invariably so high that most people can get full use only from the first shelf. So the suggestions that follow are intended to wrest maximum flexibility and responsiveness from these clumsy units.

The first task is to rearrange all the items in your cabinets to correspond with frequency of use: pieces used most often in the most convenient spaces, and so on down the line. Examine the first #1 shelf as noted on one of the wall charts, and reserve it for items that are used nearly every day. Remove all pieces that are not #1 and put them aside for the moment. This is your "unsorted pile."

Next, look through all the other shelves, pull out any #1 items, and put them into the #1 shelf space that was released. Follow this procedure for each of the #1 shelves in your kitchen until all #1 shelves contain only #1 objects, and no #1 objects are inappropriately placed. If you have room to spread out, do so, but don't worry if—the more likely situation—utensils are fairly crammed at this point. Cramming will be dealt with when we get to working out more efficient ways to use space. At present, proper placement is top priority.

Turn next to the #2 shelves and follow the same procedure:

1. Leave #2 items—things used several times a week— in place on the shelf.
2. Remove items that are not #2 and put with the unsorted pile.
3. Scout the remaining shelves for #2 items and add them to the appropriate shelves.
4. Pick any #2 items out of the unsorted pile and put them on the #2 shelves.

Shift the remaining items the same way according to this scale: #3 pieces are used pretty regularly, #4 fairly often, #5 occasionally, #6 seldom, and so on. Put the final items—the #10s, like the big once-a-year Thanksgiving roasting pan—in a #10 space atop the cabinets or on a high closet shelf.

As you place utensils, also ask yourself, "Where do I

stand when I use this object?" or "Where do I *first* use this object?" and pinpoint that location as closely as you can. Store the most frequently used serving bowls, platters, and serving spoons within the range-refrigerator-sink triangle, so food can be transferred smoothly from cooking pot to serving utensil. If you cook and serve from the same vessel, so much the better.

Materials that are used only together should be clustered together; for example, baking items like cake flour, rolling pin, sifter. Since mixing bowls are generally used for other purposes as well, store them with other bowls.

One tip: All china of the same pattern need not be stored together. Divide place settings. If, for example, you are a family of four and have service for twelve, put half of the dishes on a higher shelf, or even in a cabinet in another room.

Once utensils are properly located, consider more efficient utilization of the shelves themselves. Shelves are often too deep (a twelve-inch depth is about right) and almost always too high. One way to solve this problem is to insert portable shelf racks to make two functional shelves out of one that is semifunctional. Some shelf racks divide the space more or less evenly; others create a low space for small jars and a higher one for glasses or cans. Evaluate your shelf height and your needs before deciding what to buy. There are also revolving shelves that can hold cans, spices, or small dishes.

Dish organizers use shelf space quite efficiently. There are two styles: One type stacks small and larger plates horizontally on different levels and provides cup hooks. The other type, which I find easier to handle, stores plates in an upright position.

Other freestanding (that is, not requiring installation) "organizers" can serve a variety of purposes; for example, you can "file" those floppy pouches of beans, soups, or dried foods in a narrow box organizer. There is a useful organizer for pot and casserole covers, and holders for aluminum foil, plastic wrap, and other paper supplies. Organizers are also very helpful in putting wasted space to use, whether it's the typical cavern under the sink or an empty corner. You can get organizers for cleaning supplies and paper goods, and storage bins for potatoes, onions, canned goods, and even large pots or appliances. Some storage bins fit on runners to make drawers. Arrange them all, of course, according to frequency of use.

Also consider stackable plastic or vinyl storage cubes for dishes, glasses, rolls of plastic wrap and aluminum foil. Baskets can hold canned goods or dry food. Cluster baskets in a corner or, in a large kitchen, line them up to make a room divider. The empty sections in a freestanding wine rack could be used for rolled-up towels, napkins, or tablecloths.

Whichever organizer(s) you choose, a few unused inches often remain at the top of the shelf. Screw in some hooks for cups or small gadgets, making sure, however, that you can still remove items easily. Cramming only leads to disorganization, so if you have the space to spread out, stack no more than three pieces on top of each other.

Counters can also provide storage space if they are wide enough. Line them with canisters of sugar or flour, cookie jars, or jugs to hold "bouquets" of small utensils like serving spoons and spatulas. Small appliances like blenders will also fit on a wide counter.

Use drawers for silverware, towels, staple vegetables like potatoes or onions, or fitted as a breadbox. Keep small utensils in drawers only if there is enough space so they don't jumble. Otherwise hang them with magnetic hooks, on grids, or keep them in jugs.

Organize your refrigerator like any other cabinet, keeping frequently used items closest to hand, and grouping together similar foods such as different types of cheeses. Choose a particular corner for leftovers so that you will notice them before they spoil. If bottles don't fill your high main compartment, divide the space with shelf-makers. A shelf might enlarge the freezer capacity too. If you buy a new refrigerator, purchase one with pull-out or revolving shelves that will enable you to reach the back easily. The most convenient freezers that I have seen are at the bottom of the unit, or in compartments lining the side, rather than the traditional box across the top. With this layout the vegetable bin is placed at the top, making it much more accessible.

Making New Storage Space

If cabinets and drawers are still overcrowded after sorting and placing, hanging and shelving are two space-extending techniques.

Hangable pieces include pots and pans of every description, cups, pitchers, small utensils like wire whisks, spatulas, and slotted spoons, scissors, pot holders, paper towel holders, and even plates and platters. Almost any utensil can be made hangable. I have drilled holes in many things, including a rubber dish-drainer tray, a Dutch oven, and a small clear plastic cutting board. For one very large cutting board that was too thick to fit a hook, I put a strong keychain in the hole to hang it from.

If you plan to hang a number of items, grids, or especially pegboard, which opens a great amount of space, is the most efficient solution. It can be hung, cut to size or precut, on any flat surface, including walls, cabinet doors both inside and outside, the sides of cabinets and counters, and the undersides of cabinets. In other words, every inch of surface is a potential hanging space. It helps to paint an outline around each object on the pegboard so you'll know where it goes—and whether you've hung it up or not!

Other hanging ideas include:

1. Magnetized hooks for small utensils. Make the refrigerator door a household message center by leaving little notes under magnets. Also, dry plastic bags by slipping a small magnet inside each bag and hanging it on a metal surface.

2. Pin or hook or use a magnetic backing to affix a *permanent* pad and pen in an accessible location. Jot down any food or household item when you notice stocks running low. Take the slip with you to the supermarket, along with slips from other supply areas (see page 296).

3. Hang large pots, pans, and baskets from a cast-iron or steel ceiling fixture, or directly from ceiling hooks. One client attached a basketball hoop above the work counter, lined with "S" hooks (hooks shaped like an "S"), and hung all her spatulas and light utensils so they were easily accessible.

4. Put hooks on the underside of kitchen cabinets for cups, mugs, and small gadgets. A rack specifically for wineglasses and other stemware that attaches under a cabinet is available. The glasses are stored upside down and can be slid out. There is a similar rack for cups. There are other types of upside-down arrangements for glasses too, such as those you see in bars. They would have to be custom-made.

5. Hanging "organizers" of various kinds is useful. Here are a few suggestions: spice racks; knife holders; paper bag or garbage bag holders; paper towel holders; plastic wrap and waxed paper holders; a wire rack hooked inside the undersink cabinet door for dishwashing liq-

uid and cleansing powders. A long, narrow wicker basket of the type to hold rolls is also good for spices.

6. One tip on spices that also applies to canned goods: alphabetize them! It sounds a little compulsive, but it makes small bottles or cans very easy to find.

Creating extra shelf space is the other main extension technique. For instance, install a shelf in the gap between counter and cabinet, or between refrigerator and stove. Insert a shelf between two existing shelves if the height is unusually generous. Don't waste high shelf space that might be used for only one or two tall objects. Add another partial shelf to store small items in that space as well. Shelve a tall, narrow broom closet and hang the broom and dustpan on the wall. One client shelved a five-inch-deep indentation in the wall, creating # 1 space for canned goods.

Bulk Storage

If you have the space, buy food in quantity at a considerably lower price. To store perishables, I recommend a freezer shaped like a refrigerator, as opposed to the older style "chest" freezer. To clarify, this is not a refrigerator freezing compartment, but a full-sized appliance that freezes food for up to a year. Make sure that the freezer has pull-out shelves to keep foods in the rear from getting iced in. Try to avoid locating the freezer in a dank basement or some other unpleasant place.

Label each shelf: "meats," "vegetables," "fruits," "prepared foods." Wrap each package in freezer paper and label the outside, stating contents of the package and date of freezing. Put freshly packaged foods in the back of the freezer and keep moving older foods up toward the front.

A storeroom or pantry for dry and canned foods is a great advantage; you can sometimes buy wholesale if the quantity is large enough. At the very least, take advantage of supermarket specials, and also buy the largest size available, which is usually more economical. Divide the "large economy size" box into smaller containers that will fit on your kitchen shelves. The storeroom itself should be organized like any other shelf space.

SERVING AND CLEARING

The simplest way to swiftly transfer dishes from kitchen to table is a mobile serving cart. Load it with clean dishes to set the table, dirty dishes during and after the meal, and push it to the sink. A mobile cart, by eliminating multiple trips between kitchen and deck or barbecue, is especially convenient for eating outdoors.

Some people solve eating, serving, and clearing problems by building a connecting counter between kitchen and dining area. This is helpful only when kitchen and dining room adjoin one another so that food and dirty dishes are accessible to both locations, and can be passed back and forth easily.

A good counter can also offer fringe benefits: snack bar, storage area, and sometimes an additional working counter. These are the specifications to create these extra amenities:

1. If you would like to make it a working counter, construct two levels—a level low enough to sit at comfortably for light meals and a higher level to stand and work at. Alternatively, make the eating level a retractable shelf that you can pull out for meals. If you don't need another working surface, make the counter the lower height.

2. Figure the counter's width by measuring the thigh-joint-to-knee length of the household's tallest person, and add the diameter of your dinner plates plus a few extra inches.

3. Leave enough open space on the kitchen side for someone to sit comfortably with legs underneath as in a coffeeshop (that is, the thigh-joint-to-knee length).

4. Make the dining side into an open-shelf cabinet for storing dinnerware, possibly wine, and some serving pieces. (Reminder: Keep frequently used pieces on the kitchen side.) If you don't need a snacking counter, create storage space on both the kitchen and dining sides. Or incorporate both ideas by making a shelf that pulls out when needed for snacks and light meals.

KITCHEN TIMESAVERS

A typical up-to-date kitchen can resemble the cockpit of the Discovery space shuttle. Does all that chrome, gleam, and whir necessarily spell efficiency and organization?

Not necessarily. There may sometimes be less behind the whir and chrome than meets the eye in terms of enhancing genuine efficiency and convenience. On the other hand, many up-to-date tools can be a real boon in making food preparation simpler, faster, and more enjoyable. In order not to be seduced by fashion, however, it is worthwhile to review some of the more popular products to see whether or not they fit your needs:

Food processor. The food processor has become a staple in many family kitchens. However, a full-sized food processor has so many bowls, cutters, and attachments that use and cleanup can become a real chore.

Thus, if you mostly cook for only one or two, it might be easier to look for simpler alternatives. Some processor functions, such as pureeing, can be accomplished in a simple blender. Others, such as slicing and dicing vegetables, are just as handy using a mini-processor such as Sunbeam's Oskar. Also consider an electric knife.

Hand blender. In addition to the traditional blender, a hand blender, such as Braun's Multipractic hand blender, is a handy device. You put the blender directly into the sauce or shake or dressing that's being blended, rather than the other way around.

Coffeemaker. People get violent about their coffeemakers. If fine coffee, prepared faster than instant, is the goal, then a coffeemaker like Bunn's cold-water displacement/reservoir model might be the answer. Pour in cold water for the number of cups you want, and seemingly by magic, hot coffee comes out the other end.

Braun and Krups have "digital" models that can have coffee waiting for you at a preset time.

Countertop toaster oven/broiler. A handy-dandy product useful for heating or cooking lunches and small meals, toaster ovens are also fine for broiling. Make sure the model you purchase is heavy enough to be stable. Models that are too light can be dangerous. They tip easily and get too hot.

Microwave oven. A microwave zaps frozen foods in a flash and heats faster than anything. One cook cited these specific pleasures of the microwave: frozen bagels made ready in an instant; you can just put a potato on a paper towel and bake it very quickly without mess, fuss, or a pan to wash up; you can make a healthy and tasty vegetable dish by putting the raw vegetable in a microwave cookware container with just a touch of water. A *USA Today* survey found that 78 percent of the people polled said that the microwave oven was their greatest timesaver (August 19, 1987).

Yet, some serious cooks feel that food cooked in a

microwave never seems quite at its best, though others would give you an argument.

For those concerned with radiation, before purchasing a microwave you might want to compare radiation leakage between one brand and another. Check *Consumer Reports* and government publications. Take care, in all cases, to keep the door of the microwave clean. Dirt and grease on the door can prevent it from closing tightly, thus permitting radiation leakage.

Traditional efficiencies. An expert cook reports that she slices and dices vegetables with a knife on a breadboard in preference to a food processor because, in her view, the most efficient cutting tool of all is a fine knife weighted so as to feel good in your hand. It almost carries your hand along.

Similarly, she much prefers a hand-held can opener like Swing-a-way to an electric can opener. Says this accomplished cook, "Good good-quality implements are really the answer."

ORGANIZING INTO
A NEW HOME

Moving presents a great opportunity to organize your entire kitchen at once. In fact, this streamlined technique can be used even if you're not moving, but don't try it unless you know you won't get bogged down in the middle. Collect lots of grocery cartons and mark one box "K#1" ("K" meaning "kitchen"), another box "K#2," and so on through "K#5." Mark a sixth box "K#6 and up." Also have giveaway and throwaway boxes on hand. Go through your kitchen cabinets and drawers piece by piece and winnow and evaluate each object as discussed on page 231. Put aside enough basic pieces to use until you're set up in your new kitchen—plates, can opener, coffee, etc.—and distribute everything else: #1 pieces in the #1 box, #2 pieces in the #2 box, and so on. As you fill each box, label its contents. *Do not* combine differently ranked items in one box, even if the #2 box is full while #5 has extra space. This only creates extra work.

When you get to your new kitchen, sketch and rank the spaces as discussed on page 231, and start unpacking the "#6 and up" items first. Try to stack no more than three objects on top of each other, other than sets. If space becomes too tight as you reach the #2 or #3 items, plan how to expand the space according to the techniques discussed in this chapter, and execute the job.

14
Rooms in General

Your living room is a disaster area. The neighbors came over to see the ballgame, but only two people could watch the set at one time. The compact-disk player was on the coffee table for lack of an alternative spot, so the only place to put drinks was on the floor. Two drinks were knocked over. One of the kids racing through tripped over the Nintendo, thereby dislodging all the magazines from the top of the television set, which has become the magazine rack for your collection of *TV Guide*, *Time*, and *Newsweek*.

If anything in this story sounds familiar, you are suffering from "room overload"; the natural, though not inevitable, consequence of a room—whether called living room, den, family room, or recreation room—that functions in multiple ways. The flexibility that makes such a room the center of family operations also makes it particularly susceptible to the kind of disarray that is impractical and difficult to live with.

If room overload is your problem, use the suggestions that follow to design a workable, comfortable area. If, on the other hand, your room only has a few problem spots, read the chapter through once and then turn to page 250 for pointers on solving spot problems.

CLEARING THE ROOM

In order to come to grips with miscellaneous clutter, block out and concentrate on an area approximately five feet square. Take a critical look at every object or category of objects (except furniture) in that space to decide whether it belongs in the room at all. If the objects go elsewhere, distribute them appropriately: papers and old magazines to the desk to be sorted and integrated into the paper-handling system (see Chapter 4, page 76); toys and games to the children's rooms; rain hats to the closet. Don't try organizing the closet or shelf you're distributing *to*, just fit the items in as best you can. Put objects that do belong in the room near related objects—stack books in or near the bookcase, for example. Survey and distribute the contents of the entire living room methodically in this fashion.

Some items will frustrate you because they don't seem to have a natural "home." For example:

Alcohol and accessories
Coasters
Folding chairs
Games
Magazines

Matches
Plant-care or pet-care items
Serving trays
Snack or candy dishes

A wall system—a combination of cabinetry and shelving that lines all or part of a wall—could handle most of these items. If you do get a wall system, buy a unit that accommodates the specific articles you intend to store. If, for example, wine storage is no problem, a wine rack is wasted space. Wall units are, however, generally quite expensive and sometimes overwhelm a small room. If space is a prime consideration and you prefer more modest arrangements, see Chapter 10, page 185, for a discussion of tight-space storage techniques. Also see Chapter 15, page 271, for tips on choosing storage units.

WHAT PEOPLE DO
IN THE ROOM

An important step in organizing any room is choosing that room's appropriate functions. Often, "room overload" is a result of allowing too many activities to go on in one single room. Narrowing the list frees space and allows you to enjoy your room in greater comfort. The list that follows includes most activities that might go on in a living room:

Children playing
Computer/games
Conversation
Drinking (alcohol)
Eating (meals and/or snacks)
Entertaining a group
Exercising
Games (cards, Scrabble)

Hobbies
Homework
Housecleaning
Music playing (piano, guitar)
Reading
Telephoning
Sewing, knitting
Sleeping (nighttime—convertible couch or daybed)
Sleeping (napping)
Stereo, radio, tape, or CD listening
Storage
Television/VCR viewing
Videotaping

_____

_____

Check off the activities that are performed in your room. Use the extra lines to write in pursuits not listed.

Relocating Activities

Some of the activities listed above might be more profitably moved to another part of the house if any of the following criteria apply:

1. An activity interferes with other functions. For example, children who are playing may disturb adults.
2. An activity would be more convenient elsewhere. For example, some china and glassware may have been stored in the living room because that's where you put it when you first moved in. Ideally, it should be nearer the kitchen or dining room.
3. The activity annoys you. For example, it might irritate you to see your husband or wife napping on the couch.

Head a sheet of paper "Project List 1," and list the activity to be relocated and the specific steps necessary to do so. For example:

1. Children playing. The television set may be drawing them to the living room. If so, you might get the kids their own TV and/or VCR, or put the TV in their playroom. If books, games, and toys are stored in the living room, you might want to move them to the children's room.

2. China and glassware. Transferring these items to the kitchen or dining room is the main step, but list preliminary steps: for example, consolidating the kitchen cabinets to make additional space, or getting a new stand-up cabinet for the kitchen. (Make very simple kitchen changes at this time; just enough to accommodate the items as best as you can. You'll organize china and glassware when you do the kitchen. See page 233.)

3. Napping on the couch. If a request to nap in the bedroom isn't effective, consider exchanging the present capacious couch which invites slumber for a smaller loveseat. Alternatively, the modification may be in the bedroom rather than the living room. Perhaps the bed's satin coverlet discourages casual napping. If so, list on Project List 1 whatever can be done quickly— "buy wool throw to protect bedspread"—and postpone a large-scale bedroom planning job. This postponement is an important element of all organizing.

Principle #9 **Organize one thing at a time. Save organizing further trouble spots until later.**

In addition to moving some activities out, there are others that might be brought in. One client, for example, exercised every morning in a cramped bedroom corner only rendered operational by pushing a chair out of the way, although the living room contained a larger, more convenient open space. After our consultation, the living room became the exercise site. To make the change feasible, my client bought a tall, cylindrical basket to hold the rolled-up tatami mat, and installed some hooks inside the nearby closet where she could hang her leotard and jump rope.

Consider additional activities that might benefit you and add them to the basic activities list. List on Project List 1 the specific steps needed to make the shift.

Finally, action. Execute all the projects on PL 1 and throw the list away.

DEFINING PROBLEMS
AND SOLVING THEM

Return to the Activities List on page 247 and check off those functions that aren't working well in the room. In order to arrive at a solution, define and analyze the problem activities. Let's take two functions of our hypothetical living room as an example: conversation/small-scale entertainment, and children playing. You'll need a fresh sheet of paper, Project List 2, as your problem list.

Conversation/small-scale entertaining. Visualize your family with a guest or two sitting in the room. Are there enough seats for everybody? Must chairs be brought from other parts of the room? If seating isn't adequate, write "more seating" on Project List 2. Are the seats comfortable? What about lighting? Too bright or too dim?

Is the furniture arrangement conducive to conversation? Do people have to lean forward to hear one another? Can they see each other without obstruction? Must people balance snacks on their knees because there's no convenient place to put them? Consider the same set of questions for a larger group of people—four to twelve—if you have, or would like to have, frequent guests. Note each problem on PL 2. Don't work on solutions yet; just note that the problems exist.

Children playing. If you enjoy having the entire family together, thereby encouraging the children to stay around, there are probably going to be problems. The most likely are:

Noise, including disruptive computer games
Breakage of valuables
Spills and stains on rugs and furniture
Clutter
Interference with adult conversation and activities

List these and any other specific problems on Project List 2.

Analyzing Activities: Checklist

The two activities analyzed above illustrate a procedure that can be applied to virtually any awkward situation, whether it's a single spot problem or one of the troublesome activities on your activities list. Here is a summary of the activity-analysis process:

1. Visualize the activity in your mind.
2. Is the activity in competition with another function? For example, is game noise in competition with conversation?
3. Analyze the scene for physical comfort. For instance, are the chairs at the table high enough to permit eating in comfort? Can people easily interact with one another? Is there enough light, and is it placed properly for the activity?

4. Are people engaged comfortably with *things*? Can all TV watchers see the screen?
5. Is the furniture *appropriate* to the activity? Should a spindly-legged Louix XV ottoman hold the feet of a six-foot 180-pound man?
6. What accessories would make the activity more comfortable? A reading chair, for instance, might be enhanced by a magazine rack, snack table, ottoman, and/or adjustable lamp. And remember to keep the things you use close to hand.
7. Is the activity convenient to a related area? A dining table, for example, should be near the kitchen.

List the problem's components on Project List 2.

Making the Room Work

Most of the problems defined on PL 2 will yield any number of possible solutions ranging from clever and inexpensive gimmicks to costly new pieces of furniture. Decide in advance approximately how much money you can spend to alter the room so you can choose realistically between alternatives. Begin then with a fresh sheet of paper headed Project List 3 and list the exact steps—purchases, moves, modifications—needed to solve the problem. As you define solutions, cross the activity off PL 2. To illustrate how this process works, let's consider the two room functions discussed earlier.

Conversation/Small-Scale Entertaining

Let's assume for the sake of illustration that your present conversation area is inadequate in the extreme. These are the problems listed on PL 2:

More seating needed.

Uncomfortable upright chair.

The glass over the painting causes glare.

The couch and the chairs are too far apart; people chatting have to raise their voices.

People sitting on the couch have no place to set plates or drinks.

Step by step, list your proposed solutions on Project List 3.

More seating needed. Folding chairs is one idea, but you're probably looking for a permanent arrangement, not a solution for the occasional party or large gathering. You can enlarge the conversational area by replacing chairs with a couch or loveseat, either bought new or taken from another part of the house. Two couches facing one another, with chairs in between, create an attractive area. Use either traditional couches and chairs or modular furniture that is especially designed to create shiftable conversation groups. Alternatively, big floor pillows, if they are compatible with your decor, make attractive and handy seating. Nesting chairs are a good backup idea: light, stackable chairs, usually rattan or straw, that can be kept unobtrusively in a corner. Make two conversation groupings in a fairly large room by placing two sofas back-to-back and adding other chairs around each sofa. This can comfortably accommodate quite a few people.

Upright chair uncomfortable. Perhaps add a cushion. Alternatively, get a more comfortable seat for the conversation grouping and use the upright chair primarily for decoration.

Glaring light on glass. Try spraying the glass with a nonglare solution. If that doesn't work, consider moving the painting or the lamp.

Couch and chairs too far apart. Before you rearrange

them—the obvious solution—decide why you originally put them so far apart. Did you want, for example, to make a passageway from one side of the room to the other? If so, perhaps the entire conversation area could be moved to another spot in the room. Or the coffee table might be too big, creating the unnecessary distance. A decision is in order then: Could the table be used elsewhere? Could the furniture be arranged on two contiguous sides? Mark your steps on PL 3 and also note supplemental moves needed to accommodate the changes—moving end tables, lamps, etc.

Snacks and drinks. End tables, the obvious solution, can run into money. Try building them: wooden boxes, measured to fit the height and depth of the couch, with laminated butcherboard tops. Allow for a generous surface area. Paint the front and sides or cover with patterned Con-Tact paper. Another inexpensive idea is to build or buy small round Masonite tables and cover them with tablecloths. (See page 271 for more on end tables.) If space for permanent end tables is a problem, fit some "occasional" tables with caster wheels so they can be moved easily to serve as snack tables when the occasion arises.

Rearranging a conversational area can offer unexpected benefits. One client mentioned that his teenaged children rarely spent the evening with the family. After we rearranged the room, it became so pleasant that the children began joining in. A conversation grouping will encourage conversation.

Children Playing

Project List 2 listed these disadvantages of children playing in the living room:

> Noise, including video games
> Breakage of valuables

Spills and stains on rugs and furniture
Clutter
Interference with adult conversation and activities

Noise is a discipline problem, not an organizing problem, but if even normal noise seems jarring, check acoustics. An uncarpeted floor will sometimes cause noise to reverberate. Also check ceiling acoustics. Mark any project on Project List 3.

To prevent breakage, remove fragile items to high shelves. Sturdy furniture is imperative; an antique-filled room is not a good candidate for playroom.

You can't prevent spills or stains, but you can dilute their effect by protecting furniture with vinyls, glazed chintzes, or other relatively childproof fabrics. Sew sturdy snaps to the couch or chair in an unobtrusive site—the back of a pillow or the back of a chair—and snap on attractive but inexpensive full-sized throws. They can be taken off when you have company.

Interference with adult activities is, to some extent, what you're opting for, but don't let children take over. Stock a corner with toys, games, drawing papers and pens, and maybe a television set and VCR stocked with children's videotapes such as Looney Tunes. Line an accessible shelf or table with cork or vinyl to set glasses of milk down on. The children's corner should provide enough shelf and cabinet space to store their things. (See also "Children's Rooms," page 302.)

Checklist: Making Changes

The examples we've considered illustrate the thought processes involved in creating a functional, pleasant room. The following checklist summarizes these steps briefly.

STEP 1. Read quickly over Project List 2—your list of room activities broken down into specific problem areas.

STEP 2. Head a fresh sheet of paper "Project List 3."

STEP 3. Consider the first problem on PL 2. If a solution is obvious, mark it on PL 3. If not, ask yourself these questions:

   a. Can a substitute object fulfill the same function more effectively? For example, stretching a seating area by substituting a couch for two chairs.

   b. Could an object or piece of furniture be made more comfortable, or otherwise modified?

   c. Is a simple shifting of furniture or objects the answer?

   d. Will new furniture or objects solve the problem?

   e. If storage is your problem, will a major project like buying a wall unit or building more shelves be best, or might more modest alternatives (see pages 187 –92) answer the need?

   f. Can the problem be alleviated by creating *new* storage spaces?

   g. Would protective slipcovers or flooring help?

   h. Would caster wheels make furniture more mobile, thereby creating more space?

STEP 4. Write down on Project List 3 the exact steps needed to solve all the problem points in the first two activities. Include all relevant measurements. Cross the activities off Project List 2.

STEP 5. Actually implement all changes for the first two activities.

STEP 6. When step 5 seems well under control, define solutions for the next two activities and implement them. Continue the "define/implement" pattern until the room is completed.

PLANNING A MODEL ROOM

Although this procedure is optional, if problems are so numerous that a complete revamping seems in order, including major furniture purchases, it might help clarify your alternatives to plan everything in advance by designing a model room on paper.

The procedure calls for several sheets of graph paper, some brightly colored construction paper (get two colors), a fine-point black marker and a fine-point colored marker, a ruler, a yardstick and/or tape measure, scissors, and a compass to draw circles.

After first measuring the dimensions of your room, including alcoves and ells, outline the room with the black marker on graph paper at a scale of one inch to one foot. Also indicate to scale, with the *colored* marker, doors, windows, and structural features like radiators, built-in bookshelves, and fireplace. Note how far the radiators jut out into the room.

Figure 14 is a sample plan.

Next, measure width and length of each piece of furniture that rests on the floor. For circular furniture, measure the diameter.* Outline the furniture on the construction paper, using one color and the same one-foot-to-one-inch scale. Cut the pieces out and label each piece.

Check Project List 3 for pieces of furniture that you propose to buy. Estimate their measurements and cut them out of the other shade of construction paper. Then consult Project List 3, one activity at a time, to solve each problem by moving around the cutouts, both the existing pieces and the provisional ones, on the graph paper. Some activities

---

*To measure diameter, run a tape measure from one point on the circle to another across the center.

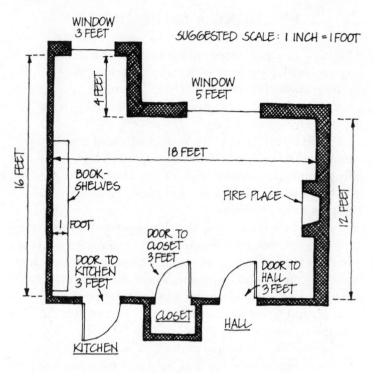

WINDOW
3 FEET

SUGGESTED SCALE: I INCH = I FOOT

4 FEET

WINDOW
5 FEET

16 FEET

18 FEET

BOOK-
SHELVES

FIRE PLACE

12 FEET

I FOOT

DOOR TO
CLOSET
3 FEET

DOOR TO
KITCHEN
3 FEET

DOOR TO
HALL
3 FEET

CLOSET

HALL

KITCHEN

Figure 14   Design a model room on paper

can be doubled up—for example, a conversation area can be adapted to snacking—but doubling is not always desirable. A large room may call for a spread-out design to fill otherwise overlarge spaces. Make sure that pathways are wide enough, and that people aren't bumping into furniture on the way from one room to another.

When the scheme seems satisfactory, attach each cutout to the graph paper with a sliver of Scotch tape and put it away for a few days. During the interval, jot down any new ideas on Project List 3. When you take the plan out again, incorporate new ideas or revise it as you see fit.

Finally, confirm the plan by evaluating it as pure design. An effective plan will always look "shapely" and should convey a sense of balance.

Even if the scheme isn't yet perfect, stay with what you have. This is an important principle:

Principle #10   **If invention has run dry, execute the less than perfect solution. A more satisfactory answer will generally come to you in time.**

Now physically execute the design in your room to conform to the plan.

THE WELL-ORGANIZED ROOM: A MASTER CHECKLIST

1. Clear the room of clutter (page 246).
2. List all the activities that go on in the room (page 247).
3. Decide which activities belong in the room and which don't, and take steps to shift them using Project List 1 (page 248). Correct the Activities List accordingly.
4. Analyze each activity into specific problem areas and list the problems on Project List 2. (See discussion on pages 250–51 and the "Activities Analysis Checklist" on page 251.)
5. Decide how much money you are willing to spend.
6. Work out solutions and list them on Project List 3. See the discussion on pages 253–54, and then follow the "Making Changes Checklist" on page 255.
7. Optional. If alternatives are confusing or if you plan a large-scale revamping, design a model room on paper (page 257).
8. Walk through the room to check that you can move

smoothly from one area to another. Also consider scale and size. Is furniture too big for the room? Is there too much furniture or too many accessories? If the flow of space is a severe problem, see the discussion on flexible rooms (page 267).

15
Rooms in Particular

Some rooms—bathrooms, bedrooms, multiple-use rooms (studio apartments or lofts), and workrooms—are used in specialized ways. This chapter analyzes layout and storage problems specific to those rooms.

BATHROOM

Many people draw a blank when they consider organizing the bathroom. What to do with all the bottles and tubes? And you can't rearrange the furniture. It is possible, however, to get around the almost invariably awkward bathroom setup by judicious use of one "bathroom aid" or another.

For bathing and showering, reduce the sense of "invasion by shampoo bottle" by consolidating all the paraphernalia on a bathtub tray, shower caddy, or shelf inside the tub. There are also shower curtains with pockets for shampoo and soap. Add no-slip stripping in the tub for safety.

If you have a small bathroom, a big family, and a shortage of towel racks, put towel hooks on the wall or create several towel racks in a limited space by attaching two one-foot panels three feet apart to the bathroom wall, and connect the panels by staggered rods, as in Figure 15.

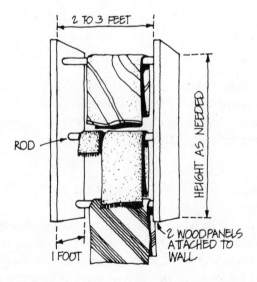

Figure 15   Increasing bathroom towel space

Bathroom Storage—
Cosmetics and Supplies

Begin by working systematically from medicine chest to toilet ledge to windowsills to bathtub to shelves, ruthlessly discarding all the items you don't use anymore—even expensive cosmetics. Divide whatever is left over into three categories: utilitarian, grooming/cosmetic, and storage.

Utilitarian products like Band-Aids, aspirin, and medicines can be stored in the medicine chest, along with deodorants and other grooming articles not attractive enough for display. Put extra supplies of any item in the storage group. If you have many medicines, alphabetize them. Arrange the medicine chest so that items used most frequently are most accessible. Also keep first-aid instructions immediately handy. Once a month, check the cabinet and throw out any product you've stopped using.

Grooming/cosmetic items include, for both men and women, skin-care products, hair products, colognes and perfumes, bath powders, and makeup. Cosmetic items can be attractively displayed on a two or three-shelf wall rack on the most accessible wall, or in an accessory shelf on the window. If these ideas are not feasible, put the items on top of the toilet ledge or on a windowsill. To expedite cleaning the ledge or sill, stand the jars up in straw baskets with sides just high enough to keep the jars from toppling over. Keep small articles like tubes of lipstick, rouge, and eye shadow in small boxes or baskets. Stand elongated pieces like mascara wands in plastic cups. (This is also a good idea for thermometers, small tubes of liniment, etc.) About once a month, when you check the medicine chest, glance over the cosmetics and throw out whatever isn't being used.

Storage items include backup stocks of toothpaste, soap, cosmetics, and toilet paper, plus bathroom cleansing products like soapsuds, powders, and toilet bowl cleaners. Utilize whatever fairly accessible space exists nearby; a linen closet in the hall, a clothes closet shelf, or even an unused dresser drawer can provide sufficient storage. If you are ambitious, build a wall cabinet or an undersink cabinet. An *ad hoc* undersink storage area can be made by lining the sink with a skirt and putting in a couple of Rubbermaid "instant shelves." The same skirted space can be used as a clothes hamper; put down a rubber pad so clothes don't get thrown directly on the floor.

Towels and linens are discussed in Chapter 16, page 295.

BEDROOM

To make the bedroom an especially comfortable haven, plan to make the bed the center of operations. First, consider the bed itself. A loft bed, double or single, practically doubles usable space in a small room by leaving space below for office, dressing room, closet, or sitting area. Platform beds, fitted with big drawers for extra bedding or off-season clothes, are coming into their own as a storage facility. If you have an ordinary bed and the room is too narrow for a bedside night table, place the bed on the diagonal and fit the open corner with shelves. It's also easier to make a bed when it's not pushed against the wall.

Next, list all activities conducted from the bed. Possibilities include:

Cosmetic operations: makeup, nails, etc.
Eating: snacking, breakfast in bed
Games or cards
Hobbies: sketching, stamp collecting, etc.
Home office: letters, bills
Intimacies

Phoning
Reading
Sewing, knitting
Stereo or radio
Television

Analyze your chosen activities according to the procedure outlined in Chapter 14, page 250, and list the various accessories you'll need. Many of them—a nail-care kit, a can of peanuts, playing cards—will fit into one or two commodious end tables, the simplest storage solution, plus a basket under the bed for projects. Baskets, either hung from a wall hook or set on the floor, are helpful for odds and ends. A wall hook is also a place to hang a mending or knitting satchel.

A handy way to accommodate spillover is an under-the-bed "dolly." Build a plywood box about three feet square with sides two inches high—just high enough so objects won't fall out. Knot a four-foot length of clothesline or light rope through a hole drilled in one side, and tie the other end of the line to the bed framework near your hand as you sit in bed. Set the dolly on casters and pull it out whenever you want it. A dolly is especially useful for items such as phone book, knitting bag, and writing supplies.

Headboards can provide storage too, from a simple set of built-in night tables to elaborate units fitted with lights, bookshelves, stereo compartment, and even a false top that lifts to reveal a storage compartment for extra blankets and pillows. The furthest extreme of headboard development is the "environment," equipped with stereo, lights, mirrors, television, and even a bar.

Failing an elaborate headboard, stand current books and magazines on the night table, toss them into a straw bedside basket, or make or buy a bed caddy: a cloth envelope secured to the bed by slipping a long flap between mattress and springs. Prop yourself up to read with a bolster, either a full "armchair" type or an abbreviated armchair. Some bolsters have pockets for pencils, paperbacks, etc. A late-night reader whose spouse goes to sleep earlier can switch from a regular reading lamp to a small, high-intensity lamp that clips to the book and illuminates only the page.

Why not set up a bedside system for simple paperwork, such as bills and personal letters? (A more complex home office has its own rules of organization as discussed in Chapter 6.) One client put two handsome pots by her bedside: The brass pot was "to do" and the copper pot, "to file." A night-table basket held notepaper, envelopes, checkbook, stamps, pens, and her organizing calendar. We hung a clipboard on a hook by the bed. File cabinets and backup supplies were in another room.

Carry out the same idea by nailing two baskets, "to do" and "to file," to the wall, using a portable caddy for the paraphernalia.

Stereos and tape decks are a problem if you want to be able to use them from the bed. Setting them on a night table blocks too much space, so build a shelf low enough that you can turn the set off just as you doze off, but placed so you don't bump into it when you sit up.

STUDIO APARTMENTS AND OTHER SMALL SPACES

Studio apartments present a special organizational challenge: how to extract full value from every inch of space in order to comfortably lead a full life in a small room that retains an open "feel." (There are also useful tips in this section for a large loft or any undifferentiated space.)

Partitions

Your first decision is whether or not to physically separate the three main household functions—eating, sleeping, and "living"—by partitioning the space. There are three styles of partitions: full and permanent, mobile, and partial. A permanent partition is usually expensive and is difficult to remove once in place. Consider this alternative only if your room is very large, otherwise you'll lose any sense of space. One permanent option is a sliding door or a roll-up, floor-to-ceiling screen, which combines certain features of permanence (it must be installed) and mobility (it can be easily whisked out of sight).

Less expensively, a bank of stacked plastic or vinyl storage cubes or a high bookcase will create separate rooms as adequately as a floor-to-ceiling partition if sound is not a factor. Paint the back of a freestanding bookcase, or

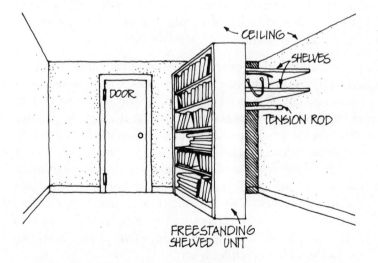

Figure 16 Use of a divider to define and increase space

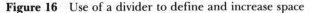

sheathe it with fabric or pegboard. To increase shelf space, shelve the back panel of the bookcase, or glue or bolt two bookcases back-to-back. There is another bookcase idea that can give shape to a featureless room while creating a coat closet and storage area. Build a floor-to-ceiling unit that's shelved on one side and flat on the other. Fit a tension rod between the flat side and the wall to make coat-hanging space. Build high shelves above the rod for out-of-the-way storage. See Figure 16 for the design.

Consider where to locate a permanent partition, and what kind to get, in terms of the following criteria:

1. "Room" size. Don't be too hasty to set up a minuscule bedroom. If a tiny room will make you claustrophobic, you might do better not to divide at all, or to divide the rooms more equitably.

2. Unfettered movement through the apartment. Make sure that the proposed partitions don't block your normal movements from area to area.

3. Light. Unless the partition can be opened, like a drape or shade, be careful to place it so as not to cut off sources of light.

Much the same criteria apply to open or partial dividers. They won't make separate rooms, but they can both unify and define areas in an attractive way. A row or cluster of large plants or baskets works well, and a serving counter between kitchen and dining area is useful for both definition and storage. Define two living room areas—a conversation/TV area and an eating section—with open shelfwork that also creates space for books, plants, and decorative pieces. The two-sided structure is handsome and useful. I've seen a freestanding fireplace accessible to both living room and dining room, each side stocked with its own wood and implements.

Light, mobile partitions that you can shift at will are

the simplest solution. One attractive variety are the opaque white screens found at Japanese variety stores. There are also burlap screens that you can cover with fabric or marbleized paper. Put screens on casters for greater mobility.

You might even have some ready-made room divisions that you hadn't thought to take advantage of. Make an alcove into a small, self-contained "reading room." Convert a hall closet into a mini-office. A wide, underused closet can be converted to a seating alcove or desk area. These are examples of what is called "adaptive re-use." If a space is obstructed by a door, either rehang the door to open in the opposite direction or remove it altogether.

Divide vertical space too. Make a loft in an old high-ceilinged house or apartment—not merely a loft bed, but an actual small room. A loft seven feet by nine feet might do for a small office; install a dining area in an eight-by-ten-foot loft, with pulleys to hoist dishes and food. Create an actual small bedroom. And of course the space below is released for whatever purpose you have in mind.

Using Furniture to Save Space

Once you've decided how or whether to partition the room, consider how to exploit space to the fullest without clutter. (See also the discussion of compact storage in Chapter 10.) Thoughtful furniture selection and placement is the key. Run through your activities as defined in Chapter 14, page 247, and list the basic furniture and accessories needed for each activity. Are there pieces of furniture on your list that can be entirely eliminated through canny storage techniques? People tend to assume, for instance, that they must have a dresser. But some of the storage techniques in Chapter 11 might create enough new shelf space to eliminate the need for a dresser. In other words, think of the function rather than the piece of furniture. Consider, too, whether you can adapt small pieces to serve the same function as furniture that may be too large for a small space. The functions of a big desk, for example, might be met by a narrower parsons table for a writing surface, backed up by a file cabinet in the closet and a portable caddy to hold supplies.

Next consider what functions can be combined in one piece of furniture. Modular furniture is the ultimate in multifunctional units: all-purpose, interchangeable modules that can be clustered into conversational groupings, opened into "pits," formed into couches or sleeping spaces, used as tables, or just about anything the imagination can devise. However, the traditional framework of tables, chairs, and couches can be extremely flexible and space saving. One single table, for instance, can triple as a dining table for six or eight, desk, sewing table, or even a bed (see bed/table below). You can get either a full-sized table big enough for all purposes or a fold-up piece. Nesting tables are, of course, a tried-and-true space-saving table idea.

The basic combination piece is the traditional convertible couch—still usually the most convenient sleeping alternative for a fairly traditional room. Another good idea is the daybed, a single bed covered with a throw and some pillows. It functions as a couch during the day and a bed at night. Some versions are fitted with a "trundle bed" that slides out to make a double bed.

Another bed combination idea is the bed/table. Measure a standard cot mattress and cut wood to that size. Set it on legs twenty-nine inches high—the standard table height. When company comes, roll out the cot mattress or a sleeping bag and you have an extra bed. Otherwise the shelf serves as combination table/buffet/desk. Alternatively, attach the bed/table *sturdily* to the wall on hinges and fold it up when not in use.

The most famous disappearing bed is the built-in Murphy bed, but I think there is somewhat less efficiency there than meets the eye. The bed's wall area is virtually unusable for anything else, and, when let down, the bed takes up considerable floor space.

Before you commit yourself to any piece that expands, opens, or otherwise changes position, particularly an expensive one, think through the space it occupies when open. Will it displace other furniture? If so, it might be worth putting either the expandable piece or the displaced pieces on casters, or choose a less bothersome alternative.

Selecting furniture or decorative pieces that can double as storage units is another way to get the most from limited space. Cluster large, covered baskets, for example, which can hold off-season clothes, linens, dry or canned foods, in a corner with plants, or use them as end tables, telephone table, or ottomans when topped with cushions. For end tables and/or coffee tables consider steamer trunks or, if your decor is contemporary, white or brightly colored lateral-drawer filing cabinets with a laminated butcher board cut to size and glued on top. It sounds unusual, but it is handsome and practical. Put heavy materials in the bottom drawer to keep the cabinets steady.

A wicker chest is another coffee table or end table idea. Covered with cushions, a wicker chest becomes a window seat. Make a more elaborate window seat by constructing a window ledge banquette that lifts up like a piano bench to provide immense storage space. Another construction idea is to make platforms fitted with huge drawers to serve as a base for seating or sleeping. Make a three-part table with a hinged top as the centerpiece that raises to reveal a bin underneath, suitable as storage for yarns, fabric, or extra bedding. See Figure 17.

If you have a table with a lower shelf, cover the table

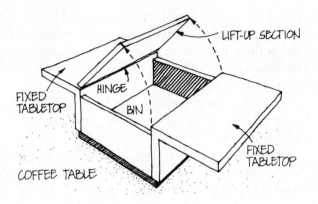

Figure 17 Multiple use of furniture

with a cloth and use that shelf to store off-season clothes or an extra blanket.

Another comparatively neglected aspect of comfortable small-space living is thoughtful furniture placement. A small room is only tolerable when there is easy movement within it, and I personally favor at least one open space five feet square. The heart of placement is to create blocks of furniture that either touch or are linked in some way, thus opening floor space. For example, back a couch with a dining table/desk as pictured in Figure 18.

Select dining chairs that don't jut out; possibly mobile stools that can be pushed under the table when not in use. The big table doubles as a coffee table and end tables, thus obviating the need for additional furniture in that area. The two easy chairs opposite the couch are linked by a single coffee table.

To define two conversation areas, place two couches back-to-back. Another back-to-back idea is a headboard substitute for a daybed. To read in bed, prop yourself against a drop-leaf table, a high-backed dining bench, the

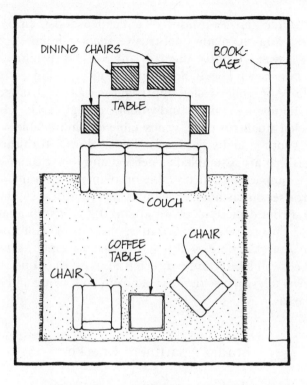

Figure 18 A furniture arrangement
for small-scale living

back of a sturdy stacking-cube storage arrangement, or the
back of a bookcase or room divider.

Consolidate furniture in vertical space as well: Hang
a swinging chair from the ceiling, and keep a wicker storage
chest beneath it. Or sling a hammock diagonally between
two corners and put a low bookcase underneath. The space
behind the bookcase could be a storage corner. Tuck mobile stools and tables under other tables.

The final element in small-space living is mobility: furniture that can be produced as needed and then deftly hidden away or made unobtrusive again. The most common answer is wheels. Virtually any piece of furniture can be set on caster wheels. Some specific ideas include: a serving table or trolley rolled out from the wall for drinks and entertainment fixings; individual rolling snack tables; wheeled stools for desk, vanity table or dining table.

Another mobility idea is "knock down" furniture— pieces that are assembled as needed and then dismantled. For example, construct a table on demand from plywood boards set on sawhorses; or top a tall cylindrical container with a round piece of plywood and drape it with a tablecloth. This same principle can be used to make a square table round. There is also the swivel principle: A long-necked wall lamp can be directed to more than one area; a swivel television set is viewable from both living and dining areas.

Studio Apartment Checklist

1. Decide whether to partition off the eating, sleeping, and "living" areas.
2. If so, evaluate the type of partition to get and its placement in terms of:
   a. "Room" size
   b. Movement within the apartment
   c. Light
   d. Storage capabilities
   e. Consider alternative partitions: closets, alcoves, vertical space.
3. Within the basic "area" divisions, or within the apartment as a whole, consider techniques for extracting full use of space:
   a. Elimination of unnecessary pieces of furniture

b. Furniture with more than one function
c. Fold-up or tuck-away furniture
d. Furniture as storage
e. Furniture placement
f. Mobility

WORKROOMS: ARTWORK, CARPENTRY, SEWING

Any workroom requires three main elements: a surface to work on, a place for materials and implements, and storage arrangements. The principles for arranging your particular setup are the same in any case, so you can generalize from the examples that follow to your own situation.

1. *Processes.* List the exact processes that are entailed in your work. Sewing processes include laying out and pinning up patterns, sewing by machine, sewing by hand. A handyman cuts wood (sawing? by machine?), hammers, drills, and paints.

2. *Work surface.* Most work requires one main work surface, although a person who sews needs two: one for pinning up patterns and one for sewing. To define the work surface(s) you require, check your process list and ask the following questions: Do I stand or sit? If you stand, make the table or drawing board high enough to accommodate an upright standing position; if you sit, the table should accommodate a comfortable, upright sitting position. If either or both, would a table that can be raised or lowered suit the purpose? Or two different tables? In that case, you might put the lower table on casters to slide under the higher table.

To define the appropriate size of the table (if it's not standard like a drawing table), consider the size of the materials you're working with: a pattern, a "mechanical" for book designers, long pieces of wood. Have the table or counter cut somewhat bigger than you anticipate needing. If several processes are involved, as in handiwork, the table should be long enough to accommodate each process.

3. *"Placement" surface.* A placement surface should be the right size to hold the tools or materials that you'll need as you work, and located so that you hardly need change position to lay something down on it. Perhaps an "ell" as pictured in Figure 19.

4. *Chair.* The chair should be comfortable, support your back, and preferably swivel so you can switch position easily. It shouldn't be too broad, or its arms, if any, too high, to scoot right into the work surface.

5. *Lighting.* Natural light, if you can arrange it, is best for your eyes. Artificial light should fully illuminate the work area without glaring. Choose a lamp—whether placed on the ceiling, table, or wall—with a mobile neck that can be adjusted to whatever job you're doing.

6. *Storing supplies.* Stand or sit in your working position and go through the motions of each process listed in step 1. Place the most frequently used supplies or tools for each

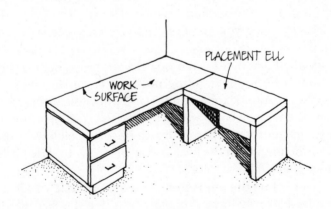

Figure 19   Increasing workspace

Figure 20 Wall storage for hobby supplies

process wherever your hand rests most naturally. To pin up patterns, for example, hang the scissors on a wall hook right by the table, or perhaps dangling from a nail on the table itself. Hang a box of pins in the same way.

For sewing supplies and fabrics there are plastic bins that fit together on runners to make drawers. Keep them under the sewing table. If you knit, hang your skeins from rods affixed on a wooden plaque that hangs on the wall (as in Figure 20) and make compartments for rolls of yarn.

The most common solution for handiwork tools is pegboard; outline each tool so you know where to put it back. The pegboard should back the work table or form an ell, whichever is more accessible. It would also be helpful to have shelves or cabinets for jars of nails, screws, and other small pieces, as well as for tools that won't hang. Shelve the

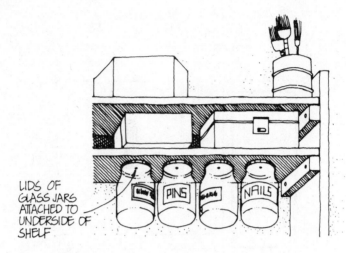

LIDS OF
GLASS JARS
ATTACHED TO
UNDERSIDE OF
SHELF

Figure 21 Increased use of limited space

wall, perhaps above the placement ell or underneath the
work surface. Another solution is a rolling cart kept under
the work counter when not in use. The cart should be high
enough to eliminate bending down for the frequently used
pieces. When you've organized your tools and supplies, fill
a few small jars with the most frequently used nails and
screws. Keep them on the work counter or nail the tops of
the jars to the underside of a convenient shelf. Replenish
the small jars from a larger jar when supplies run low.

7. *Putting projects away.* At the end of a work session,
it's depressing to leave the materials you have been working
with lying around, particularly if you're working on more
than one project. For sewing storage, buy a set of low, deep
shelves. Art supply stores are likely to have something appropriate. Attach a peel-off label to each shelf for the life
of the project and remove it when the project is finished.
To keep track of several projects, list each item you're

working on, a deadline if any, and what stage it is in. Pin the list to the wall or bulletin board and bring it up to date each time you work. The same idea applies to artwork or handiwork projects.

The plastic cabinets mentioned above are ideal for storing artwork. That is actually what they are intended for. Construction projects are bigger and thus somewhat more complicated. I suggest shelves on the wall. Use full-length shelves for large projects, and divide some shelves vertically in half, or even in thirds, for smaller projects. Label each section with the name of the project using peel-off labels. Separate bins for each project would also be satisfactory; in that case, stock each project bin with a few smaller boxes to maintain control of small pieces such as joints and hinges.

16
The
Efficient
Home

A modest degree of order in the home—a necessity for a reasonably comfortable life—consists of a moderately clean house; a simple system for shopping, food preparation, errands, and laundry; and a plan for shared family participation in these tasks for both parents and childless couples.

TASK SHARING: THE KEY
TO DOMESTIC ORDER

Maintaining the household is no longer the exclusive domain of the female. "Ask Mommy" is not an acceptable (or practical) answer for late-twentieth-century organization in response to questions like "Where do the knives go?" and "Where are my clean T-shirts?" The dream of "super-woman" has bit the dust.

Key to a harmoniously operating family are the business concepts of delegation and task sharing, translated onto the domestic stage. The great majority of organizing issues that involve conflict of one kind or another can be resolved through the adept and respectful application of delegation techniques.

Introducing any genuinely new way of doing things is rife with possibility for distress and conflict, because the seemingly strictly practical issues often shield from view deeper issues of wishes, hopes, and expectations.

In Chapter 5, mention was made of Gretta and Tom, who were running into serious difficulty because the house was not in order when Tom came home at the end of the day. Beds weren't made, things weren't straightened, dinner was never ready, a spill on the kitchen floor was still there two days later, etc. Gretta for her part felt that Tom was not taking her seriously as a professional, and got into the habit of coming back with the snappy answer "When they have you sweeping the floors at IBM before you leave at the end of the day, then you can yell at me about mopping up the kitchen."

Things had come to a pretty uneasy pass. In reality, of course, both Gretta and Tom were right. Tom was not taking Gretta's work sufficiently seriously. Gretta, on the other hand, was not taking sufficiently seriously Tom's legitimate expectation of coming home to a clean, comfortable house. So what to do, what to do?

And this is what they did: One evening, leaving their two daughters, aged eight and ten, at home with a sitter, they went out together for a long leisurely working dinner, taking with them a yellow ruled pad. They planned their evening to have three parts: the first part being a general discussion of how they felt and what their expectations were; the second part being a specific list of issues and concerns; and the third part being solutions.

In their opening discussion, they asked each other lots of questions about their backgrounds, childhood expectations, and the like. Gretta learned for the first time that Tom was not just annoyed at how sloppy things were, but he felt genuinely hurt and betrayed. His mother had been a full-time homemaker, the house was always spotless, things got done like clockwork, and to him, what he saw as Gretta's lack of care of their home represented lack of care of him and their family.

Tom for his part learned for the first time that Gretta was genuinely insecure about whether she was a "real" professional—especially now that she was removed from the office setting that seemed to validate her professionalism. So Tom's seeming disregard of her work fed right into her own insecurities, which is one reason she got so angry. In addition, Gretta's own background was similar to Tom's, and she too at some level felt she was failing in her responsibilities as a homemaker, and the consequent guilt gave her anger yet another spin.

In fact, that talk was one of the most genuinely intimate exchanges that Tom and Gretta had had for a long time.

Having come to some understanding of each other's feelings, assumptions, and expectations, they drew up a chart on the yellow ruled pad, dividing it into three columns. The columns were headed, from left to right, "Ideal," "Adequate," "Unacceptable." Then they systematically worked through, one by one, each of the questions that divided them.

To take one example, "dinner on the table" was an inflamed issue. Tom would have liked for it to be on the table as soon as he walked in the door at 6:30. That's the way it had been with his father. So they wrote in the "Ideal" column, "dinner at 6:30."

The next step was to look at the practical constraints and limitations that got in the way of that ideal. The most important constraint was that Gretta needed to keep the 5:00–6:00 P.M. hour available for clients who needed to see her after work.

Thus, dinner at 6:30 wasn't realistic, but 7:30 was reasonable—that is, an hour after Tom got home. Unacceptable was "dinner later than 7:30."

Great. So now some solutions. To make it possible to have dinner on the table by 7:30 in such fashion that neither party felt put upon, this is what they worked out: Tom and Gretta agreed to reserve three hours every weekend to cook together, preparing stews and casseroles and the like that could be frozen. Then each evening, when Tom came home, Gretta and the girls would be responsible for popping the casserole or whatever into the oven and preparing the rest of the meal, while Tom would make and toss the salad and then clear the table after dinner.

It worked out fine.

The two main organizing areas to address for solutions are *efficiency techniques* and *delegation*. Efficiency techniques are discussed later in this chapter. This section first details delegation techniques, including family delegation, outside delegation, and cooperative ventures, and includes discussion of how to realistically incorporate time constraints and financial constraints, showing how they can be adapted to a host of situations in the aid of getting things done in a timely and timesaving and comfortable way.

The Task Plan: Sharing the Work

Whether one or both parents work because of financial necessity or personal fulfillment, a side benefit is providing children with an opportunity to make a genuine contribution to the family's well-being. Many children really want to play a role in the family's functioning. Take a look at the three-year-old or four-year-old who is pleased and proud as punch when he or she can bring the dish over to Mommy or fix a simple plate of food or put something in the dishwasher. The child is proud because the task is seen as a challenge and an accomplishment, not as a screaming session.

Trouble begins, however, when chores seem to be imposed at the parents' whim, as if the child were a servant. The key to effective family cooperation is to assign to each child definite jobs with clear-cut responsibilities and let him/her work without constant supervision.

One of the reasons we have unearthed for the tug-of-war is the fact that children have frequently not been allowed to be represented in the family unit. They can make a lot of noise, but that isn't the same thing. In a workable family delegation plan, children must be recognized as, if not equal members, certainly participating members in helping to decide what gets done and what doesn't get done. It is critical that children become part of the decision-making process as well as part of the solution. Including them in the process gives them a stake in and responsibility for the orderly and harmonious working of the family.

Present your proposals in a family council, taking the tack that a well-run household is in everybody's interest. First define the extent to which each child is responsible for his own room and possessions. A toddler of two or three can pick up after himself if the room has been arranged according to his size (see page 302). A four-year-old can lightly dust and make the bed, a child of six can sweep with a small broom, and by the time he is eight or nine he can properly sweep and vacuum. See page 305 for a discussion of how to help the child help himself.

Then list all the tasks and break down complex tasks into their components. Decide as a group how to delegate and apportion tasks. If family members are consulted they'll feel better about carrying out their tasks. One way to organize the family doings is through the point system. Negotiate a weekly point value for each task based on frequency, length, and difficulty. The point system recommended by singer Peggy Lennon works well. Each person, including parents, contracts for a fixed number of points each week based on ability and fixed time demands.

Make it a game if you like by cutting chips out of construction paper. Write the job's weekly point number on one side of the chip and the job on the other. Once a week lay the chips out number side up. Each person draws his assigned points without knowing what the jobs are. At week's end, chips are returned to the "chip bowl" for another drawing. To prevent a small child from picking jobs that are too hard, put "little people" tasks on different-colored chips.

Point Value	Chore
5	Special projects: clean closet, basement, garage
4	Time-consuming tasks: vacuuming, cooking a meal
3	Simple tasks: dusting
Multiply point value by:	3 for daily work 2 for twice-weekly work 1 for once-weekly work

If you don't want to bother with chips, have the family sign up each week for enough jobs to reach their designated point quota. Keep the less desirable jobs rotating. If a child enjoys a particular task, let him or her take it over permanently.

If you like, draw up a family task chart on which chores are crossed off each week as they are accomplished.

However the jobs are allocated, clearly define the time of day when a child's job is to be completed—either before school, directly after school, or by dinnertime. Don't let tasks hang over into the evening.

As to family clutter sometimes stern measures are called for. Establish a family rule that clutter is not acceptable after twenty-four hours. Terry hid "post-twenty-four-hour" clutter in a laundry bag. Family members had to apply to reclaim left-out possessions, and those who had been particularly lax might not get their things back for a day or two.

A Note to Couples

A less complex allocation system can be used for husbands and wives who have trouble delegating the weekly housework load. The key is to view the difficulties that two people experience simply by living together, not as an arena for a test of power, but as mechanical problems. One of the most common problems is a differing standard of neatness—usually, but not always, the wife is the neater one. One husband, for example, drops his shirts where he stands, according to his spouse. In such a case take note of where he or she generally *does* stand when undressing. Put a "junk chair" (page 210) at that spot so at least all items will be in one place rather than strewn around the room.

If that doesn't work, hammer out a *quid pro quo* deal: You will put your spouse's clothes away in exchange for a service—say, washing your car once a week.

Getting husbands to share housework may also be a delicate issue. You might discuss which chores are most abhorrent to each of you and try to allocate accordingly. Respect each other's idiosyncrasies. One man, for instance, might not mind scraping the dinner dishes but refuses to put them into the dishwasher. Rather than arguing, send him up to get the children ready for bed.

To sum up, whenever a logistical problem between a couple occurs, defuse the irritation by negotiating an arrangement whereby the annoyed party receives some benefit to compensate for whatever aggravation is suffered. Don't dig in your heels on a point of principle.

THE EASY WAY: AN EFFICIENT APPROACH TO HOME MANAGEMENT

Cleaning the House

Cleaning can provide a modest sort of pleasure. It's good exercise, can be mindlessly involving, and, unlike most efforts in this complicated world, provides a clear and unambiguous sense of accomplishment.

The most crucial step is to set up a cleaning schedule that is followed faithfully. Start by setting an arbitrary hour a day, either early in the morning or later, even after work, depending on energy levels. The hour should be divided as follows:

Layer 1

These are the jobs that must be done every day: making beds, washing dishes, reducing clutter, dusting lightly, and taking out the garbage. On a sheet of paper list these jobs and the time it takes to do them. Subtract any time spent on the phone or with other interruptions.

Layer 1 tasks should take no longer than half an hour in a one-bedroom home. Add ten minutes for each additional bedroom, and ten minutes if there are two floors in your house. If there is difficulty meeting this time limit, analyze how the work might be streamlined:

1. Is one person trying to do too many of the jobs alone? Should the children, for instance, be making their own beds and picking up after themselves?
2. Are the materials and supplies needed instantly available, either in mobile caddies or strategically placed storage points?
3. How are you handling interruptions (see page 94)? Are you distracting yourself?

Here are some tips for some of the specific jobs involved in Layer 1:

Picking up. No matter how organized your home is, certain activities do create a trail of debris. Store all leftovers in one unused drawer, closet, shelf, or basket, so that all the miscellany is in one place. Anyone in the family who sees something out of place should add it to the pile for later sorting. Supply a small box for little objects like keys and jewelry.

In a two-story house, keep a basket at the top of the stairs and one at the bottom where objects belonging on the other floor can be deposited. It's always a good idea, in fact, as you move from one room to another, to pick up the items that belong where you're going.

When clutter is more than minor—guests have spent the evening, for example—tidy up "around the clock," in this way: Choose a starting point anywhere on the perimeter of the room and think of it as twelve o'clock. Straighten it up completely, move to one o'clock, and continue around the room. Then straighten up the center. It's a good idea to trundle a mobile cart along with you to collect items that belong in other rooms, saving trips back and forth.

Layer 2

These are twice-a-week (more or less) projects, including vacuuming, watering plants, wiping down the bathroom, sweeping floors. List the Layer 2's and then arbitrarily work on them in sequence for one-half hour only. Begin the next day where you left off and again work for half an hour. When you the sequence is finished once, start it over again. Follow the procedure for a week and keep track of how often each task is done. If it's approximately twice during the week, that's fine; more than twice is more often than the task requires. Gradually shorten the length of time per day devoted to Layer 2 tasks until the twice-a-week schedule is met.

Some tips follow for making these jobs easier:

Vacuuming. Using two vacuum cleaners may be helpful: a light cleaner for your weekly routine and a heavy-duty cleaner for a thorough once-monthly cleanup. If family members are allergic to dust, lint, or pet hairs, check into the powerful, built-in vacuums that suck the dirt through tubes in the wall to an outside container that is emptied about every six weeks. A big plus from an efficiency point of view is that you get rid of the cumbersome canister trundling behind. Check a local vacuum cleaner supply firm.

Always vacuum before dusting, since the dust stirred by the cleaner might land on furniture that's just been dusted.

Watering plants. Save time here by only keeping plants that thrive with a twice-a-week watering. However, if preferences range over a spectrum of plants, attach colored dots on the pots to signify each plant's watering needs: a yellow sticker for daily watering, blue for weekly, and so on. Then, depending on their light requirements, try to group plants with the same watering requirements together. Keep a *large* watering can and mister in the kitchen and, if there are plants upstairs or in other areas of the house, keep another set in a bathroom.

Try using travel bulbs. These are water-filled bulbs put into the soil to keep the plant moist for up to three weeks. They reduce the need for watering considerably, and I've been told that plants requiring continuous moisture thrive on this regime.

Bathroom. Hang a sponge on a hook right above the sink. Encourage family members to give the sink a swipe after each use.

If you take frequent tub baths, use bath salts that dissolve "bathtub ring." If you shower, cut down on residue by maintaining free-flowing drains.

Investigate toilet bowl solutions that keep toilets permanently clean.

Layer 3 and Layer 4

Layer 3 jobs are the "deep cleaning," once-a-week operations: scrubbing floors, waxing and polishing furniture, cleaning walls and woodwork, grocery shopping, errands, and laundry chores. Tackle these in several ways: Set aside several hours a week to do all the jobs at once—Saturday morning is a popular choice; add one Layer 3 job to the regular cleaning schedule each day; or when it seems necessary, add a particular task to the To Do list for the following day.

Layer 4 consists of special projects: washing windows, cleaning the stove, defrosting the refrigerator, polishing silver, and so forth. Either choose a fixed two hours a week to devote to special projects, or add them to the Daily List as they come up.

After experimenting with and streamlining a routine, write up a final cleaning schedule similar to the one below.

	What	*When*	*Who*
Layer 1:	making beds washing dishes picking up dusting taking out garbage	a half hour per day every day	List family members responsible for tasks.
Layer 2:	vacuuming watering plants wiping down bathroom sweeping floors	a half hour per day in sequence	
Layer 3:	mopping floors polishing furniture walls and woodwork groceries errands laundry	Saturday morning	
Layer 4:	special projects	on Daily List when necessary	

Meal Planning

Once a week should be often enough for the planning of family meals. Don't forget to share these tasks! You might refer to your local newspaper to see what foods are specially priced for that week. As you decide on the menus, list whatever ingredients are not on hand.

Drawing up the weekly menu/shopping list takes about an hour, but there is an easy way to reduce it to about ten or fifteen minutes by making up menu cards. Compile, from your favorite recipes, twenty to thirty easy-to-prepare main dishes. Write out or tape each recipe to a five-by-eight index card and note any ingredients you might have to buy at a special shop. Then compile about thirty recipes for side dishes and desserts, and file all the cards in a file box. Each week select as many main dish cards as necessary, mix and match them with different side dishes and desserts, and there are your menus. List the ingredients you don't have on hand, add staples like salad fixings, bread, and beverages, and you're ready for the supermarket.

Working people will find it helpful to patronize a market where all or part of a grocery order can be phoned in for later pickup or delivery. The shopping that you do yourself can be greatly streamlined by designing a categorized grocery list. Write or type the following categories on a sheet of 8½" x 11" paper, leaving some space between each category:

Dairy products
Canned fruits, vegetables, juices
Fresh produce
Fresh meats and fish
Frozen goods
Breads and baked goods
Spices and condiments
Household goods
Any other category: pet foods, etc.

Arrange the categories on your master list according to your normal supermarket route. If your first stop is the meat counter, meat is the first category on your form.

Have a trial run through the supermarket with the list, make any changes that are necessary, and then have it duplicated and made up in quantity in tablet or pad form with a hole in the top so you can hang it on a hook in the kitchen, readily available. Fill in the form whenever you notice low stock on a particular item, and complete the fill-in when you plan your weekly menus.

To further streamline shopping, unload your goods onto the checkout counter as they are arranged at home: all refrigerator items together, all canned vegetables, etc. The checker won't place them in perfect order, but there will be a rough approximation. It's surprising how much this will simplify unpacking and putting away at home.

If Betty Crocker you sometimes ain't, here are some creative improvisations that will provide you and your family with nutritious "quickmeals":

• Precook stews and casseroles, or prepackage the ingredients—each meal packaged separately—and freeze. (Freeze small leftover portions in individual containers so that you can pop them into the oven or microwave for a quick lunch or an after-school snack for the children. Label each package with freezer labels and keep packages that have been frozen for longer periods moving toward the front. Get pots large enough for quantity cooking, and be sure to have enough freezer containers. Freezing meals in freezer-to-oven-to-table ware saves a lot of dishwashing. See page 239 for some recommendations on freezers.)

• Plan your menu around a fast-food main dish such as take-out chicken or fish sticks. Combine with a side dish and salad for nutritional balance, and you've got a nice fast meal.

• Planning a dish that calls for lots of cut-up vegetables? If you live in a city where the greengrocers have salad bars, save lots of time by pulling together pre-cut ingredients in advance.

• In larger urban centers, numerous restaurants or gourmet take-out places will prepare and package real meals (not just Chinese either) that can be delivered to your home. Or you can arrange for pickup on the way home. So pick up a main dish from a gourmet take-out, prepare salad fixings and a side vegetable and some rolls at home, and you have dinner.

Shopping

If you consider clothes shopping a chore, why not plan to shop in a single department store that carries the greatest range of merchandise that appeals to you. This concentration of shopping saves time, and if you have difficulty making decisions, automatically limits your alternatives. It is especially helpful to establish a relationship with one salesperson who gets to know your style and taste. Such a relationship has many advantages and can save you both time and money. The salesperson will sometimes hold a particular item aside until it goes on sale, phone you when new shipments come in, advise you on special values, prevent you from wasting a trip to the store when there's nothing there to your taste, and even, in certain stores, select clothes to be sent to your home "on approval."

When you go to the store, take a list of planned purchases—main items and accessories. One woman I know shops by imagining occasions that will occur in the forthcoming season: a business meeting, a cocktail party, and so forth. She then examines her existing wardrobe for any article of clothing that might form a "core" piece. When she shops she takes that article and a list of the things she intends to buy to supplement the "core" piece. This system saves time and lessens the dilemma of having a closetful of clothes but nothing to wear.

Try to confine "serious" shopping to one or two expeditions at spring and fall, with occasional "fill-ins" during the rest of the year. To make the spring and fall forays even more productive, list all the birthday and anniversary presents that will be coming up during the season and buy them in advance, along with cards. Identify gifts you buy in advance by marking the recipient's initials in an unobtrusive corner.

Inventory Control: Supplies, Linens, and Laundry

Supplies

Our mothers always had lots of soap, toothpaste, or cleansing powders "laid in." We have, however, lost the knack of stocking up, largely because the storage closets that mother had no longer exist. Consequently, one can be irritated by depletion of such necessities as toilet paper and toothpaste.

The solution is twofold: First, make or find storage space to accommodate one or two months' worth of supplies. Don't feel you must centralize supplies in one single cabinet unless your house is very compact. For most dwellings, it is better to devise separate "storage depots" for different materials close to the area where they are used. One depot, in or near the kitchen, will contain backup supplies of dishwashing detergent, cleansing powders, scouring pads, sponges, and probably general housekeeping supplies. Laundry supplies like detergent, bleach, and presoaks will need a place near the washer-dryer. And there should be a bathroom supply area for extra toothpaste, toilet paper, various toiletries, Band-Aids, aspirin, and other sundries.

The "storage depot" space, which won't be used very often—thus making it a #4 in rank—can be somewhat out of the way, but not too difficult to reach. If #4 cabinet or shelf space is already available in the depot area, search no further. If not, consider less obvious possibilities: perhaps an unused shelf or two in a nearby clothes closet, or an extra drawer in a dresser. One client kept the laundry supplies inside an attractive wicker chest used as a coffee table. Another stored bathroom supplies in a cloth laundry bag hung on a closet hook. A box on the floor of the linen closet could be another container. If you are more ambitious, build shelves or a cabinet—perhaps under the bathroom sink.

Once space is set up, buy a two months' supply of toothpaste, soap, mouthwash, deodorant, cleansing powders, toilet paper, and any other regularly used item.

To maintain inventory, hook a permanent pad and pencil to the door or wall of each storage depot. Whenever supplies of any item run low—don't wait until they run out—jot it down on the pad. Collect the various depot slips when you go to the supermarket and bring stocks up to strength. You will never run out of household goods, and this system will encourage you to take advantage of sales and specials.

Linens

If the linen closet is sufficiently generous to hold both sheets and towels, that area is most desirable. If not, keep sheets in the linen closet and store towels elsewhere. If the linen closet itself is insufficient or nonexistent, use the same techniques for finding space that were discussed on page 188 or 295.

Divide the sheets according to type: double-bed flat, twin fitted, and so forth. Choosing characteristic colors or patterns can considerably simplify sorting. For instance, all double-bed bottom sheets could be white, all single-bed bottoms yellow, all single-bed top sheets striped, or whatever pleases you. Some people get proprietary about their "own" sheets, children especially. In that case, provide each bed with a three-week supply of linens that are distinctive enough to identify at a glance.

If towels won't fit in the linen closet, you might be able to keep them right in the bathroom. One client put up a pretty wicker three-shelf rack on the bathroom wall and displayed the folded towels. Another idea is to nail some ordinary plastic buckets to the bathroom door—bottoms affixed to the door—to hold rolled-up towels. Alternatively, keep them in a floor cabinet under the sink, or on a reasonably handy available shelf nearby. Try to keep a three-week supply of towels and washcloths on hand so missing a laundry does not become a catastrophe.

However you store towels, always revolve the towel pile by putting the freshly laundered ones at the bottom. The bottom towels might otherwise mildew or become musty.

Laundry

You can either choose a fixed laundry day during the week, or mark "laundry" on the Daily List when stocks get low. Neither alternative is inherently more efficient, so choose the one with which you feel more comfortable.

Large-family laundry schedules are more complex because, as one client said, "The laundry for my husband, three kids, and me would pile to a literal mountain if I saved it up. I *must* launder at least three or four times a week." In that case, I recommend that each person have his or her own hamper—a basket in bedroom or bathroom would be fine—and launder only one or two hampers at a time. This avoids collecting clothes from each hamper for each wash, sorting each person's things, and redistributing them again—an unnecessary expenditure of time and energy. Also, remember that children can take charge of their own laundry at about age ten.

Keep several plastic stackable laundry baskets in the laundry room. Sort clothes into the baskets according to the different washing types: whites, colors, permanent press. When each wash-and-dry cycle is completed, sort them back into baskets for folding according to the room or closet in which they belong. Simplify sorting white clothes or children's clothes by putting a colored dot with an indelible marker on the garment where it won't be seen, using a different color for each person.

Apartment-house laundering is slightly different. Try to do the wash in off-hours—very early in the morning or after 8:00 P.M. Stack the dry clothes in the laundry cart according to their placement in the home. If, for instance, the kitchen is near the front door, put the pot holders and kitchen towels on top of the laundered pile. Storing then becomes much simpler.

PART SIX

Family and Lifestyle

17
Children

Your child can learn to organize at a very young age. If you simply make it easy for him to take care of himself, half your job is done. It is vital, therefore, to arrange and adjust the child's room to his or her needs and capabilities. If the room is well-planned and flexible enough to adapt to the child's changing skills and needs, he or she will have to go out of his way *not* to keep the room in reasonable order. When the room is ready for the child, you can painlessly teach the methods of order.

Also discussed in this chapter are the logistics of child care: how to keep track of children's activities and mesh them with your own.

CHILDREN'S ROOMS

First, fit the closet to the child, don't try to fit the child to the closet. Line the closet with plenty of stick-on hooks at the child's eye level. When he or she can negotiate hangers, insert a tension rod—a metal rod braced with a spring—as a hanging bar. Adjust the bar over the years to the child's increasing height. For a very small child, ages two to four, who might be dismayed by the sheer size of the closet, get a child-sized wardrobe, lined with hooks. Place it, or any new piece of furniture, so as not to disturb your child's movement pattern. One little boy who used an alcove as a "cozy corner" for quiet play before bed became upset when the alcove was blocked by a new wardrobe, so it was shifted elsewhere. When the wardrobe is outgrown, switch to the closet.

Check that the clothes you buy have simple catches and fastenings the child can manage himself. Put a small clothes hamper near the closet for the child to put his dirty clothes in as soon as he takes them off. Keep the hamper in the bedroom rather than the bathroom; it's too complicated for a child to move clothes back and forth between the two rooms. Again, he should be able to manipulate the hamper himself.

Choose a low night table broad enough to allow for a lamp, perhaps a small radio, a few favorite books, a doll. Select a dresser low enough so that the child can see over the top. Be sure that the drawers move in and out smoothly without jamming and that the knobs are not too big and are shaped so that the child can get a firm grip. When buying furniture, think of the maxim "Don't give me furniture kids can't walk on." That means durable, maintenance free materials and fabrics, soft edges, and smooth shapes without fretwork that will catch dust and grit. Bunk beds are especially good space savers for older children who share a room. However, each child should have a clearly defined space: hooks with his name on them in bedroom and bathroom, separate closets or wardrobes, a desk (on hinges, to save space), even a curtain or bookcase barricade. This also helps cut down on distraction when doing homework. One frequent question when dealing with kids who share a room is what to do with one child when the other is sick. It's important then, if the illness is more than a matter of spending one night on the couch, to have an alternative arrangement prepared in advance, preferably a convertible couch or daybed that can be made comfortable so the healthy child doesn't feel shunted aside.

Play area—space, pure open space—is very important. If your child is fearless and exploratory, open the space up as wide as you can; if he or she tends to stay close to the walls and furniture, enclose the space somewhat as long as it is still wide enough to move around in. Orient the play space toward the corner of the room he tends to gravitate to. Provide enough light to read by and some floor cushions to curl up with. Also try to leave some "secret space" in the room for the child: a bed that's high enough to crawl under or a closet he or she can safely play in.

Select one corner of the play space as a "leave out" corner where the child is permitted to leave out a jigsaw puzzle or building project in progress. Otherwise all toys should be put away each day.

Many parents naturally think of a single big toy chest for the loose jigsaw puzzle pieces, blocks, torn picture books, crayons, dolls, trucks, GI Joes, and all the appurtenances of a twentieth-century child, but that is not the answer. The child gets so frustrated digging to the bottom of the chest to pull something out that everything else will be flung aside and left there until battle lines are drawn. Instead, line the play area with low shelves that create plenty of space for spreading out board games, toys, trucks, erector sets, dolls, and books. The child will have to make a special effort *not* to put toys away. I recommend adjustable shelves that can be raised as the child grows.

Line the shelves with lots of different-colored boxes, trays, and jars for loose playthings. It seems to be important to approximately correlate the size of the container with the size of its contents: small boxes for jacks, medium ones for crayons, bigger ones for He-men and toy soldiers. This idea comes from a Montessori school attended by the little boy of a friend of mine. She tells me that they shelve the room as I have suggested, and fill the shelves with brightly colored trays of different sizes. The children learn immediately that "the doll goes on the biggish green tray," "the rubber balls belong on the medium red tray," and "the jacks on the small blue tray." Alternatively, just affix bright stickers to cardboard or polyurethane trays. Also, each object should have its own space on the shelf. Kids delight in knowing where things go. There is apparently something in the young child's development that craves clear boundaries and specificity.

A Five-Point Child Checklist

Before buying anything for a young child, whether furniture, clothing, or toys, consider the following points:

1. Is it safe? No sharp angles, no small parts that a tiny child could swallow?
2. Can the child manipulate its parts, or learn to do so?
3. Is it on his scale? One two-year-old girl fell in love with a small, dime-store teddy bear, ignoring a larger pretty one. The big one was just out of scale.
4. Can it be adjusted to the child's growth? (Not always applicable.)
5. Is it dirt- and stain-resistant and/or easily washable?

TEACHING YOUR CHILD
TO ORGANIZE

As soon as your child is able to understand words, introduce one of the basic concepts of organizing: Things that are associated with each other are kept together. This is a skill that often has to be taught, ideally between the ages of three and six, when your child is most curious and eager to learn. When he or she is hardly more than a baby, invent categorizing games: Distribute a few shoes around the room and let him gather them and bring them to the "shoe place." It is important, even at this early stage, to physically set up the child's room so that he is putting the shoes *away*, not just dropping them in a pile. Use the same idea for clothes and toys.

By the age of three or four the child can grasp the grouping idea more abstractly and can probably be put in charge of his own room. Draw up a five-column chart headed "Make Bed," "Clothes," "Underwear," "Shoes," "Playthings," and cut out appropriate magazine pictures to put next to each heading if your child can't read yet. Leave the categories broad and loose; don't break "playthings" down into "toys," "books," "games," until he is older. Run the days of the week down the side. Duplicate many copies of the chart, which will look like Figure 22.

Each day at a set time keep your child company while he makes the bed and puts everything away. It will be very helpful to provide distinctive trays or boxes for different objects as described on page 304. Your child then works within each category in turn, and you can help out when necessary. Put a gold star in the appropriate box when the category is completed. If your child gets cranky and obstinate, point out the absence of gold stars for that day and leave the rest until tomorrow without recrimination. *Don't* pick up the room yourself either.

When the gold stars became routine for one little girl, the family was called together for a "Keeper of the Room" graduation ceremony complete with diploma—formal recognition of the child's first step toward responsibility and independence.

Older children, like younger ones, also delight in learning new skills. The problem is that keeping the room neat may already be an issue. Child psychologist Dr. Elaine Blechman mentions in *The New York Times* an "elegant solution" which some families have successfully used to avoid problems: The children keep their doors closed and at some point of their choosing during the day, straighten their rooms up, making them available for inspection by a certain time, say 6:00 P.M. Let the children know specifically what is to be inspected; not only making the bed and straightening up, but more precise jobs: arranging clothes in the closet according to type (see page 200); placing dresser clothes in the right drawer and pile; dividing playthings by type; cleaning jobs like changing sheets, dusting, sweeping, or vacuuming. A chart might be helpful. Make sure, again, that the room is physically set up so that your child can perform these tasks without difficulty. Ask for your child's suggestions about improvements. Encourage mastery by your enthusiastic response and by an occasional reward. When your child occasionally balks, as he will, let the room go until tomorrow but be sure to return to the routine. Your attitude is the most important ingredient. Disorder and confusion are undesirable but not a crime, so moral outrage on your part is inappropriate. Present organizing as you present reading and writing; it is simply a vital skill that must be learned.

Many children become terrific pack rats and simply refuse to throw things away, so space can become a problem. When the room looks like it's getting out of hand, sit down with your child and gather any objects that haven't

	Make Bed	Clothes	Underwear	Shoes	Playthings
Monday					
Tuesday					
Wednesday					
Thursday					
Friday					
Saturday					
Sunday					

Figure 22 Children's Weekly Chore Chart

been played with for six months or so. Pack them up in boxes for recycling; that is, bring the boxes out again in six months. Many of the toys will have regained their freshness, so you won't have to buy as many new ones, and the child will probably be less attached to the toys that still seem boring and you can get rid of them.

Adolescents pose a much bigger problem and their chaos is usually the most distressing to parents. A full-blown power struggle may be under way. Are there control problems between you that might be resolved? One teenaged girl, for instance, resented the fact that her mother opened her dresser without permission to put laundry away, and the fact that she had no clear-cut responsibilities around the house but was interrupted from her own activities at whim. She kept her room in chaos as a form of passive resistance. Perhaps helpful physical changes might be made. If neither tactic works, the most practical idea, as long as your teenager fulfills general household responsibilities and limits the chaos to his or her room, is to shut the door and resolutely turn away. Expressing adolescent rebellion through a messy room is a relatively minor problem and will probably be outgrown.

CHILD CARE AND SUPERVISION

Maintaining your privacy is vital if you are to maintain your sanity in a family of young children. In addition to the many excellent day-care centers and nursery schools, there are three more-informal ways to get the children out of your hair every so often. First, a babysitter, ranging from a doting grandmother to a high school kid down the block. Singer Peggy Lennon says, "When I interview a new babysitter, I always ask these questions to satisfy myself that the children will be safe and feel secure: (1) What would you do if the house caught on fire? If a stranger came to the door and asked to be let in? (determines judgment); (2) What would you do if a child came home crying? (determines warmth); (3) How do you plan to spend time with the children? (commits them to involvement rather than detachment)."

Give the babysitter a list of emergency numbers that includes not only the police, doctor, Poison Control Center, but a relative or close friend to turn to if you can't be reached.

Taking turns sitting with a neighbor or friend is another solution, but the group "sitting pool" is even more flexible and convenient. You agree to sit for other members' children, either in your home or theirs, no fewer than a certain number of hours per month, and you get a certain number of hours from other members.

In a play group, three or four mothers get together and each pledges to care for all the children one morning or afternoon a week. A play group is generally more than simple caretaking; the mother in charge structures the time with planned learning games, crafts, reading, and maybe field trips.

KIDDIE PAPERS

Frequently the passing of time is a great leveler when it comes to an overwhelming number of kids' papers. For example, every week or so Marnie and Simon, her nine-year-old, clean out Simon's schoolbooks and notebooks of the loose papers that he's accumulated in his school bag. They go through the artwork, the test paper results, etc., and make a very quick, independent judgment of what's interesting and what nobody cares about whatsoever. The unfinished paper with one line on it—that gets tossed. The rest goes into a plain manila folder that is kept on a shelf in his room.

They use report card time as the time of reckoning. Comes the first-quarter report card, Marnie and Simon foray back into the folders, take a second look at the material, and find that a little bit of distance helps them part with that very, very important piece of paper that isn't so important now. Before summer vacation they have a fourth and final tossing—that is, after the first-, second-, and third-quarter tossings—and this really gives you the distance you need. Because those September papers are much less entrancing in June.

What emerges then is a rather thin sheaf of papers, drawings, and artwork that they think are worth saving. This gets transferred into a manila folder labeled "Simon's third grade work" or whatever it might be, and is then neatly stored in the attic.

Let's make a distinction, however, between the kiddie lit and kiddie art versus papers you might want to save for reference such as report cards and test results. These should probably go into your regular filing system under the child's name, and you might also want to include their medical rundowns, immunization records, and information of that kind.

LOGISTICS: SCHOOL, ACTIVITIES, MOVING KIDS AROUND, AND COORDINATING

If you have a large, busy family you may find yourself constantly writing permission or absence notes of one kind or another. Why not create a "form" note and make copies. Two possibilities are suggested here:

Date _____

Please excuse _____ from class on
_____ for the following reason:
_____ Rehearsal or performance
_____ Medical appointment
_____ Other: _____
Thank you.

Signed: _____

Hope McClain

Date _____

_____ has my permission to engage
in the following activity:
Thank you.

Signed: _____

Hope McClain

Sort and handle the memos *from* school, Scouts,
church, as you would any other paperwork (Chapter 4),
but try to do it every day so nothing gets past you.

To generally keep track and control all family activities
get a *big* monthly calendar with the *biggest* date squares you
can find. Hang it where everyone will see it, probably in
the kitchen. At the beginning of each month, fill in all the
kids' regular appointments—ballet lessons, swimming lessons, Cub Scout meetings—on the calendar. As each child
tells you of special events—a birthday party, costume as-
sembly, a Brownie cookout—mark it on your personal calendar or have the child write it in. Alternatively, a
chalkboard so changing plans can be easily revised, is an
excellent idea.

Note on your personal calendar whatever preparatory plans have to be made and on the appropriate day enter them on the Daily List. Using the calendar as your guide, make chauffeuring and pickup arrangements as far in advance as you can. Work out long-term cooperative arrangements when feasible. If you live in the city, older children can often take young ones along to school or other activities.

18
Variations on a Theme: Organizing for New Lifestyles

The latter part of this century has seen a major change in the way people live their lives. Underpinning that major change has been a more broad-minded sense of acceptance of people's personal choices which now allow for other, alternative lifestyles. One of the main areas in which these changes are apparent could broadly be called new kinds of family or communal living: the single-parent family, the split family, the blended family, the cohabiting couple, and nonrelated roommates who live together to share expenses and for companionship.

All these forms of family organization have put tremendous strains on the always-intricate process of negotiating tasks, obligations, and responsibilities among people who live together.

In this chapter, we take a look at key organizing issues that pertain to each of these alternative family lifestyles, and examine some of the techniques and solutions that people have used successfully to clarify some of the confusions that can otherwise beset a smoothly functioning way of life.

THE SINGLE-PARENT HOUSEHOLD

Not only have we seen in recent years an increasing trend toward single-parent homes by virtue of divorce, but in addition, our lifestyle choices have broadened greatly, with many people now making the decision to have children alone or to adopt as single parents.

While organizing issues for the single parent share many elements in common with those of any parent, the single parent has special concerns which shift emphases to areas very specific to single parenthood.

Take the case of Ruth, a newly widowed social worker with a five-year-old son, Mark. Just taking a gander at Ruth's day is a hair-raising experience. She awakens at 5:30, before her son, in order to catch up on leftover dishes from the night before, sorting mail, putting laundry away, or doing other things around the house.

She then gets Mark up at 7:00 and walks him to school. Her appointments regarding the child are made by telephone from her office: talking to the child's teacher, setting up doctor and dental appointments, etc. Mark is then picked up by a babysitter who stays with him until she returns, which could be anywhere from 7:00 to 10:00 at night. Laundry and other household chores are basically done on weekends.

Several areas of her life suffer greatly: No way can she do any kind of systematic cleaning job, no way can she even organize her paperwork, which is still in chaos since her husband's death. There is no way to grab enough personal time for herself, and as for social life—forget it.

The techniques and approaches that follow, while no panacea, enabled Ruth to establish more order and stability in her and Mark's lives by achieving a higher degree of security and safety for Mark, and greater flexibility and peace of mind for her.

Coverage and Home Base Support

The issue of coverage has a brutal impact on the single parent. Somebody must be there for that child at every key moment during the day. He/she has to be taken to school by somebody, come home *with* somebody and *to* somebody. Someone must be with the child or available to the child at all times.

A major concern that many single parents—who are still mostly women—have expressed is that the coverage they need is frequently not your regular once-a-week babysitting routine, but flexible, "as needed" coverage.

The unexpected is a great source of fear to the single parent. "Who is going to take care of him if I'm sick? Who's going to take care of him when he's sick and I have to go to work? What's going to happen if my car breaks down?" It is critical for the single parent to develop solid support systems.

Ironically enough for these brave new parents, the enormous constraints single parents face, unless they are prosperous enough to purchase services at will, are pushing them toward solutions remindful of the old cooperative community network. The key is to have layered or redundant fail-safe systems. This means having more than one person that you can depend on.

Martha, for example, who has two children, and does have a regular full-time babysitter, nonetheless developed three alternatives. First of all, her brother and sister-in-law lived five miles away, so she had an understanding with her sister-in-law, who also worked but who was nearer by and whose hours were more flexible than Martha's, that her sister-in-law was available for problems or emergencies.

Second, a student rented a room in her home for very low rent on the understanding that he would be available for pickup and babysitting duties, and third, Martha had struck up a friendship with a nearby retired couple who minded their own two grandchildren and, just to have children around because they enjoyed them, took in six or seven neighborhood children that they also cared for during the day.

This couple became almost family members, and more than once Martha was able to call upon them in an emergency. At 11:00 one night one of her children became ill and had to be taken to the hospital, and she called up the Browns, who came within five minutes to collect the other child.

Another alternative, depending on the availability of relatives, trusted friends, and neighbors, is to develop a formal network of cooperative arrangements with other parents in the same situation as you.

The underscore here is to develop as many human relationships as you can that have an investment in you and your child so that you have at least two or three people on your list of backups. With this support, the greater your peace of mind and the better off you and your children are.

Another, and rather different, approach to developing a support network is to go where the support is—to make your home at a support base. Outside the largest urban centers, most people automatically think of living in a house. Yet it makes a lot of sense for a single-parent family to choose a place to reside that by its very nature and structure lends itself to a support base, which means, probably, an apartment, whether a co-op, condominium, or rental. This would preferably be a building where there are other parents and children. And a building with a doorman who is very invested in his tenants is a wonderful plus.

There are buildings in some major cities now which offer a whole host of social and child-oriented activities as well as some babysitting and other opportunities for cooperation. This accomplishes several things: It allows the single parent an opportunity for some recreation and social life on the premises, and it allows the child to develop some kind of support system within the building itself.

Generally speaking, the more complex the services, the more expensive the building. However, this is one of those areas in which a single parent may find it worthwhile to reevaluate priorities. It may be worth getting a smaller apartment and giving up that extra bedroom in order to buy yourself that support.

One mother, for example, with two children, who has a very limited budget, bought a very small one-bedroom apartment in a good, secure building. The children share the bedroom and she sleeps on the daybed in the living room.

And she loves it because the concierge there is able to take the dry cleaning, he is able to handle a lot of the nuts and bolts of life for her, as well as checking in with the children, who are ten and twelve, when she goes out on errands. With the concierge on watch, she feels comfortable leaving them alone for short periods of time. So, even though they are short on space, she feels that it has been a worthwhile trade-off.

So, to summarize this point, most people who are not wealthy have to have a trade-off on their home-buying dollar. Are you going to buy space or are you going to buy services? Many parents don't realize they have that option. Because they immediately think, well, I have two children, I need three bedrooms. And they remain ill at ease all the time.

The Child's Safety and Security

The child's security, as well as yours to a certain extent, is, of course, paramount. Here are some special tips:

Security systems. Many parents are using the "safe house" system, which means that, if your child walks home from school, there are houses along the way that he/she can go up to and knock on the door and say, "I'm in trouble, help me," if there's a problem, if somebody's following them, if something untoward happens.

Similarly, if there are regular routes to the playground, to the park, to the library, wherever the child goes, the child should know that there is that network out there that he or she can call on if there's a problem.

It's always wise to have two or three children walking together. One possibility if a child does walk back and forth to various places is to arrange with an older child to escort him or her.

If you live in a doorman building, apprise the doorman of your child's schedule, so if the child isn't home by 4:00 or whatever, he knows there's a problem. Let the doorman know how to contact you and what to do.

Also, make sure that a relative or trusted friend has a key to your home, so as to have access should an emergency arise.

Emergency procedures. While it's essential that all children have and memorize emergency numbers, it is especially imperative that the single-parent child be drilled and actually be coached and role-play a variety of "what-if" situations:

What if Mom is supposed to pick you up at 5:00, and Mom isn't there? Call Aunt Helen, or call Susan, our next-door neighbor. The babysitter is supposed to pick you up at 3:30 from school, and she doesn't show up. What do you do? You go back into the school office, you ask to use the phone, you call Mother at work.

Try to think of all the possibilities that could occur where your child could be left alone and what steps he or she could take. Make the rules as simple and as clear as you can.

Equipment the child should carry: (1) a phone book listing key phone numbers—the emergency numbers he is to call; (2) if he/she is old enough, a house key; (3) money, at all times—change for the telephone and perhaps enough money for a taxi.

Work Options: Selecting a Pro-parent Company

If you have options as to where you work, consider a company's pro-parent attitude. Many companies provide daycare centers and other facilities that are geared toward children, and there are also companies that are more understanding of the plight of a single parent and more flexible about your time arrangements and leave time.

Flexible time is now particularly common in certain professions such as nursing. Many single-parent nurses are opting for a three-day workweek in twelve-to-fourteen-hour shifts with four days off. Even though workdays are killer days, these parents have found it to be a lot cheaper in the long run and a lot better all around for family life to be able to have that kind of free time.

The Paperwork of Single Parenthood

If you are divorced, maintain a list of all benefits due you: child-support payments, medical insurance forms your ex-spouse is supposed to sign, etc. Keep a special folder or folders for this material, and maintain a calendar update to keep track of payments due.

If you are widowed, is your child entitled to Social Security checks? Veteran's benefits? Have you filled out the proper forms? Have you accounted appropriately to the government? Are you receiving payments at the proper time?

If something should happen to you: It is the responsibility of every parent to ensure an orderly transition should something happen to the custodial parent. In the case of a single parent, it is urgent that should something happen to you, someone—a relative, trusted friend, or lawyer—have immediate access to your will, your financial records, including bank accounts, investments, insurance, pension, and also information as to your lawyer, your accountant, etc.

It is important that immediate custodial backup is available in case, say, of accident, and that long-term guardianship is arranged for.

It is wise to let your child's school know whom to contact in case of emergency, as well as one or two of the parents in your child's play groups, someone where you work, and, if you live in an apartment building, a neighbor and your superintendent.

Somebody must be entrusted not only with your will and financial records but also with your child's schedule, his school, special medications (is he allergic to anything?), his doctors, and any other vital information about your child this person should know.

THE PART-TIME PARENT

With the increasing incidence of divorce, we have also seen an increase in the part-time parent—that is, not part-time emotionally, but in terms of being with the children only part of the time. Most often, this is the father, who winds up seeing the children on weekends and maybe once or twice during the week.

To illustrate the way it can go, let's walk through Harry's weekend visit with his two sons, Jacob and Adam. Ever since his divorce from Mona, Harry has been living in a one-bedroom apartment. The party responsible for getting Harry and the children together on the weekend has been left up in the air, which has invariably caused friction. Typically, on Friday afternoon, Harry calls Mona and says, "Can't you bring them over, Mona? I've been picking them up for the past three weeks." And Mona says, "Well, Harry, you *are* their father. I mean, it's *your* visit." And he says, "I know, Mona. But I'm tired, and I have to work late tonight. Can't you do one little thing . . . ?" and so on in that vein. This has been an insistent source of aggravation for both Mona and Harry, setting the weekend off to a roaringly chilling start.

Once the boys get there somehow, there's the inevitable question of dinner. Mona has put her foot down about endless pizza, but there's nothing in the house and Harry doesn't cook anyway, so pizza and a movie it is.

When they all get back from the movies, that is when Harry starts the unpacking. This is also, unfortunately, fraught with some degree of tension and a few teeth-gritting fights with Mona, because the children have brought over their Nintendo set and a few large trucks and other toys that are now, in the flick of an eyelash, strewn all over the living room floor.

Harry is awkwardly trying to make up the sofa bed so the boys can share it. As he unpacks, you can hear Harry mumbling, cursing to himself, because Mona forgot to include the toothbrush and the undershirts. As a matter of fact, last week he was really in a bind because one of the children developed a slight fever in the middle of the night, and he had to run out, leaving the children alone, to pick up some baby aspirin.

So the weekend is just beginning, and Harry is already disgruntled and annoyed, and the children are picking up his mood, and all in all, a great time is not being had by all. What's wrong with this picture?

Unfortunately, this is a typical picture of a weekend father who really hasn't settled into the task of being a weekend father, and who in fact perceives himself as a temporary father. However, this is the key: He is not a temporary father, but a full-time father who is a part-time caretaker on a permanent basis. If you view the situation in that light, then it becomes clear that it is imperative, organizationally speaking, that the noncustodial parent who receives his or her children regularly must begin to think in terms of providing some more or less permanent ways to provide for the children's needs once they arrive.

Let's start in order of the story:

The pickup. It seems reasonable that a certain amount of sharing of the pickup responsibility would be in order. However, it sometimes happens, because of lingering antagonisms, that one party or the other or even both, perhaps unconsciously, are sabotaging the arrangements. If that rings any bell, it is important to disconnect the question of picking up the kids from old quarrels.

Is there a third party—for example, a grandparent—available who could be counted on to take the children? Or could a student or a car service be hired to shuttle the children back and forth, splitting the expense?

In other words, it is not written in heaven that one of you necessarily has to pick up the children; much the more important thing is to use organizational skills, if at all possible, to defuse this issue of tension so that you can start off the weekend in a reasonably good frame of mind.

Making dinner. It's very important that you don't become the "pizza and Coke" daddy or mommy. If you want to take the kids out for pizza every couple of weeks, fine. But the essential rule should be, "We eat proper dinners in Daddy's house, just like in Mommy's house." Thus, organizationally speaking, when you know the children are coming, do a little advance planning. If you cook, add a special list to your shopping list that week for the children's menus. Also stock up on healthy snacks. If you don't cook, buy prepared meals from a take-out place or restaurant, but served in a "home," not fast-food, atmosphere.

Toting things. This constant toting of things back and forth is not a good thing. It has a transitory feeling to it, and creates great feelings of instability in the children.

But also, from an organizational point of view, it's a nightmare, and can create tremendous irritation in both parents. Things are forgotten; they're lost; they're not sent back; they're not sent to the weekend place. Toys are brought back and forth.

It might be worth an extra outlay of money to save an awful lot of grief to buy duplicate stocks of basic clothes, and to either buy a small wardrobe and dresser or designate closet space for the children.

Have on hand basic staples: a supply of nightwear, underwear, socks, jeans, a few shirts, a stock of T-shirts, a couple of bathing suits. So they can come pretty relieved that nothing is going to be forgotten. Have enough on hand so that they don't have to bring a suitcase—or maybe just a backpack with some special items.

Also keep basic supplies on hand. For example, Jacob got a fever, and so Harry had to run out for aspirin. There should be the baby aspirin, the toothbrush, the toothpaste . . . duplicate sets of toiletries and all the usual little staples of life.

Duplicating certain toys and games might also be in order. As expensive as it might be, it's a lot easier to spend the money on two Nintendos rather than have the child bring one back and forth.

Space and accommodation. If the kids can't have their own room, a loft bed, perhaps, in a corner of the living room might be preferable to a sofa bed. But do make sure that the kids have their own shelf space. For example, you're very irritated because the kids open their bags and all their toys promptly tumble out onto the floor. Make sure they have a set of shelves where their toys can reside.

Assign sufficient drawer space. Each child should have his or her own drawer space, whether it's real drawer space or makeshift, so the child feels at home. Again, the bottom line is to be more comfortable by being more efficient and more organized, and also to make them feel as though they're a real part of this family unit which is now your life.

Alternative arrangements. Joint custody of children is becoming more and more popular. One very positive way to approach this is to have the parents rather than the children move from house to house.

Rita and Ben's children live one month with Rita and one month with Ben. But instead of moving the children from one place to the other, it is Rita and Ben who move back and forth, while the children stay home in their own rooms, their own clothes, their own school. This setup keeps them much more stabilized in terms of the community.

Another alternative is that parents continue to live within close proximity of one another. For example, Lewis and Sue divorced, and each remarried, but they have a child in common. So now Lewis and Alice, and Sue and Tim, have purposely arranged to live within three blocks of each other. The common child, Caroline, only has to go three blocks to see the other set of parents, and she spends weekends with them. The school doesn't change, the friendship group doesn't change, and the child's flow of activity in life is not interrupted.

Sharing information. There really should be no such thing as the part-time parent. Each parent is a full-time parent, but may only have custody at various points in the week or the child's life. However, both parents need to be on top of what's going on with the children.

Even if it's not a part of your agreement, both spouses should have a file of duplicates of important papers and forms involving the children, including medical reports, an up-to-date list of doctors, dentists, other services, school, neighbors, grandparents . . . a data base on your child, so to speak.

It is also necessary to know where the valuables or important papers are, in case of the death of either parent.

THE BLENDED FAMILY

The organizing rules of a blended family—that is, a family composed of a couple and children from previous marriages plus sometimes children of their own—are the same as those for any other family (see Chapter 16), with this proviso: Experience indicates that what is required is an *absolute* scrupulousness in assuring equity in each child's chore-load and *absolute* evenhandedness in imposing sanctions if tasks are not carried out properly.

It is human nature for siblings to be preternaturally concerned that one child is favored over another. In blended families, that normal alertness is multiplied geometrically, in that one family grouping should not be favored over another. Families have been known to break up over vicious squabbling between the children over perceived favoritism. A trust on the part of all the children that both parents are absolutely fair and equitable to them all is a key element in ensuring domestic tranquillity.

COMPANIONATE LIVING: ROOMMATES AND COHABITING COUPLES

Nary a person has not had the experience at some point in life of sharing accommodations with somebody else with whom they may or may not get along, with whom they may or may not share similar values, with whom they may or may not have common understandings. So from an organizational point of view, the major concern of such relationships is to establish common ground and common ground rules. This discussion outlines some of the specific issues that arise and some approaches to finding and negotiating that common ground.

Selecting a Roommate

Cordelia and Linda discussed sharing an apartment. They liked each other very much; they had common interests, and in many ways it seemed to be a very suitable combination—except that Cordelia told Linda that she was extremely clean, that everything had to be neatened and cleaned every day to a fare-thee-well, and if not, she got very, very edgy. Linda, on the other hand, although it would not be fair to call her a slob, was, let's say, more casual in her approach to cleanliness. So, unfortunately but realistically, the two girls decided they would probably not work out as roommates for that reason.

Which leads us to the point that you should interview a prospective roommate the way you would interview an applicant for employment to establish your different levels of expectation:

1. What level of cleanliness do you require for comfort? Is it compatible with your prospective roommate's?
2. What about music? One person's cacophony is another person's symphony.
3. What are the house rules? Can the boyfriend or girlfriend stay overnight, and can friends camp out on the couch?
4. How do you feel about taking phone messages for each other? Should you share a phone, or, if one or both of you tend to have long conversations, get separate phones?

Also be aware of visual and subjective cues. Does this person appear to you to be honest, trustworthy? Does this person appear to you to be tight, to be generous, to be sloppy? Make sure you get some references.

Remember, this is a person you're going to be living with, who is going to know your most intimate habits. It's the fastest way to get on each other's nerves. So try to do a really thorough investigation to avoid some of these pitfalls.

Negotiating Your Space, or Who Gets the Big Bedroom and Who Gets the Small One?

Very often an apartment is taken by one person. If you took the apartment originally, then that gives you certain priority privileges. However, that may not be the only factor in allocating space. Personal preferences and schedules have a lot to do with it. For example, Michael and Tim shared an apartment which had one sizable bedroom and one small one. However, even though Michael had the right to choose which bedroom to take, he chose the smaller one simply because the big one did not have a big window, and Michael preferred the more open view that the smaller room had.

Another factor would be schedules. Which one of you might wind up being in the apartment much more than the other? Or which one of you might interfere with the other? Michael always gets up at six o'clock in the morning and putters around, whereas Tim sleeps in till eight. So Tim got the room that had a bit more quiet.

The key here is that you and your roommate negotiate the space, based upon your preferences for space, view, and quiet, and schedules of your daily activities in terms of apartment use.

Being Alone Versus Being Together

One of the thorniest issues that roommates have to resolve is that of preserving privacy and making time for themselves, yet at the same time arranging to spend time as friends and companions.

Brenda and Cindy shared an apartment, and they did two things which helped maintain their friendship. First, they established privacy. This was just a one-bedroom apartment, and Brenda had the bedroom, but in order to maintain Cindy's privacy, they installed a floor-to-ceiling roll-up shade which divided the living room, one part of which was Cindy's bedroom and the other part of which was their communal living room. Since their schedules were different, this worked out very well. So that was the separation solution.

On the other hand, they didn't want to feel that they never saw each other; that they were just sort of strangers passing in a bus station. So every Thursday night they made sure to have dinner together, and if they were both home of an evening, they often shared a quiet supper together as well.

Money and Possessions

The single most thorny issue that can divide roommates is that of what belongs to whom. What must be understood up front is that, when dealing with two roommates who are not related by blood or by close affectional ties, the areas of common ground are much smaller, and the definitions of what is yours and what is mine have to be much more tightly and closely defined than in a family. Call it petty if you like—it's reality.

We've all heard stories of roommates who have broken up in acrimony because Jim said that Bill kept drinking his milk or orange juice, or whatever it might be. Now, this is not the behavior, really, of grown-up people, but people become very possessive about their food and what-have-you, and this is a reality that must be accepted. It's the little things, the little infringements, that can drive people nuts.

The first question has to do with the division of food. Do you buy food together, do you go shopping together?

Or suppose one of you eats out all the time and the other one usually eats in?

The solution here is simply consistency in deciding what to do. Several different systems work, as long as both roommates agree.

One can walk around harboring tremendous anger and animosity toward someone because of the milk that magically disappears every week. Yet the terror of being thought petty makes people more reluctant to discuss these issues directly than they would be with a family member, with whom they feel more comfortable and informal.

My theory is that you shouldn't mind being thought petty. It's the petty things that can drive you mad.

So if you do agree to buy your food in common and share, then one criterion should be that you basically eat the same kinds of foods—and in these days, when people are very idiosyncratic about their eating habits, this is not so easy. If one of you only eats organic brown rice, ginger root, and tofu balls, and the other one dines on steak and Twinkies, then sharing your food is not a workable arrangement.

You may, however, decide that there are some staples you will share, such as milk, bread, and peanut butter.

Do you prefer putting money into a kitty for mutual expenses that you draw from until it is used up? Or do you split purchases as you go? Some people prefer to drop all cash register slips into a bowl, initialing the purchase, and then divvy up every two weeks or so.

Also work out a reimbursement arrangement. For example, sometimes a roommate's guests go into the refrigerator and take stuff. Of course, you can label your food, but that gets a little grim. So as long as you have a common understanding that each roommate will reimburse for or will purchase more of anything that a guest may have taken, there should be no problem.

In fact, sitting down to a weekly reckoning is an excellent idea. Just go over the foods and monitor the system and see if any problems or confusions have arisen, and clarify any misunderstandings.

In regard to household furnishings, it is strongly recommended that rather than buying in common—that is, both of you chipping in for the rug—it is a lot better in the long run if you make separate purchases—one of you buys the area rug and the other buys the pair of lamps.

Establish a mutual furnishings budget that you are both going to contribute to the apartment—you're both going to put in a hundred dollars or a thousand dollars or whatever it is—and then each item that is purchased comes out of the account of one of you or the other. Thus, when the inevitable splitting of the apartment occurs, there's no problem about who owns what.

Negotiating Chores and Responsibilities

Along with dividing up furnishings and food, task assignment is another sore spot with many roommates—who does what? The classic situation, of course, is Oscar and Felix in *The Odd Couple*. And actually Oscar and Felix came to a perfect accommodation. Oscar was a natural slob and Felix loved to clean and didn't seem to mind that he was the one who was constantly put upon. But unfortunately it doesn't usually work that way in real life, and making sure that responsibilities are allocated in a way that seems fair to both parties, and then that they are carried out as promised, is essential to a satisfactory roommate relationship. Thoughtful and considerate negotiation is the key.

For example, take shopping for the foods you have in common. One way to handle it is to take turns. That is, one person can be the designated purchaser for one week or one month and then you switch off. Or you might prefer to allocate the task along preference lines. One person may enjoy it and find it an easy thing to do, in which case the other roommate should take over another permanent responsibility that seems more or less commensurate. By the way, probably the best way to keep track of what you need is to keep a magnetic pad on the side of the refrigerator where you each list foods and household products as they get low.

Indeed, as a general rule, allocating tasks by preference tends to work better than taking turns. The idea that "I'm going to wash the dishes tonight, you do it tomorrow night" often doesn't work out. Frequently one of the roommates falls down on the job, causing tensions. If one of you really doesn't mind doing the dishes, however, then there's nothing wrong with that person having KP responsibility, so long as the other roommate clears the table and takes out the garbage.

Usually there are people who don't mind kitchen tasks or cooking, but who hate dusting and cleaning or bathrooms, and vice versa. Fine. It really doesn't matter. In other words, identify your areas of preference, balance out approximate burdens, and stick to it.

Living Together

There are important differences in establishing workable rules for living between casual roommates and people living together as lovers. The way in which life is organized around you and your lover will depend on how you define yourselves as a couple. If you define yourselves as one step into marriage or effectively married without the benefit of a piece of paper, then the same rules of household sharing and responsibilities and pooling resources that apply to a married couple would apply to you.

The other end of the gamut would be, "Come on, let's move in and have some fun together." This is a much more openly transitory situation. And then there are all shades in between.

In most cohabiting relationships, it is important that you recognize that the relationship may not be permanent. Or rather, that you have a probable assumption of impermanence. (Of course, marriages are often impermanent these days too, but you start with a probable assumption of permanence.) Thus, to the extent that your relationship seems to warrant it, it is wise to follow some of the rules discussed previously for roommates, allowing up front for the possibility of separating.

There are some areas then, applying to lovers, that are much more like a married couple, and some areas that are much more like the roommate. Specifically, togetherness vis-à-vis privacy concerns obviously will be very different between lovers. Your areas of common ground are, it is hoped, greater. You might in fact decide to be quite a bit more liberal in your notions of pooling common monies for mutual household benefit. And it's unlikely you'll be fighting over who drank whose orange juice.

However, it is recommended that whenever possible you follow the same rules with regard to furniture and major purchases as roommates—in other words, buy separately—so that you'll have some ease of separation when and if the time comes.

Afterword

Many people misunderstand the idea of organization as somehow being constraining or limiting. The truth is that, although many of the chapters involve lists, checklists, and other requirements, the bottom line of being organized is freedom from the tyranny of mess and stress.

The fact is that organization simply puts a set of tools in your hands that allows you to no longer waste energy in inefficient processes—to be able to convert that energy into useful time.

Remember that organization itself is just that—it is a tool. It is not an end in and of itself. The purpose of this book is to free you to have time and space to accomplish your goals—which is hard to do when you have to worry about when the dishes get done and where things are filed in your Rolodex and where to hang your belts. These are the kinds of things that divert your human capacity and your sense of freedom as a human being.

Further, once you get organization under your belt, once it becomes a regular tool, like any other tool—like a needle and thread, like a hammer and nails—and once you begin to see the benefits and stop seeing organization as frightening or overwhelming, then, if you have children, you will be able to pass that lesson on to the next generation, and your children will not wind up having to fight chaos as part of their life plan. It's a wonderful gift to them and you.

Bibliography

The books marked with an asterisk are those I consulted during the writing of this book. The others will be interesting reading if you care to pursue those topics.

Time

*BLISS, EDWIN C. *Getting Things Done: The ABC's of Time Management*. New York: Bantam, 1978. (Paperback)

EISENBERG, RONNI, and KELLY, KATE. *Organize Yourself!* New York: Macmillan (Collier), 1984.

HEDRICK, LUCY H. *Five Days to an Organized Life*. New York: Dell, 1990.

*LAKEIN, ALAN. *How to Get Control of Your Time and Your Life*. New York: McKay, 1973. (Paperback: New American Library, 1989.)

MACKENZIE, R. ALEC. *The Time Trap*. New York: AMACOM, 1990. (New Edition.)

MAYER, JEFFREY J. *If You Haven't Got the Time to Do it Right, When Will You Find the Time to Do it Over?* New York: Simon & Schuster, 1990.

Money

MUNDIS, JERROLD. *How to Get out of Debt, Stay out of Debt, and Live Prosperously.* New York: Bantam, 1988.

Decorating and the Uses of Space

CONRAN, TERENCE. *The House Book.* New York: Crown, 1982.

*KATZ, MARJORIE P. *Instant-Effect Decorating.* New York: M. Evans, 1972. A very direct, common-sense approach to decorating and utilization of space.

*LIMAN, ELLEN. *The Spacemaker Book.* New York: Viking, 1977.

*LIMAN, ELLEN, and PANTER, CAROL. *Decorating Your Room: A Do-It-Yourself Guide.* New York: Franklin Watts, 1974. Although purportedly written as a primer for children, many grown-ups will find this basic information useful too.

MCALISTER, MARCIA. *With House in Hand: Organize Your Decorating. A Step-by-Step Planner for Home or Office.* Marcia McAlister Enterprises, 1984.

*STODDARD, ALEXANDRA. *Style for Living: How to Make Where You Live You.* Garden City, N.Y.: Doubleday, 1974. Stoddard's approach to decorating is very similar to my approach to organizing. Find out what pleases you most and work around it.

VARNEY, CARLTON. *Room by Room Decorating.* New York: Fawcett Columbine, 1984. (Paperback)

Reader's Digest Complete Do-It-Yourself Manual. 1981. (Distributed by Random House.) If you plan to do your own work, this "handyperson's how-to" will be useful.

Home and Family Management

*BRACKEN, PEG. *I Hate to Housekeep Book*. New York: Harcourt, Brace & World, 1962. (Paperback: Fawcett Crest, 1965.)

*EISEN, CAROL G. *Nobody Said You Had to Eat off the Floor . . . The Psychiatrist's Wife's Guide to Housekeeping*. New York: McKay, 1971.

*LENNON, PEGGY. *On the Homefront: Speaking for the Management*. Published by Kentucky Fried Chicken, 1976. No longer available.

*SKELSEY, ALICE. *The Working Mother's Guide to Her Home, Her Family and Herself*. New York: Random House, 1970.

Kitchen

CONRAN, TERENCE. *The Kitchen Book*. New York: Crown, 1984.

*U.S. DEPARTMENT OF HOUSING AND URBAN DEVELOPMENT. *Designing Kitchens for Safety*. U.S. Government Printing Office, Washington, D.C. No longer available.

Other

*KOBERG, DON, and BAGNALL, JIM. *The Universal Traveler: A Soft-Systems Guide to Creativity, Problem-solving and the Process of Reaching Goals*. Los Altos, Calif.: William Kaufmann, 1974. (Distributed by Crown.) Organizing difficulties are often linked to problems with general decision-making. This book offers some useful insights into the process.

*TOFFLER, ALVIN. *The Third Wave*. New York: Morrow, 1980. (Paperback: Bantam, 1981.)

Reference to Elaine Blechman, *The New York Times*, September 2, 1977.

Reference to Jane O'Reilly, *New York Magazine*, January 17, 1972.

Reference to Mimi Sheraton, *The New York Times*, April 20, 1977.

Figure 16 (coat-hanging space design) from an idea in *Better Homes & Gardens*, July 1977.

Index